# Waste and Wealth

# Waste and Wealth

An Ethnography of Labor, Value,
and Morality in a Vietnamese
Recycling Economy

MINH T. N. NGUYEN

New York    Oxford
OXFORD UNIVERSITY PRESS

Oxford University Press is a department of the University of Oxford.
It furthers the University's objective of excellence in research, scholarship,
and education by publishing worldwide. Oxford is a registered trade mark of
Oxford University Press in the UK and certain other countries.

Published in the United States of America by Oxford University Press
198 Madison Avenue, New York, NY 10016, United States of America.

Library of Congress Cataloging-in-Publication Data

Names: Nguyen, Minh T. N., author.
Title: Waste and wealth : labor, value, and morality in a Vietnamese
   recycling economy / Minh T.N. Nguyen.
Description: New York : Oxford University Press, [2018] | Series: Issues of
   globalization : case studies in contemporary anthropology | Includes
   bibliographical references and index.
Identifiers: LCCN 2018028851 | ISBN 9780190692605 (pbk.)
Subjects: LCSH: Recycling industry–Social aspects–Vietnam–Red River Delta. |
   Refuse and refuse disposal–Social aspects–Vietnam–Red River Delta. |
   Informal sector (Economics)–Social aspects–Vietnam–Red River Delta. |
   Migration, Internal–Social aspects–Vietnam–Red River Delta. |
   Ethnology–Vietnam–Red River Delta.
Classification: LCC HD9975.V53 R43 2018 | DDC 338.4/76284458095973–dc23
LC record available at https://lccn.loc.gov/2018028851

9 8 7 6 5 4 3 2 1
Printed by Sheridan Books, Inc., United States of America

*To Linh and Thomas*

# TABLE OF CONTENTS
........................

# PREFACE

I first came to Spring District[1] in Vietnam's Red River Delta during the fall of 2011. My first visit to the district was an eye-opener, because the living standards there did not match what I had expected. Previously, I had been conducting ethnographic research among waste traders in Hanoi.[2] Many of them were from Spring District, and they commonly told me how "miserable" life back home in the countryside was. The reality was quite different. When we met during a village meeting, Mr. Quan, an articulate eight-five-year-old resident of Spring District's Green Spring commune, said, "Our village used to deal in shit, and now we are rich!" (*Làng mình ngày xưa chuyên đi buôn cứt, thế mà giờ lại giàu đấy!*) Then he laughed heartily, amused at the boldness of his own statement. By various standards, however, Green Spring commune is wealthy. Its roads are wide and well-paved, and its kindergartens and schools are comparable to high-quality urban facilities. It is not uncommon to spot villas surrounded by manicured gardens, some imperiously overlooking canals and green rice fields.

Mr. Quan was not joking about Green Spring villagers "dealing in shit" in the past. In the early twentieth century, many villagers went to work for the colonial Hanoi Sanitation Company under the patronage of an influential native villager, Mr. Năm Diệm, who became its director (DiGrigorio 1994). As I got to know Mr. Quan's family better, he and his wife, Ms. Quyên, were happy to share their memories of older times. Mr. Quan's father had worked for the sanitation company in the 1930s, and as a child, he had picked trash in Hanoi together with his siblings; his father had also introduced many relatives and fellow villagers to the company. Once married, Ms. Quyên and Mr. Quan worked together in the sanitation company for a while (his wife's beauty as a young woman was "just about decent," Mr. Quan said with a wink). Then he switched to working as a cyclo driver—he said he could no longer stand the filth—before getting involved in revolutionary activities and later joining the Vienamese army. Ms. Quyên kept on doing the work, however.[3] Her task was to collect night soil (human waste) for Hanoi householders, who made monthly payments to the colonial administration for the service. "The French then made fat bucks from the sanitation fees", said Mr. Quan.[4] The workers were given a pushcart with six buckets to replace those that had been filled; bigger families would use more than one bucket. The workers' payment was meager, and it was often deducted on account of the urban householders' complaints to the authorities about their service. Yet they made additional money from selling the night soil to farmers in the surrounding areas of Hanoi. After the French left, many continued to work for the sanitation company under the socialist government; their family members initially worked in the municipal dump as trash pickers and later established a niche in the waste trade, capitalizing on their relatives' access to household waste.

The Quan-Quyên family returned to their home village by the end of the 1950s. Mr. Quan then went away as a soldier, and Ms. Quyên stayed home, being in charge of the family. When Mr. Quan came back from the army in the early 1980s, chronic hunger was prevalent—"How terribly hungry we were (đói rài đói rạc ra)," he said—in an economy ravaged by war, inefficient central planning, and international isolation. Green Spring had seven hundred households then, and only three of them had a brick house (the rest were mud houses). While Ms. Quyên had occasionally engaged in waste work during the collective period, she became a full-time waste trader following the return of her husband, travelling to other northern provinces to trade waste together with two of her children and one granddaughter, and sometimes taking along others from the village. They would take the local train to the surrounding provinces on their buying trips, then bring bags of waste back to Hanoi to sell to waste depots in Ô Chợ Dừa, now a modernized central district that used to be a slum-like area populated by migrant laborers and poor urban residents (see DiGregorio 1994 for a description of the area during the late 1980s and early 1990s). The common waste items she traded in then were poultry feathers, animal bones, broken glass, rags, copper, and aluminum. In the late 1980s, she opened her own depot in Hanoi, buying from itinerant traders, often women from her district who walked around Hanoi neighborhoods purchasing recyclable wastes from urban households. In the more thriving economy following the reforms (*đổi mới*), her business had just started growing when her youngest daughter died in an accident. Broken with grief, she went back to the village and has not left again. Yet her children and grandchildren, like thousands of other people from Spring District, remain active in the trade today—her family altogether owns seven waste depots in Hanoi and Hải Phòng. The networks that villagers like her initiated have become part of a waste economy that spans major cities, involving tens of thousands of people (DiGregorio 1994; Mehra et al. 1996; Mitchell 2008, 2009).

Spring District is situated in Vietnam's populous Red River Delta, about 140 kilometers from the capital city of Hanoi, 1,500 kilometers from Hồ Chí Minh City (HCM City), the other major urban center (see Figure P.1 for a map of mainland Vietnam). The district has nineteen communes, with a total population of 180,000 people and a population density of 1,600 persons per square-kilometer; the average household size is four to five persons. Rice farming was the main agricultural activity in the district, alongside small-holding crop cultivation and sericulture. Because of the Red River Delta's high population density and limited farmland,[5] labor migration has long been important to local livelihoods. During French colonialism (1884–1945), peasants took up seasonal farm work away from their villages or migrated to other parts of the country to work in mines or on rubber plantations; some were even recruited to work in other French colonies (Gourou 1955). In the four decades of state socialism that followed, people continued to migrate for work, albeit on a smaller scale due to strict mobility restrictions. Since the mid-1980s reforms, however, the loosening of formal mobility constraints have made it easier for people to be on the move, while urbanization and in-dustrialization have accelerated, creating livelihoods opportunities that had been hitherto unknown. Although local people generally prefer Hanoi be-cause of its proximity, younger people are also migrating to other urban cen-ters to trade waste, including the more distant HCM City and its surrounding industrial regions. The trajectories of Spring District people are in many ways similar to those of millions of Vietnamese with rural origin who have em-braced mobile livelihoods in response to political-economic shifts in the last three decades. The dynamics of mobility, change, and continuity that I por-tray in this book resonate with the experiences of peasants elsewhere in Viet-nam and Asia and by no means are confined to this community (see, e.g., Taylor 2007, Luong 2010 , Vu 2013, Rigg et. al 2014). What distinguishes the case of Spring District is the role of waste, both as a global commodity and as a social category that suffuses these dynamics with particular meanings for the creation of value and the remaking of the social and moral worlds.

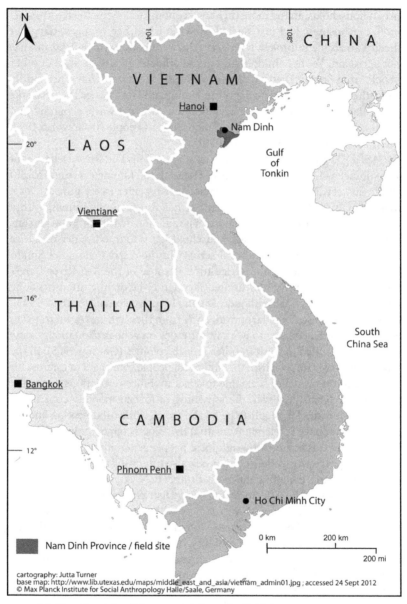

FIGURE **P.1 Map of mainland Vietnam and the major field sites.**
Source: Courtesy of Jutta Turner.

# Field Research

The main bulk of field research for this book took place in Hanoi and Spring District from July 2011 to July 2012. In 2015, I conducted more than two months of follow-up research, during which I also visited migrant waste traders from Spring District in HCM City. In addition, I visit the country every year for about a month, staying in touch with some informants and keeping an eye out for the general development of the waste trade. During the fieldwork, I stayed with two host families in the district and was able to connect with their migrant family members, relatives, and neighbors in Hanoi and HCM City. I attended as many events in the district as possible, from weddings, death anniversaries, and funerals to religious festivities. The opportunity to observe the interactions and behavior of the same people in different settings of the city and the country allowed me to identify translocal dynamics of social performativity and connectivity in local people's mobile life. Participant observation was the primary research method, yet I also conducted eighty interviews with waste traders or their family members and organized a number of focus groups. I chose these informants for interviews based on the likelihood that their household trajectories might bring further insights for the research. In most cases, we already knew each other, and the interviews were largely semi-formal, taking place in people's homes or lodgings during their leisure time. My research partner, Tạ Thị Tâm,[6] and I administered a household survey among three hundred households in 2011 to gain a broad understanding of the local patterns of mobility and livelihoods, and we formally interviewed a range of local cadres and officials.

In the local administrative system of rural Vietnam, a district is divided into communes, which are further broken down into villages or hamlets. The commune is the lowest level of formal administration, whereas the village is governed semi-formally, staffed largely by voluntary local leaders who receive token remuneration for their work. As elsewhere in Vietnam, the administrative units referred to as communes in Spring District today were called villages during and before the colonial period. While the communes have expanded over time due to population growth, local people continue to identify with the commune as if it were a village community, rather than thinking of it in sterile terms as an administrative unit. Indeed, when talking about "our village," people commonly refer to the name of the commune. This affective, village-based connection to the homeplace explains why rural networks of migrants in urban centers are often traceable to particular communes. Migrant waste traders in Hanoi nowadays come from all over Spring District and other places in the Red River delta, yet the pioneers of the trade originated from Mr. Quan's Green Spring commune. Previously among the poorest in the district, people from this commune have introduced the trade to the locality, turning it into one of the most viable forms of migrant livelihood for peasant households. My study focuses on two communes of Spring District, Green Spring and its neighboring commune, Red Spring. If Green Spring people are predominantly waste traders, many of whom have become wealthy depot owners, Red Spring's population is more diverse as it has higher concentration of government offices and public facilities, plus a small township with a large market, due to its central location. While many peasants from Red Spring work in the waste economy, a sizable number of people from the township have relatively high academic achievements,[7] a factor that features in the local valuation of waste work. In this book, I refer to Spring District when discussing general local patterns, and to each of these two communes when emphasizing their particularities, especially regarding local people's participation in the waste economy and their identification with waste work.

The book touches briefly on HCM City and other urban regions, yet the main urban site for my analysis is Hanoi, a growing city of 7.5 million people (Figure P.2). For many, the capital city represents not only the center of state power, but also a place of high culture, civility, and intellect. There is an enduring cultural distinction between urban residents, especially the "original Hanoians" (*người Hà Nội gốc*) and whoever comes from outside the city (*người ngoại tỉnh*) in terms of perceived cultural sophistication, politeness, and manners. The "country bumpkins" (*người nhà quê*) are often a target of derision by urban people, who deride what they consider to be migrants' crude appearance, uncultured habits, and lowly minds (Chapter 4, Nguyen 2015b). In the last decade, Hanoi has expanded to include several outlying provinces in its metropolitan region, and its population has grown exponentially, changing what it means to be a Hanoian. Most Hanoi residents today migrated from the countryside at some point in their life, and many retain significant rural connections. Although rapid urbanization has induced nostalgia for the rural idyll, the cultural distinction continues to hold sway, now often invoking the gap between rural migrants and the urban middle class regarding awareness of law, order, and civility. In their life and work in Hanoi, migrant waste traders from Spring District are confronted daily with these deep-seated social boundaries.

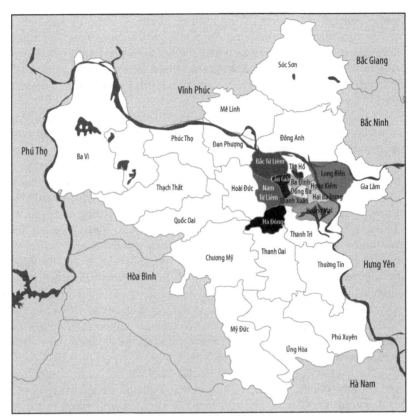

FIGURE **P.2  Administrative map of Hanoi.**
Source: Courtesy of Hanoi People's Committee's official website at https://www.thudo.gov.vn/hnmap.
aspx (downloaded with permission on February 1, 2018).

## Researching People on the Move

I hope that this book conveys my deep respect for Spring District waste
traders as sophisticated, reflective, and resourceful social actors, even if
I might at times portray events and situations critically. Armed with
theoretical categories developed in other empirical settings, I emphasize connections and associations that local people take for granted,
and I sometimes interpret events differently than they do. Such a schol-
arly approach is not meant to dismiss their narratives as irrelevant or
misguided. During my research, I regularly met highly articulate men

and women whose story-telling skills I admired and still somewhat envy; they often have convincing narratives of their lives and their homeplace. But my task as an ethnographer is to stitch individual stories together, connecting them to my observations of their life and work, drawing out the differences and similarities, and trying to understand why they exist.

I myself come from the countryside. My early childhood was spent in a village not far from Spring District, and I grew up in a small city with state-employee parents whose close relatives remain in the village to this day. Like Spring District people, I have led a mobile life, first as a student and then as a researcher for institutions abroad, coming back and forth to do my work and live my transnational life. Also like them, I have lived between places, experienced the ambivalence and conundrum of maintaining social relations on the go, and sometimes felt left behind by a place that one has left. Yet the research has also made me keenly aware of the difference between our trajectories. At the most basic level, my mobility has been much less circumscribed by either citizenship or financial constraints. Academic work is precarious, but the precarity differs greatly from that of a migrant waste trader in Vietnamese cities. In other words, we traverse different "regimes of mobility" that are shaped by our positioning in the global order (Glick Schiller and Salazar 2013).

However friendly we became, social distance lingered between me and the informants. For many, I was at best a quaint species: my repeated explanations of what an anthropologist does made little sense to them, and anthropology itself seemed an occupation that did not fit the categories sensible to them. Although they seemed to perceive me a "learned person" (*người có học*), I did not operate like a journalist or a government cadre "from above"—that is, like other "learned people" who on other occasions would most likely be inclined to enquire about their lives. I asked them questions, but unlike the others, I came back repeatedly, staying for weeks at a time and hanging around with what seemed to them like no apparent purpose. In the beginning, some people suspected that I might report on their lives in the newspapers with the often half-pitying, half-condescending tone that they had come to associate with journalists, which made them uncomfortable and led them to keep their distance. Others thought that I might be a salesperson for an insurance company or a pyramid scheme. As I went about observing and probing into people's lives, they also observed me and Tâm, my research partner, intensively. We made good topics for conversation in the village; our behavior and habits were analyzed, compared, and wondered about, often with bemusement. Over time, their suspicions and speculations were laid to rest as people came to know more about our whereabouts and families, seeing that we did not intend to make their lives into front-page news items (which, however, did not prevent some from continuing to call us "the two journalist ladies").[7]

Social research in Vietnam is strictly regulated; access to research sites and participants requires various kinds of permission, especially in rural areas. Employed by a foreign research institution, even as a Vietnamese national, I had to obtain formal approval from the Vietnam Academy of Social Science and an affiliation with one of its institutes. For long-term stays in Spring District, I had to gain permission from the provincial and district administration, which referred me down the administrative hierarchy to the village level. This might seem cumbersome, but it actually facilitated access to the field site. If I had descended upon the village with no official recommendations, I would perhaps have been chased out in no time for asking strange questions. And while not automatically instituting trust, the introduction by the authorities gave me some legitimacy in the eyes of local people and cadres, who understandably would not want to run into trouble for having talked to the wrong kind of stranger. I already knew the matriarch of my host family well from my previous research; she used to extend invitations to me to visit her home and village. When I chose Spring District for the study and asked her for permission to stay with her family, she insisted that I ask the commune administration to inform the village leaders that I came to her family as recommended by the authorities rather than because of our earlier acquaintance. As such, nobody could question her motive in admitting a village outsider into her home.

Although I worked with people both in the city and the country, the access I gained to individuals and families in the countryside was crucial. That I had met people in the village before visiting them or their relatives in the city made a difference. There was much less suspicion and guardedness—the specific knowledge about their home village and family connections there helped to create rapport with local people, who perhaps found in it some recognition for who they were. Amidst the alienating effects of mobility, identification with the homeplace seemed like an anchor for many, and the simple fact that somebody knew about it in some detail seemed comforting for them. The research design also allowed me to examine individual trajectories as part of whole families, sometimes of whole lineages whose members lived and worked in different places at the same time. In this way, I was able to see people's actions in a different light—namely the social value created across geographical locations. In the book, I use the term *local people* to refer to people from Spring District, whether they are in the city, on the move, or in the village. This is not to deny that some of them have and will become local in the city, but to emphasize the homeplace as an important part of their migrant identity and also as an anchor for myself in researching a mobile community.

## Credits and Acknowledgements

I carried out the field research for this book as a Research Fellow at the Max Planck Institute for Social Anthropology between 2011 and 2016. Parts of the book are based on material that I included in several journal articles:

> Nguyen, Minh T. N. 2014. Translocal Householding: Care and Migrant Livelihoods in a Waste-trading Community of Vietnam's Red River Delta. *Development and Change* 45(6): 1385–1408.
> Nguyen, Minh T. N. 2016. Trading in Broken Things: Gendered Performances and Spatial Practices in a Northern Vietnamese Rural-Urban Waste Economy. *American Ethnologist* 43(1): 116–129.
> Nguyen, Minh T. N. 2018. "In a 'Half-dark, Half-light Zone': Mobility, Precarity, and Moral Ambiguity in Post-Reform Vietnam's Urban Waste Economy. *TRANS (Trans-Regional and -National Studies of Southeast Asia)*.

The material in these articles has been extensively reworked and reshuffled according to the book's structure and arguments. All of the photos in the book are mine, unless otherwise indicated, and all the direct quotes from Vietnamese sources are my own translations.

The most rewarding part of ethnographic research is the opportunity to know people beyond the surface—people whom one would otherwise hardly meet on a personal level. Meeting the research informants has not only broadened my intellectual horizons, but also enriched my life in many ways. Although the encounters were not always easy, I was fortunate to have met all of them. Many were open and easy-going, but even the not-so-friendly informants taught me important things. Again and again, I was surprised by how some of the most profound conversations emerged during casual interactions with informants. They include my two host families who took me in with trust and hospitality, who extended warmth yet allowed me the space I needed, and who taught me about the intricacies of reciprocity, an art that I shall never master as well as they do; the female traders who invited me to lie down with them on the pavement during their lunch break; the depot owners on the highway of Hanoi, who offered me meals and sometimes rice to take home, along with their fascinating stories; the young male traders who let me in on their conversations during their time together in the village; the village leaders and local cadres who worked at the intersection between state structures and community relations, and who accorded me the necessary distance required by their formal responsibilities but nonetheless treated me with respect and humor; and, all the others who spared their time with me and who I am not supposed to name here in order to protect your privacy and identity. I am thankful to you for everything that this book is about.

To write a book is to become indebted to many people for their time, critiques, and ideas—the gift of people's intellect and scholarship. Since the book draws on several journal articles that benefited greatly from anonymous peer reviews, I would like to thank the strangers and hidden colleagues who have constructively engaged with my writing over the years and provided me with precious suggestions and feedback. The multiple reviewers commissioned by Oxford University Press, all of whom graciously agreed to be identified, gave extremely helpful suggestions for shaping up the book: Catherine Alexander, Durham University; Erik Lind Harms, Yale University; Heather Hindman, University of Texas at Austin; Ann Marie Leshkowich, College of the Holy Cross; Reece Jon McGee, Texas State University; Carrie L. Mitchell, University of Waterloo; Jonathan Padwe, University of Hawai'i at Mānoa; Josh Reno, Binghamton University; Christina Schwenkel, University of California, Riverside; and Sophia Stamatopoulou-Robbins, Bard College. You were encouraging, while your rigor and high standards positively challenged me. That said, I am responsible for any errors and slippages in the pages that follow.

Thank you so much to the following scholars who have critically engaged with my various writings related to the book from an early stage; I have learned a great deal from your feedback and your own inspiring works: Catherine Alexander, Kebeet Brenda-Beckmann, Charlotte Bruckermann, James Carrier, Meixuan Chen, Kirsten Endres, Chris Hann, Erik Harms, Michael Herzfeld, Ann Marie Leshkowich, Catherine Locke, Hy Van Luong, Marek Mikus, Dominik Mueller, Andrew Sanchez, Nina Glick Schiller, Oliver Tappe, Sarah Turner, Roberta Zavoretti, and Li Zhang. Kirsten and Erik heroically read the whole manuscript under time constraint, giving me the best feedback that an author could get, insightfully critical and yet generously encouraging. Other colleagues provided helpful comments through seminar discussions, especially at the Department of Resilience and Transformation in Eurasia, Max Planck Institute of Social Anthropology; Institute of Anthropology and Institute of Cultural Studies, Vietnam Academy of Social Science; Institute of Anthropology, University of Zurich; and School of International Development, University of East Anglia.

I am indebted to a number of institutions and people associated with them. Anyone doing field research in Vietnam knows how important institutional support is. I would like to thank the Institute of Anthropology, Vietnam Academy of Social Science, for formally sponsoring my research. Thank you to Nguyễn Thị Thanh Bình, Nguyễn Văn Minh, and Vương Xuân Tình of the institute for their friendly backstopping. Tạ Thị Tâm from the institute provided highly competent research assistance with tact and good humor. During my follow-up research in 2015, I was also helpfully assisted by Nguyễn Viết Phan, a promising student anthropologist at the Department of Anthropology, HCM City National University. At Oxford University Press, the editors and staff were extremely constructive and professional. Their excellent standards are difficult to meet but rewarding to follow. Special thanks to Carla Freeman, Meredith Keffer, Sherith Pankratz, and Li Zhang for their patience and encouragement. Thank you to Wesley Morrison, Patricia Berube and others in the production team for their efficient and high-quality work. The Max Planck Institute for Social Anthropology continued to generously provide me with office space beyond my employment contract. The institute's library is a gem, well-resourced and staffed by the most helpful and friendly librarians I have ever worked with, especially Anja Neuner and Anett Kirchhoff. As the institute's Working Paper series editor, Bettina Mann provided excellent editorial inputs for three of my papers that eventually made it into the book in revised form. Jutta Turner helpfully provided the map of mainland Vietnam, and the Hanoi People's Committee's Information Gateway kindly permitted the use of the administrative map of Hanoi. The German Academic Exchange Service (DAAD) and the Association for Asian Studies (AAS) generously granted the funding that enabled me to present a chapter at the AAS conference 2017 in Toronto.

This book was written during a period of unemployment and health crisis in my family—it would have been impossible to keep writing without the kindness of many people, so many that I am not able to name them all. People generously offered practical help, heartfelt words of encouragement, and assistance with job applications; some wanted to give me money and to come from afar with a helping hand. Kindness, I think, is what sustains us, and the knowledge that there are people who care about you turns things around and makes life meaningful. Thank you for your kindness, Gunes Tetik Aslan, Bùi Minh Hồng, Đặng Minh Lý, Đào Minh Trường, Annuska Derks, Hoàng Dương, Konstanz Eckert, Kirsten Endres, I-Chieh Fang, Janet Fisher, Mathias and Antje Gastersted, Nina Glick Schiller, Ildiko Beller-Hann and Chris Hann, Erik Harms, Ann Marie Leshkowich, John McDonagh, Nghiêm Phương Tuyến, Nguyễn Thị Hương, Nguyễn Thị Loan, Nguyễn Thị Vân Anh, Nguyễn Thu Hải, Nguyễn Tường Vi, Ly and Quynh Nguyen, Natasha Pairaudeau, Phạm Thu Hằng, Ahsan Rana, Helle Rydstrøm, Christina Schwenkel, Martin Slama, Oliver Tappe, Trần Hoài, Roberta Zavoretti, Samia and Mark Zeitoun (the names are alphabetically listed; surnames in Vietnamese come first). In the family, my parents Nguyễn Chấn and Trần Thị Thành, Nguyễn Huy An, Nguyễn Trần Thìn, Nguyễn Văn Hiếu, Khổng Thị Tâm Hằng, Olivia Diem, and Martin Sikor gave moral support that deeply moves me.

I dedicate this book to my daughter Linh Sikor and my husband Thomas Sikor.

A monk in Spring District said to me, "People in this region do not have any proper job; they just do waste work, the most low-down kind of work in society" (*cái nghề mạt hạng nhất của xã hội*). When I asked how local people had become rich from this kind of work, he answered that they were just lucky. And at my suggestion that waste work seemed a "proper job" to me, he replied, "No, it is not really a job; it is just something you do out of desperation" (*cùng đường rồi thì mới làm*). Yet later in our conversation, he pointed out, and without seeming to connect with what he had said before, that all the villas and big houses in the area had come from waste work. Something he did not say then also became clear to me later on: much of the money spent on renovating his pagoda also originated from waste work—and from the people doing it whom he so disdained. Contrast the monk's remark with Mr. Quan's statement in the Preface that his village has become "rich" even with a history of "dealing in shit." While both men refer to the local occupation with waste work, the first statement is a disparagement of local people notwithstanding the wealth they have generated, and the second is a slightly self-deprecating yet triumphant pronouncement of how much they have been able to transform from a humble beginning. These differing statements suggest contradictory valuations rooted in multiple value frameworks that people draw on from their social positions. They also point to the struggles that Spring District waste traders face to gain social recognition and maintain dignity even as they work in an economy filled with dangers and uncertainties.

This book tells about the people of Spring District and their complex negotiations with political-economic forces to remake their economic, social, and moral lives from a marginalized position as migrant waste laborers. It reveals not only their creativity and resilience but also the contradictions and ambivalence in their everyday practices of dealing with waste, caring for each other, and maintaining communal lives across locations and spaces. On another level, the book illuminates the little-known mobility of labor and material and the value creation in the waste economy, which is often considered as peripheral but in fact is integral to global consumption and production. Addressing the opportunities, dangers, power, and limits of remaking in this economy, it shows how local women and men seek to construct viable livelihoods and meaningful lives in the face of stigmatization, uncertainty, and precarity, as well as the uneven outcomes of their actions. Further, it highlights how market rationalities, moral economic ties, and socialist structures of feeling intermingle in people's practices of labor and livelihoods, care, and consumption to implicate on the remaking of gendered personhood and moral life.

*Waste and Wealth* contributes to studies of human economies and post/late-socialist transformations, showing how the forces of globalization blend with local historical-cultural dynamics to shape the ways in which people lead their economic and moral lives. Apart from the mobility of people and material—a central theme of globalization—here is also a story of globalization that is less tangible: how people's actions, and the moral meanings of their actions, rework market relations and capitalist motives. When converting the gains of their labor and mobility into locally meaningful values, the people of Spring District incorporate the logic of the market into their moral world, at once redrawing and reproducing the parameters of both. This process of remaking produces winners and losers, giving rise to new kinds of social relations in the local society and generating a great deal of anxiety, yet it is nonetheless one in which local people locate their value creation. These dynamics are complicated by the Vietnamese party-state's long-standing intent of molding people into certain kinds of moral personhood for its development agendas and the commodification of state power.

## Migrant Labor under Market Socialism: The Rise of the Peasant Entrepreneur

It has been more than three decades since pro-market reforms were formally introduced to Vietnam in the mid-1980s, eliminating much of the central planning, collectivization, and subsidization that had been the mainstays of state socialism. From a country with more than half of the population living in extreme poverty during the early 1980s, Vietnam has made substantial gains in economic development and general living standards. It has joined the ranks of middle-income countries, with an official rate of poverty about ten times lower than before the reforms and an expanding middle class. Although slowing down, the economy has still grown at seven percent, on average, in the last decade and a half. Urbanization, industrialization, and wealth concentration are occurring faster than ever, with rapidly changing patterns of production, consumption, and property ownership. These systems are now globally connected and financialized through the penetration of foreign capital and corporations, the rise of national capitalists, and Vietnam's participation in international trade agreements. Meanwhile, inequality is growing between social groups differentially positioned in the new economy, whose opportunity structure increasingly favors those with access to political power (Gainsborough 2010, Hayton 2010).

In Vietnam today, people live their lives more and more on the move and between places. Urbanization and industrialization around major urban centers have drawn millions of rural migrants, as agriculture-based livelihoods alone no longer sustain the growing costs of household reproduction. As elsewhere in East and Southeast Asia, labor migration has become one of the most common livelihood strategies for rural households (Fan 2008, Rigg and Vandergeest 2012). The normalization of mobility requires continuing adaptation by rural households (Resurreccion and Hà 2007, Hoang and Yeoh 2011, Vu and Agergaard 2012, Locke et al. 2014). Translocality, a process in which the household forms and sustains itself across multiple locations, has come to define rural people's mobility, much like it has elsewhere in Asia (Douglass 2012, Nguyen and Locke 2014). As we shall see, the people of Spring District have long engaged in translocal householding, adapting their mobility patterns to the care needs of household members over their life cycles and to the demands of their livelihoods. This process is intimately linked to distinct modes of circulation shaped by local men and women's shifting participation in the waste economy, intra-household negotiations, and the changing structure of the labor market.

Migrant labor has been essential to post-reform development, catering to the myriad needs of an expanding urban society. Yet the place of the rural migrant is uncertain in that society, where class distinction now takes for granted the privileges assumed by the urban middle class (Nguyen-Marshall et al. 2012, Nguyen 2015b). As providers of labor for manufacturing and urban services, rural migrants predominate either the informalized and personalized activities of self-employment and family businesses, or the rigid production regimes of global factories (Chan 2011, Tran 2013, Endres and Leshkowich 2018). Even as their labor is indispensable for maintaining urban lives and urban development, rural migrants are viewed as transgressors into urban society or, worse, as polluters of urban social and moral order (Leshkowich 2005, Turner and Schoenberger 2012). In the official rhetoric of urban order and civility, the presence of rural migrants in urban spaces is undesirable and needs to be done away with—as can be observed in the openly heavy-handed approach to street vendors during city beautification campaigns. Despite the easing of regulations, the household registration system (hộ khẩu), a socialist instrument of control, continues to limit people's mobility and social life. Similar to the Chinese hukou, it ties a citizen's social, legal, and political entitlements to her or his formally registered residence, restricting rural migrants' access to urban properties and services and formally categorizing them as outsiders in the city. The state's continued resistance to abolishing this divisive system suggests its interest in retaining the categories that have been produced for discipline and control.[1]

In the meantime, urbanization and industrialization have generated diverse spaces of livelihoods hitherto unavailable to people of rural origin, giving rise to "peasant entrepreneurs." Unlike the much-lauded postreform entrepreneurs who populate public imaginations as wealthy owners of companies and businesses, the peasant entrepreneurs tend to operate in small-scale ventures that are labor-intensive, requiring relatively little capital investment and based on rural networks. They provide the city with services of all sorts, such as street vending, catering, transport, and construction in the underbelly of the urban economy (see Zavoretti 2016 for a good discussion of the Chinese peasant worker as part of similar dynamics). While they are not as visible in public discourses as those entrepreneurs owning bank accounts and stock-market shares, the goods and services they produce are essential to the functioning of the urban economy and indeed urban life (see also Endres and Leshkowich 2018). In this manner, peasant households from Spring District, such as that of Mr. Quan and Ms. Quyên described in the Preface, have turned the waste from urban consumption and construction into a long-lasting enterprise. Here, waste trading is not just a seasonal activity for some. It has become a full-time occupation for many, something that local people identify as their "traditional trade" (nghề), to be mastered with skills and knowledge that can only be learned through experience and insider networks.

Yet the trajectory of prosperity that Mr. Quan assumes for his offspring and his village is by no means certain—it is in fact deeply dependent on processes that are beyond their control. For his village, now a commune of seven thousand people, to be wealthy as it is, for it to become "rich" with a history of "dealing in shit," has been not such an easy leap as it appears in his statement. It has required long years of local people's hard work and persistence in an economy at the shadowy edges of urban society, where they continue to struggle with dangers of all sorts and the inferior status of migrants working with waste. It has demanded their resilience against the ups and downs of the global waste trade, which is closely intertwined with volatile global production and consumption cycles. It has also required the continual reshuffling of care within and beyond the family, so that women and men could come and go to engage in migrant waste work. And their occupation with waste has not been without consequences. The stigma of working with it haunts people, leaving its marks on their gendered personhoods and on their social and moral lives.

Nonetheless, these peasant entrepreneurs from Spring District have formed trading networks stretching between city and countryside that are rooted in moral economic ties yet involve social relations reaching far beyond the district's boundaries. *Waste and Wealth* analyzes the ways in which the moral and social lives of these translocal networks are simultaneously transformed by, and are themselves constitutive of, political-economic processes under market socialism. At the center of these networks is waste. Rather than just the material basis for local livelihoods, waste constitutes a social category that shapes social relations and gendered moral personhood through the values and anxieties generated for the people and communities working with it.[2] Such dynamics of value creation are part of what I term "the political economy of remaking," a process in which the valuation of material, labor, and people is interwoven with hybrid moral ideas and paradoxical ideologies of development to implicate on economic and moral lives. This process is embedded in the material revaluation underlining the expansion of the recycling industry in many parts of the world (Gille 2007, Gill 2010, Alexander and Reno 2012, Parizeau 2013, Millar 2018). The outcomes of remaking are not just changing economic life and practices, but also a moral personhood that simultaneously references reciprocal ties and obligations, neoliberal ideas of the self, globalized aspirations, and socialist structures of feelings. These elements are continually reinvented in people's work of sustaining moral life and social relations, their labor and entrepreneurship, and their engagement with the state, the market, and other institutions. Their actions generate values that defy the devaluation of their labor and personhood yet are concurrently grounded in the moral ambiguities prevalent under market socialism. Before laying out the theoretical basis for the political economy of remaking, let us take a look at how waste and recycling have turned into central issues of globalization.

## Waste Global: Geographies of Recycling and Human Economies

According to a powerful argument in environmental studies, the waste of the North gets dumped onto the South as a result of global inequalities; waste is thereby viewed as a problem of overconsumption for the North and of poverty and urban management for the South (Gregson and Crang 2015). Global inequalities notwithstanding, waste collection and recycling are among the most important sources of livelihoods for millions of people around the globe, especially migrant and low-status laborers in the South (Sicular 1991, Medina 2000, Goldstein 2006, Wilson et al. 2006, Gill 2010). Waste economies, rather than being insular systems that concern only the poor and the marginalized (Birkbeck 1978, Sicular 1991), are integral to the global economy. In fact, the very construction of waste economies as somewhat peripheral to global capitalism undergirds how they function (Eriksen and Schober 2017). Even as these economies remain relatively hidden, waste has become a "prime fodder for privatization, an unregulated commons to which informal recyclers and larger firms struggle for access" and involving major global transactions (Alexander and Reno 2012: 20).

The global waste trade has been rising sharply alongside the high demand for recyclable material in emerging industrial countries, especially China (Goldstein 2006, Tong and Wang 2012, Minter 2013). In 2010 alone, China imported about 7.4 million tons of discarded plastic, 28 million tons of waste paper, and 5.8 million tons of steel scrap (Moses 2013). In the United States, hundreds of Chinese waste dealers tour scrapyards at any time, sending containers of waste metal worth tens of thousands of US dollars to China, where the imported waste trade is a high-level playing field dominated by powerful individuals and groups (Minter 2013). Official figures such as these likely are underestimated, however, if one takes into account the potentially huge amount being traded through informal cross-border trade between China and its neighbors. In Vietnam, Chinese waste dealers frequent recycling villages and urban depots throughout the country to buy pre-processed waste for cross-border export.[3]

As an industry, waste recycling has ramifications for the global system of production and consumption that China increasingly dominates. In *Junkyard Planet* (Minter 2013), Adam Minter provides a fascinating account of how the global waste market fluctuates according to the ups and down of the world economy. According to Minter, "[I]f manufacturers aren't manufacturing, the scrap dealers are among the first to feel it"; at his family's scrapyard in the United States, they always had the feeling that they "knew the direction the economic breeze was blowing months ahead of time" (2013: 231). During the global economic downturn in 2008–2009, prices for waste metal went down by eight to ninety percent worldwide, affecting millions of recyclers and trash pickers all over the globe (Thorpe 2009). At the end of 2008, as Chinese ports were "jammed up with thousands of devalued containers of American scrap metal that nobody wanted to claim as their own, much less pay for," waste traders from Spring District suffered the greatest losses in their history (Minter 2013: 235). Many depots were closed, with owners who had hoarded large amounts of waste metal losing hundreds of million đồng. Similar to the Chinese scrap traders in Minter's book, the waste traders in Vietnamese cities perhaps knew little about Lehman Brothers and its undoing, but they experienced first-hand its effects on the world economy. In another development, the Chinese government banned waste imports in 2018, sending shockwaves to rich countries that were used to shipping their waste to China, earning foreign exchanges while assuring consumers that their waste will be recycled. In my opinion, this ban is likely to cause a global reshuffling of the waste flows rather than halting them: the waste will instead go through other countries before they reach Chinese producers in preprocessed forms. The environmental costs of recycling will thus be shifted elsewhere, even as Chinese industries retain a stake in the global waste trade – the scenario would be congruent with China's rise in the global order.

In Chinese cities, meanwhile, migrant waste traders, who operate in similar ways as people from Spring District, carry on with what they have been doing for decades despite tighter government regulations (Mosbergen 2018). Waste work is not simply a frontier of livelihoods for large sections of the world's population (Gill 2010, Gregson and Crang 2015). As a human economy in which people are involved in tangible acts of labor (Hart and Sharp 2015), it fuels the very development of the kind being witnessed in emerging industrial countries such as China, India, and Vietnam. People's continued pursuit of economic activities such as waste trading, which are often seen as peripheral to or even as a shortcoming of the national economy, signals the viability of the economic life of a place, a city, a country, or even the global economy. Nevertheless, this should not prevent us from asking questions about the unequal power relations and broader forces that shape its unfolding. This book portrays waste as a vibrant economic domain that enables marginalized groups to gain access to the national and global economy, but also shows how exclusive political-economic processes and cultural distinctions lead to ambivalent and differentiated social outcomes (see also Gill 2010, Parizeau 2015, Millar 2018). Subsisting on the precarious existence of rural migrants in urban centers, the waste economy of Vietnam is subject to an institutional framework that hinders their participation in urban social life and the urban economy on equal terms with urban actors. Some households in Spring District successfully move up the hierarchy, capable of accumulating wealth, acquiring urban properties, or sustaining livelihoods and family life; others become indebted or bankrupt because of price fluctuations, accidents, tenure instability, or legal problems. These patterns of mobility engender anxieties and changing aspirations in local lives, generating social differentiation across rural and urban locations.

## The Political Economy of Remaking

In a forceful critique of globalization, sociologist Zygmunt Baumann (2004) views waste as the flipside of consumption and progress. For him, waste is not just the debris of objects and material, but also human beings made superfluous through the so-called progress: the unemployed, the refugee, the migrant, and so forth, categories of people who are made scapegoats for modern life's anxiety and the fear of becoming waste oneself. Baumann's metaphor of waste is powerful, yet it leaves little space for the agency and creativity asserted by the humans who are deemed as waste in the global order. Indeed, people working with waste, often marginalized social groups (the wasted humans, in Baumann's terms), have been shown to be politically active in the global processes of remaking involved with waste recycling (Alexander and Reno 2012, Gregson and Crang 2015, Millar 2018). Research has demonstrated that major economic categories such as labor, property, and value are reworked through these processes, involving intense moral and political struggles among individuals, social groups, industries, and nations over the valuation of waste and waste work (Alexander and Reno 2012). The exoticized figure of waste pickers and their devalued labor often contrasts with the "surprising significance of apparently small and undignified acts of collection and revaluation" (Alexander and Reno 2012: 19). People who work with waste reject the devaluation of their labor and personhood and demand recognition for their contributions (Fredericks 2012, Millar 2012). Yet their practices also reveal moral ambiguities arising from daily exposure to waste and from the ambivalence of waste as an in-between category (Reno 2009). In the work of recycling, therefore, not only are waste objects and material remade and revalued, but also the social relations that waste economies are part of—relations of gender, family and kinship, citizenship, and belonging.

Concerned with how such global dynamics play out in the Vietnamese waste economy, the political economy of remaking is a process in which, through the labor and mobility of the traders, waste generates value for families, communities, and regions as well as the social status and gendered personhood of attendant actors. This process, I will show, is implicated in the politics of morality and value emerging from Vietnam's political-historical context in which enduring cultural forms come into play with globalized imaginaries about the future. The process is thus not just political-economic, but also deeply moral. Therefore, why not call it "the moral economy of remaking," the reader might be wondering.

## Morality and Political Economy

Spring District is in the same region inhabited by the early twentieth-century Southeast Asian peasant communities that James Scott (1976) analyzes in *The Moral Economy of the Peasant*. Based on Edward P. Thompson's (1971) work on eighteenth-century rural England, Scott identifies reciprocity and the right to subsistence as the two central moral principles of Southeast Asian peasant politics.[4] These moral norms shape the economic relationships between people of differential standing in village societies, creating a whole spectrum of patron-client arrangements. Although these arrangements shift according to the power relations between rural elite and peasants in local societies, the two principles generally provide moral resources for the latter to negotiate their livelihood goals with the former. A violation of these principles, Scott argues, would lead to resentment, resistance, or even actions to usurp the existing social order. While Scott foresaw the likelihood of greater migration out of these rural communities, the peasants he wrote about were much less mobile than today's villagers. Spring District's rural networks now span Vietnam's major urban centers, and the waste economy that they are part of is a vast economic system connected to the global market and the main sectors of the national economy. The notion of moral economy thereby remains useful for understanding how these translocal networks are sustained when people are on the move. It is also good for thinking about "value as morality" (Otto and Willerslev 2013: 15)—that is, how the value of economic practices is defined through the moral world in which they are embedded. As we shall see, subsistence and reciprocity (sometimes metamorphosing into the language of care) are frequently evoked by the waste traders to make claims or to justify their actions.

Nevertheless, moral economy as a concept does not capture the ways in which the moral world is continually remade by political-economic forces and people's reflexive engagement with the structural conditions of their life. It provides little scope to consider how market rationalities and state development ideologies are incorporated into people's lives through the existing moral repertoires of local societies (Muehlebach 2012, Nguyen et al. 2017). Indeed, the Vietnamese moral framework today mixes and matches neoliberal ideologies with socialist values and enduring cultural norms; local people draw on this hybrid framework to evaluate their actions and make social claims, albeit with much ambivalence. It is through such exercises of "moral reasoning" (Sykes 2009) in a world full of contradictions and uncertainties that the moral becomes deeply entangled with the political.

The notion of "the political economy of remaking" foregrounds my argument that the moral is constitutive of political economy. It does not just evoke norms-based mechanisms that provide people with the resources to correct or resist the effects of political-economic forces (Scott 1977, Fassin 2009) or represent a dimension of the economy (Hann 2017). The moral, I argue, is a driving force that shapes how the political economy of Vietnam today has been unfolding. As powerful social institutions seek to mold a certain kind of moral person that suits the new economy, the people of Spring District, like other Vietnamese, pursue their own project of self-making that encompasses acquiring a better life and remaking their place in the social order. In doing so, however, they partake in fashioning a moral personhood that is suitable for the governing approach of market socialism, one that combines privatization with authoritarianism. The political economy of remaking, therefore, captures both the production of economic value and the production of the moral person as part of social relationships, economic networks, communities, and nation. In the waste economy, it begins with the mundane act of recycling by the migrant waste traders and their daily engagements with their social and political contexts. Underlying the multilayered production is the centrality of waste labor and its social valuation.

## Waste, Labor, and the Politics of Value

It is a truism to say that waste has a value, in the sense that a monetary value can be derived from waste through its reincorporation in productive cycles as recycled material. As David Graeber (2001) points out, however, value can be understood as that which drives people to actions and gives meanings to these actions; it is what makes life worth living. Nevertheless, the creation of value is never straightforward—it is a deeply contested process socially, politically, and morally (Appadurai 1986, Myers 2001). Considering waste recycling as a process of value creation reveals the transformative powers of the people working with it: the values that they create from waste are consequential not only for family and communal life, but also for the economy and society as a whole. As we shall see, however, the value creation at times occurs at the very moment their labor and personhood are degraded, and at times it is sustained by moral ambiguity in people's dealings with power. The meanings of waste are thus deeply interwoven with the social status of the people working with it, at once shaping their economic and moral lives.

### *Revaluing Waste*

Waste can be defined as that which is no longer wanted—objects and material that people want to dispose of, to make disappear and out of sight, either because they cease to be useful, meaningful, or functional. It is "both an unwanted, unintended side effect of human activities, and inevitably also a social construct," that emerges out of the human need to be assured of the existence of social order (Eriksen and Schober 2017: 283). Not only do waste items become useless and valueless for the people who discard them, but they might also turn into disturbances and threats. Through the act of disposal, waste assumes the character of dirt: it represents social disorder, its presence threatens the stability of established social patterns, and according to Mary Douglas, it is "essentially a question of matter out of place," so removing it protects the social order (36). What counts as waste in a society is determined by the particular social relations that define the appropriate order of things, relations that "impose system on an inherently untidy experience"; the presence of waste therefore signals transgression of social boundaries (1966: 4). In *Rubbish Theory*, however, Michael Thompson (1979) suggests that social boundaries do not remain unchanged: they shift, they blur, they become noticeable within contexts, especially through the exchanges between people of different worldviews. This observation dovetails with Appadurai's idea that objects and material move between "regimes of values" (1986: 15), systems in which specific political, cultural, and social mechanisms define the value of things. In this way, waste can also be thought of as a stage in the "social life of things," to use Appadurai's words, when objects undergo a period of value ambiguity, being reassessed to be disposed of or re-created. It is "part of an ongoing social process" involving "complex social arrangements that enroll a broad range of institutions, regulations, and technologies in [its] circulation and transformation" (Reno 2009: 30–31).

The contributors to Alexander and Reno's (2012) important volume on global recycling economies suggest that such valuation of waste is inseparable from struggles over the value of the people working with it, whose existence is often constructed around tropes of the abject outcast or the social parasite. Waste workers, traders, and trash pickers are commonly perceived as dirty and morally dubious, as a menace to the public, and historically, this perception has been conflated with the depiction of people working with waste as a potential source of harm and pollution (Cohen and Johnson 2005, Zimring 2017). For the workers themselves, however, the implications of waste and their relations to it are manifold, simultaneously offering and limiting the scope for transformation (Reno 2016, Millar 2018).

In Spring District, these social relations evolve out of local people's long-term engagement with the waste economy across rural and urban spaces. Even as waste represents the debris of rising consumption and obstacles to civilized living for urban people, it constitutes a material and symbolic base for the migrant waste traders, both abject and desirable, from which men and women build their lives, care for their families, and craft their identities. In their practices, local people do not just create the economic value of waste, but also transform it into social values important for sustaining family and communal life, thus remaking their place, and the place of the countryside, in the social order. Yet waste is also problematic as a social category entrenched in constructions of gender and class, based on which social and spatial boundaries are erected to mark the pure from the impure, the moral from the immoral, and the messy from the orderly (Douglas 1966, Thompson 1979). In Vietnam today, waste is indicative of the moral danger perceived by the urban middle class in the presence of the migrant laborer, especially that of the female laboring body, seen as disrupting the urban order in both public and domestic spaces (Leshkowich 2005, Nguyen 2015b).

## The Labor of Waste: Gender, Class, and Performance

In *The Social Life of Things*, Appadurai (1986) states that the value of commodities is not determined by the sum of labor necessary for their production, but largely arises from cultural and social valuation. While also highlighting the cultural and social valuation of waste, I shall maintain the Marxian view of labor as the primary source of value. In the waste economy, labor is the precondition for the removal of waste's ambiguous status and turning it into a commodity—hard, tedious, and often exhausting labor that collects, buys, cleans, weighs, sorts, classifies, packs, presses, loads and unloads, transports, strips, disassembles and reassembles, and so forth. This is bodily labor that is visible and even measurable by time units. Yet waste work also involves other forms of labor. Chapter 2 describes the labor of performing a certain persona for the purpose of getting through a transaction: waste traders tend to downplay the value of waste vis-à-vis the urban public, at times along with the value of their personhood, in order for waste to generate economic value. Chapter 3 shows the labor of maintaining relationships with diverse actors in the recycling economy, such as urban householders, local authorities, or policemen, which involves the intricate act of negotiating power imbalances, often through gift exchange and patron-client networks. In short, labor, in all its bodily, performative, and relational dimensions, is central to the creation of value from waste.

Rather than being confined to the economic realm, however, the valuation of labor itself depends on cultural-historical contexts. The market economy has brought with it significant shifts in the value of labor (see also Nguyen 2015b). During state socialism, labor was celebrated as the primary resource for socialist construction, embodied by the honored and relatively protected socialist working class. Even waste labor was given a high social and political value, as indicated in a school textbook poem by the influential socialist poet Tố Hữu that glorifies the street sanitation worker; depicted as "like iron, like bronze," she is immortalized for her labor of cleaning up the streets of Hanoi (Box I.1). However, in a society now much more preoccupied with consumption and class distinction, labor has come to be associated with the body of the rural migrant, as the urban middle class distinguishes itself through an orientation toward work related to the mind (Nguyen 2015b). This turn is closely linked to the global devaluation of labor resulting from the increasing disconnection between production and the accumulation of wealth (Li 2010, Ferguson 2015).

As we shall see, when performing as the abject rural migrant or the self-sacrificing mother, men and women from Spring District deploy ideal categories of class and gender for their own purposes, thus creating differential value for their gendered personhood. Whereas such strategies are productive for their livelihoods and eventual social mobility, they also help to essentialize the very categories that define them as the lowly Other. Likewise, when maintaining patron-client relationship with powerful actors, waste traders carve out spaces for their actions, yet concurrently reproduce the very power structure that sustains itself on the basis of their marginalization.

The creation of value in the waste economy is therefore defined by the traders' gendered positioning in social hierarchies. In this vein, Fred Myers (2001) writes about a *politics of value* that refers to the fraught process of value creation by actors who occupy different locations in the social order. It concerns not only the value of objects and material, but also that of persons, of citizens, and of social relationships, which is "never simply defined, but is always involved in global as well as local circuits of exchange" (Myers 2001: 8). More than just the appropriation of value by social actors, however, a politics of value is ultimately about the definition of what value actually is (Graeber 2001). Chapters 5 and 7 show how the Vietnamese party-state seeks to set the benchmark for personhood and development while holding local people accountable for its development goals. In Spring District, the values generated from migrant waste work are actively mobilized for state projects such as the New Countryside Program, or the "socialization" policy that shift responsibilities for care and well-being on individuals, households, and communities. This takes place along with tacit disapproval of waste trading as a form of migrant livelihood, something that is deemed as socially and morally destabilizing for rural communities and as infringing on urban aesthetic (*làm mất mỹ quan đô thị*). Local people often voice skepticism and contestations of state

---

**BOX I.1    THE SOUND OF THE BAMBOO SWEEPER**

| | |
|---|---|
| Summer nights | Winter nights |
| When the cicadas | When the storm subsides |
| Have gone to sleep | I see |
| I hear | On the cold street |
| On Tran Phu street | The female sanitation worker |
| The sound of the bamboo sweeper | Like iron |
| Rustling through the tamarind trees | Like bronze |
| The sound of the bamboo sweeper | The female sanitation worker |
| In summer nights | In winter nights |
| Whisking away garbage... | Sweeping away the trash. |

---

Source: Extract from *The Sound of the Bamboo Sweeper* (*Tiếng chổi tre*), Tố Hữu, 1961 (author's translation) Gió lộng. Hanoi: Literature Publishing House.

discourses, but equally often, they willingly consider themselves as having a role in realizing the state-initiated goals of development. To a certain extent, therefore, their practices help to foster the ideas of self-enterprise and self-reliance promoted by the post-reform state, which seeks to "socialize" as much as possible its responsibilities. Such politics of value are inseparable from the politics of morality I will turn to next, political-cultural dynamics that betray an uneasy mixture of older notions of moral order, socialist principles, and neoliberal moral logics.

## Exemplary Society and the Politics of Morality

Originally thought of as a series of measures to lift the country out of economic stagnation, the economic reform program known as đổi mới (renovation) has been followed by significant political transformations. Despite the continued political monopoly of the Communist Party, the state's interventions in private and social life have shifted in both nature and intensity. Under what is now known as market socialism, neoliberal principles mix with socialist institutions and practices, forming techniques of governance that appeal to citizens more through moral means than via coercion. The particular mixture of authoritarianism with liberalism produces a moral subject who is self-choosing and self-responsible yet remains politically governable by the state (Schwenkel and Leshkowich 2012, Nguyen-Vo 2008, Nguyen and Chen 2017). While people are left alone with their own consumer choices and to their own devices, there is an ever-present will to control society by the party-state, in ways similar to those that Li Zhang and Aihwa Ong (2008) have written about in post-reform China.

Social control in Vietnam, however, has often been exercised via cultural means, be it under any political system. Similar to China, Vietnam is an "exemplary society," one that builds its social norms on "memories of the past and dreams about the future," according to Børge Bakken (2000: 72). These two backward-and forward-looking elements blend and transform each other, so that the memories are invoked not just to revive traditional ideas and practices, but also to control the present and justify certain visions of social order. They form what Bakken terms "exemplary norms" (2000: 9), or norms that are deployed to simultaneously discipline and educate people. Therefore, rather than just through punishment and coercion, social control is instituted through models of learning that cultivate the moral behavior necessary for an orderly society while rendering social change predictable.[5] Here, Bakken articulates a distinct idea in the Chinese society that is quite similar in Vietnam—the idea that people are inherently able to learn from models and that models are necessary for fashioning people's actions toward social goals. This idea is a key cultural norm that links the moral basis of individual and group actions with how these societies have been governed. Throughout different eras, moral education in Vietnam has often been modeled on narratives about the good deeds/sacrifices of the exemplary persons, which often oscillate between myths and real life (Jamieson 1993, Malarney 2007).

The exemplary persons of market socialism differ from the model workers, soldiers, and agricultural producers of state socialism—the citizens who were ready to sacrifice individual interests for socialist construction and national defense (MacLean 2013). In the new economy, they are the successful male entrepreneur, the civilized urban citizen, and the middle-class woman who excels professionally yet remains devoted to her family (Nguyen-Vo 2008, Nguyen 2015b, Jacka 2017). Embodying the desired prosperity and development of the nation, these new exemplary persons are educated, civilized in habits and lifestyles, and global in outlook while having compassion for the disadvantaged. Unlike the poor or the rural migrant, they are able to navigate the human capital demands of the new economy. Above all, they embody a moral order amidst the anxieties generated by marketization and encounters with global forces (for a discussion of similar dynamics in China, see Anagnost 2004).

Post-reform exemplary norms are epitomized in the discourse of *dân trí/trình độ dân trí* (intellectual level of the people), which categorizes people and regions according to their levels of human capital. Although semantically different in meaning from the Chinese term *suzhi* (human quality),[6] *dân trí* similarly suggests a gradient of human development measured on people's educational level, their knowledge of science and technologies, their social behavior, their awareness of the law, and so forth (see also Gammeltoft 2015, Harms 2016).[7] In the party-state's view, to raise the level of *dân trí* is essential to developing the human resources needed for industrialization and modernization of the nation.[8] In popular discourse, areas with a high concentration of educated, middle-class people are said to be of high *dân trí*; rural and mountainous areas are poor, because they have low *dân trí*; and people commit crimes and violate the law for the same reason. Like the discourse of *suzhi* in China (Anagnost 2004, Kipnis 2007), *dân trí* is supposed to have a causal correlation with human development. Because one has low *dân trí*, one is poor and unruly, and vice versa; low *dân trí* thus is deemed both the cause and the effect of poverty, disorder, and underdevelopment. And as long as a community has high *dân trí*, its members are supposedly able to overcome unemployment, rising cost of living, a volatile market, and unequal life chances in order to succeed. In other words, if you emulate the actions of the exemplary persons, you can attain their achievements, thus helping to improve the "intellectual level" of yourself, your community, and your country.

The exemplary society will become visible through this book's discussions on how waste traders from Spring District engage with state narratives of development such as that of a "New Countryside" (*nông thôn mới*) or of "socialization" (*xã hội hóa*). Whereas the New Countryside refers to a modern form of rurality, socialization centers on a doctrine that individuals and families are primarily responsible for their own well-being, while communities, social organizations, and private entities participate in provisioning for those incapable of doing so. These policy narratives are at once weaved out of neoliberal notions of self-enterprise and self-responsibility (see Rose 1999) and an enduring moral order in which "harmony, stability, cohesion, constancy, sacrifice, control of self, and attachment to the groups are story-lines again and again" (Bakken 2000: 170). The practices of Spring District waste traders are shaped by hybrid forms of subjectivities and social relations that draw on the exemplary norms of market socialism. In their stories lie the production of success and failure that not only involves a capacity to make a living, but also the ability to transform it into social recognition, through caring and being cared for and through consumption and aspirations for a good life. These stories are about the struggles to be and to become a certain kind of moral person in the face of the contradicting demands of market socialism—demands for order and stability at the same time as demands for prosperity and development (see also Nguyen-Vo 2008). These struggles give rise to a politics of morality in which moral economic ideas and state agendas clash and mesh with each other in ways that are meaningful for people, but also invoke in them subtle forms of resistance, irony, or ambivalence.

I use the terms *morality* and *ethics* as distinct from each other. Morality here refers to locally meaningful systems of value that guide people's social conduct and their ways of being in the world—for example, the inside/outside categories (*nội/ngoại*). In Vietnam, these value systems culminate in the twin concepts of *thành người* (becoming human), or becoming a fully developed social being through acquiring the attributes necessary for conducting a moral life (see also Gammeltoft 2014), and *làm người* (doing human), or living the moral life of the person (see Chapter 4). Ethics, meanwhile, is about ways of acting on the world by social actors who are often confronted with moral challenges or dilemmas in everyday life—for instance, the ethic of risk-taking embraced by the waste traders who operate under conditions of uncertainty and ambiguity (see Chapter 3). Clearly, these two notions are intertwined and at times might not be distinguishable (Lambek 2010, Stafford 2013). Often, however, there is a tension between them, requiring people to make compromises or to engage in efforts aimed at restoring the moral categories that they have transgressed as a result of adopting certain ethics in their daily actions.

## Desires, Aspirations, and Fictional Expectations

In Vietnam today, questions of value and morality are invariably connected to what the sociologist Jens Beckert (2016) terms *fictional expectations*. Evoking Benedict Anderson's (2006) notion of *imagined communities*, which underscores how social imaginaries about the past and the present have produced the nation-state, Beckert argues that global capitalism has been driven by imaginaries of the future as inhabiting limitless economic opportunities. Fictional expectations refer to this temporal orientation in which actors form images of future development, outcomes of their actions, and trust in the value of goods and money to "orient their decision making *despite* the incalculability of the outcomes" (Beckert 2016: 9, emphasis in original). These expectations are fictional since they exist as mental, and sometimes emotional, representations that give actors the confidence to act as if certain outcomes are assured—for example, the expectation that investment in the stock market will eventually pay off, or that higher education will bring about better income and social status—even if there is evidence otherwise. Often, the powerful—the state or global corporations, for instance—influence the expectations of others through defining imaginaries about the future. These actors relentlessly vie to craft the most convincing narrative of a lifestyle, product, or development goal, thereby creating fictional expectations among citizens and consumers. In this struggle, power is derived through the very uncertainty of the future, and while these expectations are fictional, they have real consequences for people's lives.

If socialism has always been oriented toward imaginaries of the future in which collective well-being and social harmony predominate, the fictional expectations Beckert refers to are premised on consumption and private accumulation of wealth. In Vietnam today, both kinds of imaginaries can be detected in social and political life, although the latter holds increasingly greater sway. They are entangled with aspirations for cosmopolitan experiences and global valuation of personal and national identities, akin to what Lisa Rofel (2007) calls a "desiring project" in China. As privatization becomes further entrenched, such desires and aspirations are embraced by people of all walks of life to varying degrees, even as the gap between them widens.

In her influential analysis of precarity in post-industrial societies, Lauren Berlant (2011) describes a situation of "cruel optimism," in which people's fantasies of the good life turn into sufferings, given that this promise has lost much of its foundation in "the precarious present." This precarious present contrasts with a past in which social mobility and secure employment were the norm, and people in these societies are poignantly trapped by their attachment to these ideals. Like for many others in the South, however, for the people of Spring District, precarity has always been a normal part of life, including at the height of state socialism. Desires and aspirations can be treacherous if their objects—in this case, dominant ways of living the good life—are meant to be elusive, especially for people like the waste trades, who are working in an economy heavily dependent on the booms and busts of the global market. Some of them have come to realize that long years of investment in their children's higher education do not necessarily lead to the desired white-collar jobs that might help the latter graduate from waste work. Others struggle with indebtedness; with loss of livelihoods due to health problems, accidents, and legal troubles; or with a vicious circle of family separation. The perils of disenchantment are around the corner, spawning imminent anxieties over falling through the cracks, not being cared for, children turning bad (hồng), and being deemed the outcast—anxieties that are inseparable from the moral implications of waste. Nonetheless, desires and aspirations, rather than hindrances, drive their actions and shape how they make sense of these actions—indeed, the very valuation of their lives. These desires and aspirations are a moral force that guides them in their negotiations with the uncertainties of the waste economy. As we shall see, when weaving the "fictional expectations" of global capitalism into their project of remaking, local people also domesticate them through the logics of care, belonging, and communal life.

## Overview of the Chapters

The structure of this book mirrors the two components of the political economy of remaking. In Part I, "Waste," I discuss the patterns of labor mobility, the spatial and social dynamics of the urban waste trade, the ways in which men and women conduct their trading activities, and how they negotiate with the precarious conditions of the waste economy. In short, Part I is about how people generate economic value from waste in the face of fluctuations in the global market, and how their actions thereby remake ideal categories of class and gender and their place the urban order. In Part II, "Wealth," the chapters grapple with how value is created in and through practices of care, consumption, and local development, and with how the uneven process of value creation is underlined by the politics of value and morality in the remaking of social and moral life.

Chapter 1 characterizes the variable patterns of gendered mobility, household organization, and migrant networks of Spring District people in the last several decades. The chapter shows that these have shifted alongside the expansion of the urban waste economy, but also remain rooted in the enduring gendered binary of inside and outside (*nội/ngoại*). Waste work is at the center of a process of translocal householding in which men and women from the district have been alternately partaking, carrying out their livelihood activities and familial duties from different locations. In this process, their orientations toward the inside or outside are varyingly performed and enacted by different generations of men and women who reproduce normative ideas of gender when on the move, while acting in ways that transgress the boundaries between the two domains.

Chapters 2 and 3 concentrate on activities within the urban waste economy, highlighting how local people build networks, appropriate urban spaces, and how they deal with the risks of waste trading, thereby remaking the urban space and order. Chapter 2 characterizes how local women and men carry out their trade through gendered performances of social roles that both play into and undercut urban stereotypes of migrants working with waste as dirty, pitiable, and morally dubious. Chapter 3 goes further into their negotiations with other actors within the waste economy. Wherever they carry out their trade, dangers loom in a zone of ambiguity, "half-dark, half-light," with illicit dealings and patron-client ties in which they are often in a position of lesser power. This chapter highlights the moral ambiguity underlining practices and linkages within the economy, showing that the waste traders play an active role in reproducing it through an everyday ethic of risk-taking. Together, these two chapters highlight the opportunities and the dangers that arise from uncertainties in the global economy and urban development, the marginal status of migrant laborers, and the commodification of state power.

If Part I demonstrates urban class dynamics that devalue the waste traders' labor and personhood, Part II shows how they seek to create value for their actions through practices of care, consumption, and local development, and how these practices are fraught with anxiety and tension. Their project of remaking is at once shaped by globalized desires for urban middle-class life, the state-initiated discourse of "intellectual level of the people" (*dân trí*), and their interpretations of expectations within family and kinship. Chapters 4 and 6 suggest that waste-generated money enables local women and men to carry out their obligations of care and reciprocity while pursuing their aspirations for the good life. Yet the social implications of waste often undermine the outcomes of their endeavors. Quite a few are unable to make the transformation; their problems attest to the anxieties of translocal householding and the moral dangers of waste.

Chapter 5 and 7 examine how the waste traders position themselves vis-à-vis state development projects and discourses, how they draw on these for evaluating their actions, and how they participate in the moralization of success and failure that punishes failing as an individual matter. Chapter 5 demonstrates how the entrepreneurial pursuits of a number of returning waste traders play into the state vision of a "New Countryside." Seeking to distance themselves from waste and driven by aspirations for "civilized living" in the home place, some have taken advantage of the limited opportunities for land use and market access created by the absence of villagers who remain in the waste trade. While seeing through the self-responsibilizing logics of the state's development goals, they also find in these a space of social recognition. Meanwhile, the pitfalls of rural entrepreneurship and the limit of their aspirations reveal the uncertainties that reverberate across the city and the countryside. For these households, urban waste work keeps lurking in the background as a fallback option, indicating the deeply translocal character of the rural household today. Chapter 7 juxtaposes the construction of a local exemplary waste trader with that of people who have fallen through the cracks and links these constructions to the moral logics of the state's "socialization" policy. The chapter highlights the making of the striving individual who is driven by the dream of success and the fear of falling, a process that is co-constituted by state, market, and moral economic institutions. The process results in a punitive evaluative framework for those who fail or who choose to act otherwise.

The Conclusion reflects on how the dynamics of the waste trade tie in with global processes of labor mobility, material remaking, and neoliberalization to shape the remaking of gendered moral personhood and social relations. This chapter also considers how global ideologies are domesticated by moral economic ideas and the post-reform party-state's governing approach, especially the deployment of exemplary norms for its developmental agenda. The political economy of remaking, I argue, signifies how marginalized people and communities all over the world have been engaging with the uncertainties of the economy and politics to generate values and sustain moral lives.

Finally, a note on how I address people in the book: informants who are older than me are referred to as Mr. or Ms., whereas those who are about my age and younger are referred to with their first name (I will be in my early forties by the time this book is published). This is an effort to reflect the hierarchical system of address in Vietnam in which people are varyingly addressed depending on their age, gender, and the social relationships they have with others, and my place in the system.

Waste, unsorted.
Source: Author's photo, Hanoi, 2012.

# PART I

# Waste

## CHAPTER 1

# Mobility, Networks, and Gendered Householding

M s. Lan sets the handful of freshly cut green bananas from the garden beside newly filled cups of rainwater on the family altar and lights the incense sticks. Once the incense sticks have died out, she goes out into the yard, sets alight the paper money that had been displayed on the altar, and mumbles some prayers as it burns. It is an offering to the ancestors, so that they will protect her during her next trip. "I'll have to leave at exactly ten past twelve. One should always depart past the hour, for good luck," she says. Neatly dressed in dark green jeans and a patterned, synthetic, long-sleeved shirt, she has a backpack on and carries a heavy bag containing homegrown rice and vegetables. She looks ready to go: "I always have to dress myself properly when I leave. One should not look too sloppy when one goes outside." At ten past noon, I take her by motorbike to the bus stop, where a group of villagers with similar bags of rice are waiting to leave for Hanoi. The trip takes about three hours to the main bus station, and then she travels another half-hour to reach the run-down and crowded lodging, hidden within a dark and narrow alley in central Hanoi, that she shares with other villagers from Spring District, most of whom are itinerant waste traders like her. (Figure 1.1 depicts the typical sleeping and living space of itinerant junk traders from Spring District like Ms. Lan; this particular room is shared by four women.)

Her departure is a snapshot of the comings and goings of men and women in Spring District over the past three decades. In her mid-forties, Ms. Lan is a married woman with two grown children from Red Spring

FIGURE 1.1  Inside the rental lodging of migrant junk traders.
Source: Author's photo, Hanoi, 2012.

commune, the neighboring commune of Mr. Quan's Green Spring. During the 1990s, she took some time to follow in the footsteps of Green Spring people, initially being concerned about the moral dangers of "going outside" to work away from home and the status implications of waste work. We shall see that the varying mobility trajectories of her family members indicate the ways in which waste networks from the district have evolved along with the rising consumption and construction in Vietnam's expanding urban centers. As the networks grow, local households extend their spatial and social boundaries to meet the demands of migrant livelihoods, much like in other places of Asia (Douglass 2012, Nguyen and Locke 2014). This chapter shows that mobility continually remakes local ideas of gendered spaces and reciprocity at the same time that these notions shape local people's lives on the move.

Until recently, migration scholarship has predominantly assumed a dichotomy between migrants and left-behind family members, based on a static notion of the household, for which migration is abnormal to its organization. The fixation on a presumed division between migrants and those left behind, however, obscures the ongoing processes by which the household organizes and deploys its labor for multiple purposes in response to shifting systemic conditions. It fails to account for past migratory trajectories, life-cycle dynamics, and ways in which households increasingly operate across geographical locations (Rigg and Salamanca 2011, Huijsmans 2014, Jacka 2012). According to geographer Mike Douglass, processes of forming and maintaining households have to be seen as projects sustained across multiple locations and through varied social formations as households seek solutions to "local disjunctures" underpinning global movements of labor and persons (2012: 12). These disjunctures include issues such as population aging, changing marriage and childbearing patterns, and declining public social provision. Earlier writings on transnationalism also emphasized the "processes by which immigrants build social fields that link together their country of origin and their country of settlement," maintaining economic, social, and political ties that extend beyond borders (Schiller et al. 1992: 1). While these authors are more concerned with cross-border mobility, the same can be said of processes taking place within countries with differential regimes of mobility, such as Vietnam and China (Nguyen and Locke 2014). In this book, I use the term *translocal/ity* to refer to mobility trajectories in which household reproduction occurs across locations and spaces, regardless of whether these are translocal or transnational.

Since the last century, authors from various disciplines have paid special attention to the household and its dynamics (Thorner et al. 1966, Folbre 1986, Sen 1990, Agarwal 1997). Anthropological research, in particular, has long gone beyond viewing the household as either a unified unit of altruism and cooperation or a site of patriarchal oppression and conflict (Moore 1994). It recognizes that the household features "shifting relationships of authority, influence and emotional solidarity" (Yanagisako 1979: 185), constituting "a locus of competing interests, rights, obligations and resources, where household members are often involved in bargaining, negotiation and possibly even conflict" (Moore 1994: 87). Thinking about these complex dynamics through the householding framework allows us to consider the household's multidirectional and transboundary trajectories today, trajectories that in turn remake the moral categories guiding the mobility of household members.

## Householding, Networks, and Reciprocity

As privatization becomes further entrenched in Vietnam, the rising cost of living, dispossession of landed properties, and shortage of local employment opportunities make it imperative for rural households to embrace migrant livelihoods (Nguyen and Locke 2014). Householding is foregrounded as much by these post-reform political-economic conditions as by men and women's practices of mobility and the meanings of these practices for family life. In Spring District, householding is profoundly implicated in migrant waste work as the mainstay of migrant livelihoods.

## Cities as the New Economic Zone

A local joke in Spring District refers to Hanoi as its "New Economic Zone." The joke is an inverted reference to the fact that hundreds of households were sent to New Economic Zones in remote areas as part of the state resettlement schemes in the 1960s–1970s. Historically, such movement typically flowed from the delta to distant frontiers, but in this joke, the capital city is made into a frontier site. The joke also refers to a contemporary reality: in recent years, labor migration has been taking place alongside a steady stream of high-school graduates migrating to gain a higher education, many with a view to settling in the city or returning home to work in the local government. This other stream of migrants largely originates from areas such as township centers, where local government officials and employees are concentrated.

The modesty of itinerant waste traders such as Ms. Lan and the apparent cheapness of the waste in which they trade disguise a thriving economy that has been alternately enabled and caused to fluctuate by the changeable political-economic conditions since the reform (đổi mới). I shall specify the practices and social relations of this economy in the next two chapters. For this chapter, however, it is important to point out the main activities in the waste trade and how they have come to shape household trajectories. These include engaging in itinerant trade (door-to-door buyers, a predominantly female occupation), operating fixed-location depots (typically a household business), and driving transport vehicles (typically male owners of minitrucks who transport waste from depots to large buyers or recyclers), though a few households have become large-scale dealers. By the late 1990s, the number of itinerant waste traders in Hanoi from Spring District and other localities had reached tens of thousands (see also Mitchell 2008). Hundreds of households from the district, especially from Green Spring, have switched to operating urban waste depots, buying waste from businesses and itinerant junk traders. A waste depot is potentially more profitable but demands greater capital and labor inputs; thus, both spouses tend to migrate together. A transport vehicle is often an extension of a waste depot that has accumulated sufficiently to expand into waste transport, an operation entirely performed by men.

The difference between itinerant and fixed-location waste trading (waste depots) shapes the mobility patterns of men and women from the district and their positioning in the householding project. Table 1.1 summarizes the major local household trajectories of Spring District migration during the last several decades; the time division indicates when a particular trajectory became common. Until the mid-1980s, it was more common for men to migrate, either to the city for any kind of manual work or to gold mines in remote regions; in addition, most adult men were in military service for several years. In the stagnant economy of that time, the mobility of adult male members did not make a difference to the household economy. Toward the end of the 1980s, however, women—who had been in charge of household affairs in their husbands' absence—started to go to Hanoi in greater numbers to work as itinerant waste

TABLE 1.1 **Household Trajectories of Migrant Livelihoods in Spring District**

|  | UNTIL MID-1980S | LATE 1980S AND 1990S | LATE 1990S AND 2000S | FROM 2000S |
|---|---|---|---|---|
| **Role of Migration** | Migration not significant for household livelihoods. | Circular migration significant for household livelihoods. | Circular migration a major component of household livelihoods. | Permanent migration by some households; circular migration still important. |
| **Popular Migrant Activities** | Gold digging, manual labor, junk trading. Remittance insignificant; agriculture main income. | Junk trading combined with cleaning (women), motorbike taxi (men). Remittance significant. | Recycling depots, transport vehicles. Remittance decisive. | Successful depots shift to other urban small enterprises. Remittance main income for elderly. |
| **Dominant Household Division of Labor** | Husband migrates; wife stays home to do agriculture and care for children and elderly. | Wife migrates; husband stays home to do agriculture and care for children and elderly. | Husband and wife migrate together; children live with grandparents. No agriculture (land is loaned or rented). | Whole households migrate to cities; elderly stay. No agriculture (land is loaned or rented). |

Source: Author's compliation.

traders (like Ms. Quyên in the Preface). As the waste market started to expand alongside growing urban consumption and construction in the 1990s, urban waste trading surpassed agricultural production in terms of contributions to household income. For many families, the waste trade has now developed into household businesses that require both men and women to be on the move, leaving children with grandparents and sometimes abandoning agriculture altogether. Since the 2000s, a number of households have settled in the cities, either running successful depots or having shifted to other urban small businesses while retaining property and kinship ties to the village.

## Waste Networks: Money, Reciprocity, and Distance

With more households from Spring District entering the depot business, Hanoi and other northern cities are showing signs of saturation, while urban developments are pushing out depot operators in central locations. Therefore, southern industrial provinces, such as Bình Dương, and the largest urban center, Hồ Chí Minh City (HCM City), have become attractive locations. Whereas Hanoi is relatively close, allowing the circular migration that many itinerant traders from the district are practicing, HCM City is more than a thousand kilometers away. Spring District families choosing to go to HCM City thus tend to relocate together, often to set up a waste depot in one of its outlying districts (waste depots are banned in the inner districts). Whereas itinerant traders in Hanoi are from Spring District or provinces near Hanoi, itinerant traders in HCM City come from the central coast, northern mountains, and southern regions (e.g., Thanh Hóa, Vĩnh Phúc, and Vĩnh Long provinces) (Luong 2018). In addition, the itinerant traders in Hanoi regularly go back and forth between the city and their home village, unlike the itinerant traders from these other regions, who as mentioned tend to migrate together with their family to HCM City.

As a result, the waste trade in Hanoi centers on denser networks of kin and village ties. In HCM City, the networks are more diffused, in many cases featuring depot operators from Spring District dealing with people having various places of origin. Reciprocity thus works out differently in the two locations. In Hanoi, itinerant junk traders tend to sell their purchases to particular depot operators who in turn maintain loyalty of the junk traders through home visits to the village for family events or gifts of rice and homemade products. The truck operators in Hanoi cultivate regular contacts with a number of depots or recyclers through similar reciprocal acts. In HCM City, however, the relationships between depots, itinerant traders, and dealers are governed almost entirely by money and pricing. When opening a new depot there, the family needs to buy waste at high prices for some time to attract the itinerant traders, even if this means that they have to forego any initial profits. It is a tacit agreement that for every million Vietnamese *đồng* of waste sold, depot owners are obliged to "gift back" about two percent of the transaction at the end of the year, topped up by money for an air ticket home for frequent sellers. Spring District depot owners often express exasperation at how upfront the itinerant traders in HCM City are in demanding their year-end bonus, a practice that does not exist in Hanoi. This bonus averages three to five million *đồng* per year, amounting to twenty-five million in one particular case, and indicating the much larger volume of waste traded in the south. Some itinerant traders in HCM City "surf" (*lướt sóng*) among depots, selling their purchases to as many as possible in order to maximize the bonus— although some depot owners do make sure that the "surfers" know such behavior is not welcome.

In Hanoi, waste transporters tend to be men from Spring District whose families own a waste depot; a transport vehicle is often an added-value extension to the depot after years of saving. The men operate their own vehicles and hire additional labor for loading when necessary. In HCM City, meanwhile, the truck drivers tend to be hired laborers themselves, with their employers owning a fleet of vehicles and dealing in a much greater volume of waste. In HCM City, I met a Chinese dealer during his tour of the waste depots as he sought to buy plastic waste for direct export to China via informal cross-border trade. Quite a few large-scale dealers in HCM City are Vietnamese Chinese people who have long been in the waste trade. Depot owners there seem to have more straightforward transactions with these dealers and are rather uninterested in their personal and familial backgrounds. In contrast, the cultivation of personalized relationships in Hanoi's trading networks is more emphasized—for example, through attending customers' family events. Delayed payments are also common in Hanoi because of these more personalized ties within the network.

In short, Spring District waste networks are shaped by distance and the mobility patterns of the attendant migrants. The farther south Spring District people are, the less their networks depend on home-place ties and the more they function based on the mediation of money. In either case, the uncertainties of setting up shop in a place far away from home does not seem to deter these families, for whom the globalizing HCM City has become a new frontier. Nhung, a female depot operator in HCM City's

District 12 and the mother of two small children, told me that her parents had decided to go south in 2004 because of their slack business in Hanoi at that time. Having mobilized sixty million *đồng* from the extended family, her father had declared to the relatives that they were determined to make it work and would never return in the case of failure. By the time I met Nhung in 2015, several other families from the extended family had followed in their footsteps, operating waste depots in different parts of the metropolis. The necessity to adapt to new places is taken as given; as Nhung said, "Each place has its own customs. When entering a family, one has to do like others in the family do (*nhập gia tùy tục*). But we have our craft trade (*nghề*); we are not afraid. Wherever we go, we'll find a way to do our trade." In Spring District nowadays, peasant households talk about packing up and going to another city to open a waste depot (*mở bãi*) with an air of nonchalance. Of course, they plan and strategize for such mobile ventures—it just seems an obvious move that no longer requires much justification. The normalization of mobility, however, does not preclude household politics and negotiations around the mobility of household members, for whom modifications to gender norms have to be carefully managed.

## Staying at Home and Going Outside: Choice, Decision, and Power

The scholarship on migration has established that gender, along with class, ethnicity, and other categories of difference, both shapes and is shaped by mobility (Elliot 2016). Men and women embrace different trajectories of mobility, having different experiences, being confronted with different social constraints, and achieving different social outcomes for their mobility. The householding dynamics in Spring District suggest that the mobility of local men and women shifts along with changes in the gendered structure of opportunities created by new patterns of urban consumption and waste generation. Essentialized gender roles are, however, reproduced in people's daily practices, even as these sometimes depart from normative structures (see also Leshkowich 2014).

### Inside and Outside: The Gender of Space

Pierre Bourdieu's (1990) well-known description of the Kabyle house in Algeria suggests that gender relations and practices are structured according to the spatial division of the house as a basic unit of the social world. Men and women are supposed to dominate in some spaces and cede control in others, and gender characteristics are ascribed to different spaces within the house: "[T]he low, dark part of the house is also opposed to the upper part as the female to male" (Bourdieu 1990: 273). Yet together, they hold up the house and reproduce the gendered moral order of a society. Gender and space are thus mutually constituted, a crucial linkage as far as the crossing of spatial boundaries is concerned. The spatialized meanings of the Kabyle house offer a parallel to the importance of the Vietnamese division between the inside (*nội*) and the outside (*ngoại*).[1] As some authors have pointed out, this division structures not only kinship but also community and nation, although its meanings are flexible given the co-existence of contrasting kinship models (Luong 1989, Harms 2011). In Part II, I will show that the inside/outside division also matters for the creation of value from waste through migrants' investment in the patrilineal kinship and home village as the place of recognition and belonging. Here, I focus on how the mobility of local men and women into the urban waste economy and their practices of mobile householding are foregrounded by their consistent reference to these gendered categories of space.

Important for this question are the social meanings of men and women's movements between these spaces as the locus of kinship value and as the domains of gendered work (Brandtstädter 2009). The inside is the realm from which men originate and over which they hold control. As Susanne Brandtstädter writes about the same inside/outside notion in China, the inside is the "male world of inherited kinship property and of kinship bonds that formed a bounded center" (2009: 162). In this male-centric perspective, the inside is the core of one's identity, the place where life springs forth as a continuation of the family and where the most important social ties are located (Rydstrøm 2003). The outside domain is where women come from; it is the realm of the stranger, the unknown, the unruly and undisciplined, dangers that might threaten the moral order of the inner realm. Women's incorporation into the inside realm through marriage is therefore necessary for the sake of their morality and well-being. Coming from the outside, a woman has to be domesticated into her role of "supporting the inside" (*nội trợ*) from the very beginning; according to a Vietnamese adage, one should "teach the children when they are small and teach the wife when she barely arrives."[2] Her virtues lie in remaining within the bounds of the inner realm, devoting her life to it and not venturing away from it, since doing so would risk a disgraceful return to the outside. The man, in contrast, is charged with both overseeing the moral order of the inner realm and maintaining relationships with the outside. The underlying idea is that men alone have the moral caliber and the authority to deal with dangers outside the home.

Such ideals underline, rather than contradict, the seemingly reverse spatialization of gendered work. Women's work is that which "produced familiarity" within the inside, whereas men's work "produced the non-familiar (politics, strangers and, by extension, the state)" in the outside, a distinction that aligns with the domestic/public divide (Brandtstädter 2009: 162). Despite her lesser position in terms of kinship value, a woman finds her place in the world within the inside realm through her work of reproducing it. The married home is a sphere over which she could wield her power, a power invoked in the popular reference to a married woman as "the general of the domestic space" (*nội tướng*). In this way, like the Javanese women Susanne Brenner writes about, a Vietnamese woman accumulates status for the family, while her husband "performs status," through their respective occupation with the two gendered domains (1998: 154).

As we shall see, there is constant flipping of these spatialized binaries in people's practices and interpretations, making what otherwise seem to be rigid structural opposites into playful sites of social navigation.[3] Yet the categories remain enduring as the central components of a moral framework that informs people's actions. They continue to hold sway even after decades of the socialist state's rhetoric of liberating women from the domestic sphere and fully incorporating them into the public sphere of productive work and political affairs (Drummond and Rydström 2004, Leshkowich 2011). In Spring District, these gendered categories of space carry on to shape the mobility of men and women between the village and the city, even as their networks stretch far beyond the village and their practices entail relentless transgressions of the boundaries.

## "Going Outside" and Remaking Gendered Spaces

Ms. Lan has been making the trip to and from Hanoi for the last two decades, since her eldest son was less than a year old. The early separation from her small children caused tremendous emotional dislocation that she still recalls. Her daughter was born two years after she first went away, and she left again, working both as an itinerant junk trader and as a cleaner for urban households in central Hanoi, six months after the child's arrival. Her husband, Mr. Mạnh, cared for the two children when they were small. Once they were six and four years old, however, Mr. Mạnh left them with his widowed father, who lived close by, and went to Hanoi to work as a manual laborer and earn additional income to pay off the debt incurred by the construction of their house. Some months later, when the grandfather's health declined and, according to Ms. Lan, their son "wanted his dad back home too much," Mr. Mạnh returned and stayed. The grandfather was taken ill, and until he died six months later, Mr. Mạnh took turns with his two brothers, whose wives were also circulating between Hanoi and the village, to care for him.

Before Ms. Lan first left, Mr. Mạnh had, in his words, "been everywhere possible and done everything possible" before he became "fed up with going." He had been in the army for three years in the early 1980s before their marriage, and like many other men in the district, he had gone prospecting for gold in the mountainous regions during the mid-1980s. These trips left him with painful memories of failure and disappointment: he had often returned empty-handed, with debts on account of his travel and food costs that burdened the family. He said he had been fortunate to have avoided drug addiction, as many gold diggers took opium during their stay at the mining sites to cope with the hardship. Once, Mr. Mạnh left his pregnant wife to go south for several months and look for a job with a fishing fleet. Failing at that, he went to Hanoi to work as a bicycle transporter for about a year, during which time he made just about enough to cover his living costs. Mr. Mạnh's narrative of his past mobility is deeply melancholic; he frequently mentions having had thoughts of death when the fruitlessness of his efforts or the desperation of waiting in vain for work became too much to bear. He depicts his past returns to the village with a sense of loss and incompetence:

> I remember coming back from a gold digging trip. I had only two thousand [đồng] left in my pocket, then enough to buy a cup of [rice] wine and some roast peanuts. I didn't come home right away, but stopped by the little pub at the village entrance. I spent the last of the money on a cup of wine and peanuts. I just sat there, thinking about "carrying my face home" (vác mặt về nhà) and the likely reactions of my wife upon knowing that I had failed, that the money we had borrowed for my trip was all gone . . . I just sat there . . .

Like the other male villagers of his generation, Mr. Mạnh stayed home in the end, so that Ms. Lan could leave. The decision was made after Ms. Lan suggested the idea and, despite his initial resistance, convinced him that it was the best option for them as they were poor, heavily indebted, and "indescribably miserable."

Ms. Lan's first departure was in the early 1990s, when the market economy was beginning to evolve following the economic reforms of the mid-1980s. Leaving was difficult, not only because her first son was small but also because of her unfamiliarity with waste trading. When Ms. Lan first left, she was accompanied by a relative from Green Spring who took her to the migrant lodging in Hanoi and acted as her guide during the first days.

By then, it had become normal for women in Green Spring to leave for Hanoi, yet people in her Red Spring commune were still suspicious of such female ventures beyond the village—"to go outside" (*ra ngoài*) was a bold move for any woman at the time. She resentfully recounts people saying, "These women must be working as hookers in the city to leave their husband and children like that!" Yet she had been determined to do something about their poverty and indebtedness, and the successful engagement of Green Spring people in the waste trade had encouraged her to take the risks. Some years later, all of her seven sisters had followed in her footsteps, combining waste trading with cleaning for urban households.

Unlike her husband's previous departures, which had been hampered by the economic stagnation before and immediately after *đổi mới*, Ms. Lan's migration was facilitated by the opportunities of the emerging market economy that her predecessors had taken advantage of and passed on through their rural networks. Although a number of men were involved in itinerant waste trading and other forms of migrant work, it was common for men in the district to stay home. The women's combined income from junk trading and cleaning work—which the men are reluctant to undertake—tends to be steadier than the income of the men (see Chapter 2). The normalization of female migration, meanwhile, has also been facilitated by women's traditionally active roles in petty trading, which allow them some leverage over their mobility. That local people refer to itinerant waste trading as "going to the market" (*đi chợ*) seems a way of coming to terms with the mobility of married women. Even though they move beyond the space of the home, they remain in the space of the market, one of the few public spaces in which female activities are traditionally sanctioned (Leshkowich 2014). Despite the uneasiness stirred up by the migration of the first women, the initially "strange" household arrangements like those of Ms. Lan and Mr. Mạnh have become part of life in the district, and their children have grown up and embarked on even more complex householding trajectories. Such normalization of female mobility notwithstanding, acts of transgressing gendered boundaries must be made up for.

## Negotiating Boundaries and Remaking Gendered Ideals

Recent studies suggest that female migration has somewhat modified the gendered division of labor in Vietnamese rural households, with men undertaking more domestic duties as their spouses migrate for work in the cities or even overseas (Agergaard and Vu 2011, Hoang and Yeoh 2011, Vu and Agergaard 2012). While recognizing the flexibility of these households, authors have noted conjugal anxiety over the lost status of the husband as a result of their lesser economic role (Resurreccion and Hà 2007, Trương 2009). In my study, however, men and women continue to uphold gendered expectations by referring to ideal categories to evaluate their actions, even as these actions take place outside the designated space for each gender. When Mr. Mạnh left, for example, a normative arrangement was in place, with Ms. Lan staying at home, or "inside," and when she left, the norms were somewhat upset, hence the moral uneasiness that she noted. As she "went outside" and became mainly "concerned with economic matters of the family," both of which had been considered male domains, Mr. Mạnh assumed responsibility for "taking care of the basics at home." These basics include not only care of children, the elderly, the house, and the ancestors, but also paddy cultivation, keeping livestock, and sericulture. "I have to stay at home to look after them, otherwise they will all be in disarray. There is always so much work to do," Mr. Mạnh said to me on several occasions. The silkworms require feeding hourly, and he wakes daily before 5 a.m. to feed the livestock or do some work in the field. He also produces the households' rice, food, and fuel, some of which Ms. Lan takes with her to consume in Hanoi.[4]

When talking about his daily life at home, he downplays the "womanly work" (việc đàn bà) that he does, such as caregiving and housework, while emphasizing his productive and symbolic roles. "The house, the garden and the field, and the ancestors' grave" that he claims to take charge of make up the material and symbolic structure of their household, the realm of the inside. Admitting that his wife's migrant income is essential to sustaining this structure, he stresses that he is the one who ensures its continuation for the sake of the family's moral stability: "Wherever one goes, the father's home place and the ancestral land are one's roots (quê cha đất tổ là cái gốc của mình)—one can never abandon them." Even as Ms. Lan's mobility brings her work beyond the boundaries of the home and the village, to the outside realm, it helps Mr. Mạnh to realize important male roles rather than undermining them. During our conversations in Spring District, men like to make the following joke: "We middle-aged men now stay at home to keep the goal (giữ gôn)." The masculine football analogy refers to their charge of the inside realm, even though the charge includes care and domestic work in their spouses' absence. For these men, not acting as the income earner does not imply a reduction of their status, which, similar to that of the Javanese men discussed by Brenner (1998), is evaluated through other aspects of manhood that are not confined to breadwinning. If Brenner's male informants obtain status through cultural refinement and ritual potency, then these Spring District men's role as patrons of the inside realm sustains their status. Recasting it as that of being the "goalkeeper," they maintain the ideal of manhood as the protector of the family's hierarchy, morality, and its link to the ancestors; the goalkeeper metaphor seems a reinvention of this ideal in the time of mobility.

As much as Mr. Mạnh identifies with his symbolic roles in the inside realm, Ms. Lan seeks to hold on to domestic duties in her mobile life. Her behavior in this regard is not unlike the successful female professionals or entrepreneurs who understate their success as being secondary to their roles as wives and mothers (Chapter 5-Nguyen 2015b). In the beginning, she made sure that her migrant work was a gradual transition for the family; initially, she came back about every ten days, despite the great difficulties in using public transport then, and increased the length of her absence slowly. This contrasts with Mr. Mạnh's previous month-long sojourns due to long distance and poor communications. Further, Ms. Lan comes back regularly or "whenever there is anything"—a wedding, a funeral, or someone falling ill—and stays at home for a week or two each time. "He is very thorough and was good with the children [when they were small], the fields and the silkworms, but how can men be as attentive as us women?" she muses. And whenever she comes home, the division of labor assumes clear gender boundaries again, with the domestic tasks of cooking, cleaning, and washing up returned to her.[5] Now that their daughter has a small child, Ms. Lan asks them to come over for a day or two during her visits home so that she can "hold the grandchild" (bế cháu), "otherwise people will ask why the maternal grandmother does not care about the grandchild." Apart from dealing with social duties as they arise and taking part in regular agricultural activities, Ms. Lan washes large loads of bed sheets and mats in the nearby river, often complaining loudly as she hangs them up: "How lazy men are, leaving the sheets to stink like that!" Before departing, she makes sure that there are sufficient supplies of instant noodles, spices, toiletries, and other essentials in her absence, a fact that she refers to with satisfaction. These acts signify her care for others in the family while assuring them and herself of her femininity.

By fulfilling these duties, Ms. Lan retains control over matters regarding the reproduction of the inside realm, normatively seen as womanly matters, and thus her status in the family and the village. This is especially true in her relationship to her children. Explaining the need for her to remain active in their education, Ms. Lan depicts herself as the parent of greater authority:

> In my family, I am the one who is strict with the children; Mạnh is
> very tolerant toward them. They are more afraid of me than of their

dad. I just have to say one sentence and they have to listen to me. Thus I have to be back frequently to have words with them about their behavior.

The separation was emotionally difficult for her, and her self-portrayal seems a way of coming to terms with not having been there for them as normally required of a mother. This statement indicates that Ms. Lan seeks to relate to her children by means of parental authority to compensate for her absence. And while her description appears to contrast with the ideal of male authority in the family, Ms. Lan, in our conversations, often emphasized its importance: "A man's voice is necessary for the family; without it, the family would be in disorder. Even if he doesn't speak much, his mere presence is reassuring." She also said that the children used to ignore her whenever she came home and are now closer to their father than to her as a result of her earlier separation from them.

## Gendered Mobility and Generation

The normalization of female mobility notwithstanding, negotiations regarding who stays and who "goes outside" remain open-ended and are equally shaped by the intergenerational dynamics of the household. While both young men and women migrate for work in the urban waste trade, their mobility differs in the level of parental control and gendered expectations, as the relationship between Ms. Lan, Mr. Mạnh, and their children suggests.

### Sons, Daughters, and the Limits of Mobility

Ms. Lan's daughter Duệ started going to the market with her at sixteen after withdrawing from school. Her parents then considered it "quite alright" for her to accompany her mother for some years before returning home to get married, the primary goal for young women. When I started my fieldwork, Duệ was eighteen years old, married to a man twelve years older than her from the same commune, and had a six-month-old baby. After working as an itinerant trader for some years, her husband became a taxi driver in Hanoi. Duệ and her son lived with her in-laws, her husband's grandmother, and three of her husband's nieces, whose parents were all migrant waste traders. Duệ said she would like to resume waste trading once her child was about one-and-a-half years old, for "one feels restless staying at home without earning any money"; she was also keen to join her husband in Hanoi. However, her father-in-law had said that he would not let her go anywhere until the child was at least three. Her son was the only male offspring among the six grandchildren of her parents-in-law, who had been "longing for an heir" and were simply overjoyed with his arrival. Her father-in-law, an articulate local cadre, insisted that she stay home to care for her son. As head of the parents' associations at his grandchildren's nursery and school, he believed that motherly care was necessary for the healthy development of the child, although his wife and his elderly mother were also involved in caring for the baby.

Duệ saw his unequivocal attention to her son as an indication of her special status in the family. She pointed out with pride that her father-in-law did not ask his other daughters-in-law to stay at home with their small daughters, who had been cared for by his wife since they were babies. Yet she was frustrated by the restrictions on her mobility, which she often jokingly referred to in her father-in-law's presence to test his reactions. Since her husband rarely disagrees with his father, the negotiations about her mobility rest between Duệ and her father-in-law rather than between her and her husband. When I met Ms. Lan again in Hanoi about two years later, she told me that Duệ was pregnant again. "It will be a long time until she can go out again," Ms. Lan said.

Before her marriage, Duệ's mobility had been under the purview of her mother. Joining her mother in the city as an itinerant waste trader thus was not much of a step outside the boundaries of the inside realm, given that these boundaries had already been reconstituted through her mother's mobility. But for Dân, the son of Ms. Lan and Mr. Mạnh, it was an entirely different matter: young men are on the move with much less restriction and parental supervision. After finishing lower secondary school, Dân had been following friends several years older than him, first to Hanoi as an itinerant trader and then to HCM City as a truck driver for several years before returning to get married in 2011. Unlike young women, whose mobility invokes anxiety about their moral propriety, young men are emboldened to "go outside," embracing adventures and trying things out, even if these sometimes might challenge parental authority or conventions. Yet like Dân, most men eventually "straighten up" and "settle down," establishing a family and in so doing meeting their patrilineal expectations and duties (Nguyen 2018). In Spring District, such a return to the male obligations of consolidating "the inside" often signals a turning point in how local households engage with the waste trade.

## Waste as a Frontier of the Patrilineal Family

Whereas itinerant junk trading is individual work mostly done by women, operating a waste depot is a household venture often undertaken by married couples, sometimes involving their children, parents, or other relatives.

In the early 1980s, central Hanoi contained only a a small number of waste depots (DiGregorio 1994); today, they can be found in almost every residential quarter and along most major roads. The main requirement for opening a depot is storage space accessible from the main road, such as undeveloped plots and rundown houses, sites that can be rented cheaply from urban people. To start a depot is referred to as *mở bãi*—literally "opening a site"—a term that implies expanding to new frontiers. I shall go into further details of waste depot operations in the next chapter. Here, it suffices to say that the depot business is risky due to market fluctuations and instabilities in land tenure, and many households end up failing and indebted. Nevertheless, *mở bãi* has come to assume the same importance once played by paddy production; in fact, it provides the scope for the extension of the patrilineal family here. Families with several siblings running separate depots in different cities are common in the district. If parents previously sought to give a newlywed couple a piece of residential land or a house, many now try to provide their sons with funds to set up an urban depot, often after years of saving their incomes from migrant work. Long-standing depot operators will sometimes start an additional depot in anticipation of their son's marriage. The ideal bride for these families would be a woman who, besides usual feminine qualities, should be familiar with the waste trade. In our conversations, Ms. Nga, a depot owner who had been in the trade for more than three decades, often expressed her satisfaction at the trading skills and the household managing abilities (*khả năng thu vén gia đình*) of her daughter-in-law. Despite not coming from Spring District, she said, the latter used to be an "excellent itinerant trader" recommended to their son by a relative. Once the union had been agreed upon by both families, the young woman came to live with them in their depot for a full month before their marriage in order to learn the ins and outs of depot operations.

Mr. Mạnh and Ms. Lan would not open a waste depot themselves, yet they made sure that Dân and his wife would. Upon marriage, Dân did not want to continue in his driving job, as his wife was concerned about the womanizing reputation of truck drivers. Yet his parents' influence was central to their decision; Mr. Mạnh and Ms. Lan offered them 70 million *đồng* (about US$3,500) for the purpose of opening a depot, on condition that the money was not to be used for anything else. Shortly after their wedding, the young couple searched for a suitable location in Hanoi. Failing to find one after two months, they went to H-CM City and then settled in the central province of Lam Dong, where a distant relative was operating a depot. When I last saw Mr. Mạnh, he was preparing for a trip to Lam Dong to help construct fences for the depot. He told me that if there were too many transactions for the couple to handle, he would stay for some months to help, and might perhaps do the same every year. When the couple had children, he said, the children would go back to the village to live with their grandfather in their early years. Ms. Lan would continue "going to the market," as she was still fit and her "lucky streak"[6] had not run out, but she too would have to think about retiring if needed at home to care for their grandchildren. In any case, this peasant household clearly anticipates that its translocal operations will continue, requiring the flexibility of individual members while remaining rooted in local understandings of moral obligations, a theme to which I will return in Part II.

Such characterization of the translocal household does not imply that people are forever on the move. A small number of waste traders from Spring District have managed to buy residential land and, as such, have become official or unofficial urban residents in Hanoi or HCM City (see also Nguyen et al. 2012, Karis 2013). According to district records for 2008–2011, more than a hundred people from the district—twice as many as in previous years—have changed their residential registration to other provinces, including Hanoi. Others have shifted the focus of the household economy to the country, through new forms of agricultural production; these families continue to assume a translocal outlook in which the potential mobility of some members or of the whole household is taken as given (see Chapter 6). Even when migrants move their household registration to a city, it is not certain that they will remain there permanently; some get registered in Hanoi in order to buy residential land, planning to retire in the countryside when their children are set up.

## Conclusion: Translocality, Networks, and the Remaking of Gendered Spaces

The translocal household has become part of life in Spring District. The comings and goings of women and men are but part of the householding project that is subjected to open-ended negotiation between genders and generations. Their trajectories, which appear idiosyncratic when examined in isolation at a particular point in time, indeed blend into each other to shape the changing pathways of the household as a whole over a longer period, even across generations. Household dynamics are not just "influenced by extra-domestic politico-jural considerations" (Yanagisako 1979: 191) but are integral to broader processes of change. These household trajectories of migrant livelihood have evolved out of the changing political economy of post-reform Vietnam—one in which rural people are drawn into the underbelly of enlarging cities to service urban economies and urban people, yet also one in which new economic and social forms emerge out of people's practices as they are on the move. The urban waste networks formed around the mobility of Spring District households provide the structure for their urban entrepreneurship.

As men and women participate in the translocal householding project, they are certain to negotiate the boundaries between gender appropriate spaces (i.e., the inside and outside). Household relations remain defined by both contestation and cooperation but increasingly center on an interpretation of needs and rights that is embedded in unequal power relations, with varying outcomes for gendered persons within the household. As evidenced in the Lan-Mạnh household, there are differing ideas about who migrates (i.e., "goes outside",) how a person migrates, how labor and resources should be divided among male and female members, and the purposes of their migration, depending on age and gender. As "specific sorts of persons with particular rights and needs" (Moore 1994: 93), household members interpret these rights and needs from different power positions. Such negotiations are also foregrounded by the varying ways in which household members perform their gendered identity, thus reproducing normative ideas about what it means to be a man and a woman. When Ms. Lan insists on fulfilling her domestic roles during migration or Mr. Mạnh emphasizes his productive-protective role at home, both are drawing on normative categories of gender to deal with the moral travails of mobile householding. Concurrently, their gender identity is reinvented via alternative discourses, such as the authoritative migrant mother, and new metaphors, such as the goalkeeper of the family.

As such, gender relations remain embedded in normative categories that are intertwined with the changing intergenerational obligations generated by mobility. Following Henrietta Moore (1994), men and women construct gender identities within dominant categories of gender; even when some defy such categories and expectations, they remain within the bounds of their effects. Via such construction of identity as gendered "persons with specific attributes in ways that are congruent with socially established patterns of power" (Moore 1994: 93), the household not only is reproduced, but also reproduces society as its operations reach across spatial and social boundaries. In redefining the boundaries of the household through their mobility, people also remake the boundaries of their village as the inside realm, which is now expanded to encompass rural networks in urban centers. These networks are fluid: they function based on moral economic ties characteristic of the village and yet are flexible enough to accommodate newcomers, new practices of reciprocity, and to extend over greater distances. The spatialized categories of inside and outside have been remade through translocal householding, but they remain consequential in structuring the mobility of men and women.

As we shall see, these categories are equally important for the valuation of waste labor, shaping the social outcomes that men and women are able to gain from the waste economy. The next two chapters home in on local people's day-to-day dealings with waste in urban spaces and their negotiations with the social ambiguity of waste, and with their marginal status in the urban society.

CHAPTER 2

...........................

# Labor, Economy, and Urban Space

Not far from Hanoi's central Thống Nhất Park lies a quiet street that I sometimes go to chat with some female itinerant junk traders. On hot days, there is a good spot on one side of the street for a midday nap, under the cool shade of old trees outside a colonial-style villa (the cement surface feels rough, though, as I found out when once trying to lie down among the women during their short nap). On the other side of the street is an apartment building. Without the ubiquitous shopfronts of most other central Hanoi streets, where owners would not allow them to sleep outside their stores, the junk traders could spend their lunch breaks here without being harassed. As well, they are on good terms with the live-in domestic worker of the family living in the villa and with the residents of the apartment building, who regularly sell them castaway, recyclable household items. One of the junk traders said to me, "It's wise to make friends with the maids. They often work for wealthy families which consume more and thus produce more junk. Usually we split the earnings; they get their share and we get our share. In this way, we cooperate well, and nobody is disadvantaged." For the traders, therefore, locations like this spot are both good resting places and points of business. Similar gathering points for female junk traders can be found throughout central Hanoi. (It would be more difficult to find male junk traders in such spots, since they rarely assemble in open spaces as the women do. The male traders operate in entirely different manners, as I will show later.)

This chapter demonstrates that women and men from Spring District have been appropriating urban spaces to make a living and generate wealth from an ambiguous social positioning as rural migrants working with waste. It shows that their creative potential "unsettles the associations often made between [waste and] garbage and marginality" (Millar 2012: 165), as they use the flexibility enabled by that marginality to advance both socially and economically. In doing so, they engage in performative acts that draw on deeply gendered social meanings of dirt and labor (Douglas 1966). Such performances are simultaneously strategic and contingent on their class position, which they seek to transcend with varying outcomes, all the while helping to shape a vibrant waste economy linked to broader systems of production and consumption. Viewing their performative practices as spatially embedded allows us to recognize that gendered and classed subjects, although constituted within dominant discourses, can appropriate the discourses for their own purposes. In this chapter, I connect such practices to an ongoing process of class spatialization in urban Vietnam, a process in which class takes on spatialized meanings through urban housing, architecture, and zoning (Zhang 2010). I show that waste traders' performances are part of a multitude of everyday place-making practices, for which the creative deployment of stereotypes is central (Nelson 1999, Herzfeld 2005). These practices in turn remake the urban space and the social relations that they encounter, in ways similar to those of other peasant entrepreneurs yet underscoring their distinct relation to waste and its social implications.

## The Itinerant Junk Trader and Changing Urban Waste Production

Đồng nát means "broken things" in northern Vietnamese (the southern equivalent is ve chai, and recyclable waste is formally referred to as phế liệu). I translate it as "junk," using the phrase "itinerant junk traders" to refer to people who go from door to door to buy waste for resale to waste depots. "Waste traders," meanwhile, indicates a whole spectrum of actors involved in the waste trade, including waste depot operators and wholesale dealers. In Spring District, people say đi chợ (literally "going to the market") when talking about the work of itinerant junk trading in the city. In ways that never fail to attract attention, the itinerant junk traders make themselves known on their itineraries by singing catchy rhymes, which reveal the changing range of tradable wastes over time (see Table 2.1).

TABLE 2.1   Itinerant Junk Traders' Rhymes[1]

| VIETNAMESE | ENGLISH |
| --- | --- |
| Lông ngan lông vịt | Goose feathers, duck feathers |
| Các cụ ăn thịt còn lông | Meat already gone, feather left uneaten |
| Túi bóng ni lông | Nylon bags |
| Đồng chì nhuôm bẹp | Castaway copper, lead, and aluminum |
| Dép nhựa đứt quai | Torn sandals |
| Mang đổi kẹo đêêê! | Bring them here for candy, pleeease! |
| | |
| Can làn mũ nhựa | Plastic bottles, baskets, and hats |
| Dép nhựa đứt quai | Torn sandals |
| Mảnh kính mảnh chai | Broken glass |
| Chai xanh chai đỏ | Red and green bottles |
| Chai bỏ từ lâu | No longer to be seen |
| Chai rượu chai dầu | Old alcohol and oil bottles |
| Mang ra đổi kẹo kéo nàooo! | Bring them here for candy, pleeease! |
| | |
| Bàn là quạt cháy máy bơm | Iron, electric fans, and water pumps |
| Tivi cát-sét nồi cơm đầu màn | TV, cassette players, rice cookers, and DVD players |
| Ắc quy loa bục mỏ hàn | Batteries, loudspeakers, and welding guns |
| Hỏng không dùng nữa thành hàng bán đêêêê! | Broken and useless, why don't you sellll! |
| | |
| Ti vi tủ lạnh đầu dàn | TV sets, refrigerators, and stereo players |
| Dùng lâu đã hỏng thành hàng bán điiii! | Broken and useless, why don't you sellll! |

[1] Itinerant waste traders in Hanoi sing these rhymes as they make their rounds. The first and second rows date from before the mid-1980s; the rest appeared later.

Source: Author's collection.

Itinerant junk traders are not new in Vietnam; they had operated long before the mid-1980s reforms, albeit on a smaller scale. Because of shortages under state socialism, the state encouraged recycling, although it never reached such an ideological status as it did in socialist Hungary (Gille 2007). Until the 1980s, the junk traders mostly bartered, such as exchanging a new pair of plastic sandals for some used ones or some rice or candy strips (*kẹo kéo*) for a kilo of waste metal or plastic; nowadays, they offer cash. The waste they purchase varies over time according to consumption patterns and market demands, which before the reform were largely driven by local and national industries. Today, it reflects the global demand for recyclable materials, such as plastic, paper, and stripped metal. The waste also signals the national demand for second-hand household goods, for which Vietnam has a vibrant underground economy, one that already existed during the central-planning period.

Until the 1990s, many, including better-off households, sought imported secondhand household goods. Since the 2000s, as people have begun to consume more electronic goods, there has been a rapid increase in the scale of electronic waste, which traders purchase either to resell secondhand or to strip for metal.[1] Although imported secondhand items are still traded on the market, locally produced goods have also entered the secondhand trade, which has become geared toward low-income households.

In 2011, Hanoi produced more than 2.3 million tons of waste, and that amount is growing each year by fifteen percent (Ministry of Natural Resources and Environment (MONRE) 2011). About eight to twenty percent of that waste, including ferrous metal, plastic, and paper is recycled (MONRE 2011; World Bank, MONRE and Canadian International Development Agency 2004). Managing and treating waste in Vietnamese cities is largely performed by the state-owned Urban Environment Company (URENCO). Although URENCO has a subsidiary that trades and recycles waste, it tends to indiscriminately transport most of the material it collects to landfills on the outskirts of Hanoi, where one can find scavengers who make a living by retrieving recyclables. Within the city, migrant waste pickers form patron-client networks with URENCO employees to access the waste containers of businesses and offices, often by performing some tasks for the latter without pay.

In recent years, private companies have become more involved in managing urban waste; in Hồ Chí Minh City, a multimillion-dollar private company has been operating. Because these companies have sorting and recycling facilities, they might affect the livelihoods of scavengers and trash pickers working at dumpsites and landfills. Waste traders from Spring District, however, often buy recyclable waste directly from households and businesses that separate it themselves. These traders then transport the waste to recycling facilities in traditional craft villages around Hanoi that used to produce products such as paper, copperware, and work tools but have now switched to recycling. Although some of the recycled material is consumed by local industries, a large part of it, especially plastic and copper, is exported to China via informal cross-border routes. These waste traders are therefore less likely to be affected by the privatization of waste management and more by changing patterns of urban construction, consumption, and state regulation.

## The Waste Hierarchy and the Promiscuity of Waste

The itinerant junk traders are known to the urban public through their frequent interactions with urban households, while waste depots are less visible, often half-hidden in non-descript places. Both occupations, however, are part of a complex, hierarchical waste system ranging from scavengers and trash pickers, who operate at dumps and waste-collection points, to itinerant traders, depot owners, transporters, and large-scale dealers (DiGregorio 1994; Mitchell 2008, 2009). In the outlying regions of Hanoi, a number of villages specialize in industry-scale waste dealing—for example Quan Độ village in Bắc Ninh province, where villagers secure large orders for handling the waste of corporations such as Samsung or Vietnam Post and Telecommunication. The waste trading performed by Spring District migrants is small-scale in comparison, yet it feeds into the hierarchy of waste work mentioned earlier, a hierarchy that, similar to many other regions of the world, is embedded in local social relations (Li 2002, Hayami et al. 2006, Masocha 2006).

Spring District waste traders distinguish between their relationship with waste and that of "waste harvesters" (Masocha 2006), such as the scavengers working in municipal dumps (người bới rác) and the trash pickers (người nhặt rác) operating around city collection points. The waste traders often emphasize that their own activities require them to invest money and develop trading skills that the other waste workers do not possess, a deficiency that in their view explains why the others have to be more exposed to dirt in their work. Ms. Mai, a 45-year-old female junk trader, stresses exposure to dirt as a central element that defines their differing relationships to waste:

> Scavengers go for the trash bin wearing masks and poking wherever there is garbage. That would be too dirty for us junk traders. We just buy clean things. They [scavengers and pickers] don't even know how to buy things, because they either are afraid of overpaying or do not have the money to buy. Occasionally a scavenger informs me that so-and-so is selling things. I'd go to buy them, and if I get a good deal, I'll give something back to him or her.

In this construction of difference, the waste traders come into human contact with their customers, unlike the waste harvesters who work directly with dirt. The traders' relationship to waste is mediated by not only the capital they have at their disposal, but also the social ties they build through transactions. The exposure to dirt, associated with lowliness and destitution, largely defines the social and gendered boundaries of the harvesters' place in the hierarchy. This is the case even though many people from the district themselves used to work as scavengers and trash pickers (or "shit dealers," to go further back). The junk traders, in distancing themselves from "waste harvesting" and emphasizing the commercial aspects of their network, seek to redefine their social positioning based on distance from dirt. Mary Douglas's (1966) conception of dirt as central to constructing the social order is pertinent for understanding this redefinition—by dwelling on the social implications of dirt, the junk traders themselves participate in consolidating it as an indicator of social status.

In so doing, however, the junk traders inadvertently reinforce the discourse underscoring the association of dirt with the waste they trade and, more importantly, with their personhood. Following Douglas (1966), dirt is not only socially but also morally meaningful—moral impurity is often internal to the construction of dirt. Historical examples of this abound, from the colonial construction of the unhygienic colonial subjects, to the bourgeois imagination of the urban poor in early industrial Europe, to the association of cleanliness with whiteness in America until today (Stallybrass and Allon 1986, Cohen and Johnson 2005, Zimring 2017). In northern Vietnam, people commonly perceive the junk trader as a cunning yet pitiable rural person, and urban parents sometimes use the junk trader as a negative example with which to discipline their children: do well in school, or you might end up being one. Like the street hawkers who sell cheap goods in urban centers, junk traders provide a service that responds to urban needs, yet urban people often consider them a nuisance to public space and a menace to household safety (Anjaria 2006, Milgram 2014, Endres and Leshkowich 2018). A strong urban stereotype holds them to be polluters of the urban space with their uncivilized habits and inclination toward dishonesty. "These countryside breeds, they are so dirty and messy (*Cái giống nhà quê nó bẩn mà nhếch nhác lắm*). And one needs to watch out not to be too careless with one's things, lest they steal them in the wink of an eye," said an acquaintance of mine, a retired woman who used to work in a state hospital, upon hearing that I was researching the waste trade. She went on: "You know, they live together like a herd in the 'rat-hole areas' (*khu ổ chuột,* the Vietnamese term for slums), husband and wife and children, all eating and living like that. Disgusting (*kinh lắm*)!" As if to back up her assessment, she then mentioned having seen some photo reportages on the life of the waste traders in the city.[2]

Many among the urban people I know would be more cautious in making such a statement; even as they might complain about the habits of rural migrants, many would express sympathy for their hard life. My acquaintance's vehement expression of contempt and her association of ruralness with dirtiness are a little puzzling: she herself came from the countryside, where some of her close family members still live. Perhaps she was seeking an alliance with me through evoking the class-based construction of the rural Other, or simply wanted to show that she had something important to say on the matter. In any case, her statement reminds one of the stereotypes of immigrant Jewish scrap dealers in the United States during the interwar period as the "mysterious un-scrupulous foreigners" ready to make their gains through swindle and dishonesty (Zimring 2017: 129).[3] The association of low morals with exposure to dirt is indeed widespread, occurring in different times and places (Campkin and Cox 2012). In Vietnam, this is compounded by the dominant view of rural people as uncultured and backward. While Spring Distract waste traders acknowledge that not all urban people treat them with disrespect, the intimate experience of stigmatization is recurrent enough for them to perceive it as a general pattern in their daily urban encounters: "There are all kinds of people wherever you are, but we frequently run into those who treat us as if we were scum-bags. This work can be quite humiliating sometimes (*Làm cái nghề này nhiều khi cũng tủi lắm em ạ*)," said Ms. Hương, a long-time itinerant trader from Red Spring.

## Waste, Migrant Labor, and the Spatialization of Class in Hanoi

As the capital city, Hanoi, along with Hồ Chí Minh City, is the primary location for the Vietnamese state to realize its modernizing agenda; in the official rhetoric, it is to be "modern and civilized," with "green, clean, and beautiful" spaces. In a move similar to the creation of metro-politan centers in China and elsewhere, Hanoi was expanded to incor-porate outlying regions into a Hanoi Metropolitan Area in 2008, doubling its population to more than six million. Writing about similar dynamics of urban regeneration in China, Li Zhang (2010) points out a process of "spatialization of class" in the creation of new urban spaces that is driven by the urban middle class' desire for owning private homes as a site of consumption and self-realization, a sort of private paradise. As has also been noted in Vietnamese urban centers, class distinction is externalized in the privatized architecture and zoning of residential quarters and in the establishment of public spaces where middle-class consumption is at once conspicuous and exclusive (Douglass and Huang 2007, Drummond 2012, Harms 2016). This urban order is dominated by a state-sponsored notion of beauty that is infused with ideas of orderliness and civility and that acts as an instrument of social control (Harms 2012).

Although their labor is crucial to how this urban order functions, rural migrants are seen to upset it through their unruliness and out-of-place existence; their presence in the urban space is considered the antithesis of beauty. Like street vendors, itinerant junk traders have been targeted by various municipal actions—for example a regulation in 2009 that bans street vending in 62 central streets of Hanoi.[4] Junk traders have occasionally been evicted from the city center during beautification campaigns, but their trading activities defy easy categorization. Unlike the street vendors, they pose a problem for the police seeking to fine them since they do not keep their purchases for long; as soon as their baskets are full, they unload them at the waste depots. In addition, the waste they carry appears to have little value, so there is little incentive to confiscate it, a common municipal measure against street vendors (Endres and Leshkowich 2018).

Unlike China, where urbanization has been more drastic and uniform, urban Vietnam has remained relatively fragmented, allowing the popular sector to thrive in yet-to-be-planned urban spaces, even in the city centers. This has so far allowed the waste trade to expand. The conditions in Vietnamese cities are gradually changing, however, and operating as waste traders in the inner city will likely become more difficult. Urban waste depots are explicitly regulated by environmental legislation as business, and owners must submit an environmental impact assessment and register if they deal annually in three thousand tons or more of waste.[5] Most depots trade a smaller volume, though, and their turnover is in any case difficult to monitor. Therefore, they tend to operate largely without registration, quietly doing business and trying to maintain good relationships with local government officers and their neighbors. As one depot operator said, "As long as one knows how to 'make law' [làm luật; i.e., pay enough in bribes], there should not be much of a problem" (see Chapter 3 for a discussion of "making law"). There are, however, increasing calls for stricter regulations of waste depots. The following extract from an entry on the Communist Party's daily is an example of how waste depots are portrayed as disturbing urban beauty and order:

> Most of the waste depots do not have business registrations. Many encroach onto the sidewalk, affecting the traffic. Some that are located in dense residential areas are creating environmental pollution due to failure to treat waste. Along the National Highway Number 5 from Hanoi to Hải Phòng, there are more than fifty waste depots; along the thirty-kilometer-long Highway 21A from Sơn Tây to Xuân Mai, there are more than a dozen of depots where waste and garbage are piled high, overflowing onto the sides of the road, which looks very unaesthetic. (Vu 2011)

Although the waste economy's informalized spaces represent a source of income for local government and law enforcement agents, the waste piling up in urban depots is beginning to disturb the urban planners and residents. Media reports of occasional accidents involving waste traders handling undetonated explosive devices salvaged from former war zones further heightens the public perception of waste depots as disturbing the urban order.[6] Waste and waste traders pose challenges not only to the maintenance of urban and order, but also to the hierarchical spatial ordering of market socialism, one in which those who do not belong should be kept out of sight, so that they do not infringe upon the sensibilities of the urban public. As I will show, however, this spatial ordering can be as enabling as it is constraining for the waste traders from Spring District. Like migrant laborers elsewhere in the South, whose practices often blur the boundaries between legal and illegal and re-chart the city's marginal spaces as productive for livelihoods and social life (Karis 2013, Rao 2013, Milgram 2014), their strategies simultaneously play into and undercut the spatialization of class in Hanoi.

## Gendered Performance of Class as Access to Urban Spaces

A gendered performance of class underlines the itinerant junk traders' transactions with urban people; in differing ways, men and women traders emphasize their social inferiority to mask the value of the waste items. This performance corresponds to the kinds of waste they choose to specialize in, based on gender norms that delegate to men the public and "big matters" of the household, which are distanced from dirt, and that assign to women the domestic and "small" details of homemaking, which are considered as dirty and impure.

## The "Miserable Migrant": Stereotype as Bargaining Chip

Imagine that you live in central Hanoi and call in a female junk trader who is passing by. You pile all your unwanted items in front of the modestly dressed woman, who likely wears a conical hat and has a carrying pole across her shoulders; Figure 2.1 shows a typical female itinerant trader on the streets on Hanoi. The trader carefully examines each item, sorting the "goods" (*hàng*) from the undesirable items. Once the sorting is over, she asks for your price. If you name an amount, she likely says, "But I myself can't sell them at that price. You know I am just selling my labor (*lấy công làm lãi*). There is a profit of only a couple cents per kilo of paper. And these unwanted things would just make your house messy if you don't get rid of them." If you hesitate or ask her why anyone would work for such little profit, she tells you there is no other work in the

FIGURE **2.1  A female itinerant trader in central Hanoi.**
Source: Author's photo, 2012.

country other than planting paddy (*làm ruộng*), which at best can only provide enough rice to eat, and every cent she makes in the city is necessary to feed and school her children. It is "miserable in the countryside," and peasants like her have no other option than to come here to make a living. Otherwise, she says, "Who would ever want to do this kind of work?" At this point, you might say, "OK, give me whatever you think is appropriate," and she replies by stating her price, adding that you are certainly not taking a loss by selling your junk to her. Alternatively, you are so moved by the hardship in her life that you give her the items for free, and the subsequent feeling of having done something charitable leads you to do the same next time.

Now consider the following narrative of Danh, a nineteen-year-old male junk trader who bikes around Hanoi buying used and broken appliances. A cheerful, sociable, and respectful young man, Danh is also a savvy trader who has mastered the art of bargaining. During a family lunch that I attended, he told this story when the conversation shifted to the bargaining skills necessary for trading in electronic waste:

> Once Hưng [his friend] and I were called in by this middle-aged man who wanted to sell us two used air conditioners. The conditioners were not really broken, and I was sure that they would fetch at least one million *đồng* [about US$50] from a secondhand appliance dealer. After having a look at it, I said to him, "Uncle, there is not much life left in your air conditioners, and all we can do is to break them apart and sell the parts inside. So we can give you at most 300,000. We are not even sure if we could sell it for a profit at that price, so we are taking a risk (*liều*)." After some haggling, we got them for 350,000. Some hours afterward, I told Hưng, "Let's come back and try something!" So we came back, and I was putting on this crying face (*mếu máo*), saying to the man, "Uncle, we were mistaken about the price of your old air conditioners. The dealer would give us only 300,000 for them. We are taking a loss, and we are not going to have anything to eat today. Please consider our circumstances." In the end, he gave us 60,000 back. We sold the conditioners for 1.2 million that day.

Central to Danh's narrative, and the earlier vignette of the female traders' practices, is the performance of a naive and inferior persona that appeals to the sellers' social status. In referring to their lower-class position, the junk traders put a claim on the sellers' probable compassion and their obligations as people who are higher in the social hierarchy. By reminding the latter of an object's worthlessness, they subtly tell the sellers that it would be unworthy of someone with their status to haggle. The purposiveness of such performance is highlighted through a contrast between their dealings with customers of the middle class and those with customers of the laboring class, such as hotel housekeepers or office cleaners. For example, the alley leading to my former apartment in central Hanoi faces the back of a midrange hotel, where I could observe junk traders' daily transactions with the hotel's service staff as they negotiated over a variety of items, including plastic water bottles, newspapers, cartons, toilet-paper-roll tubes, and large amounts of broken water taps or plastic items. Certain junk traders know the hotel staff; others do not. They come at intervals and wait at the fence around the time the hotel staff finish cleaning. These transactions, in which the junk traders do not perform the "miserable rural migrant," invoke less social distance and are more focused on prices.

Similar accounts of performances shifting according to context and social relationships in urban Vietnam suggest that female traders tend to draw on gender as a naturalized category in order to facilitate their trading activities (Leshkowich 2005, Harms 2011, Leshkowich 2011, Hoang 2015). Under the guise of dominant assumptions about class and rural-urban identity, these women traders frequently invoke sacrifices for their children and their difficulties in maintaining family livelihoods as bargaining chips in their dealings with customers and state officials. In these practices, the women instrumentalize, internalize, and thus sustain normative categories of gender and class. By juxtaposing the female traders' performances with those of their male counterparts, we see more clearly that the class-based performance of gender is also a gendered performance of class. Both men and women refer to their rural and class-based disadvantages, but the men do not usually evoke the vulnerability of the selfless parent as much as the women do. As we shall see, male and female practices are mutually constituted in reproducing ideal categories of class and gender, which in turn account for the junk traders' differential access to urban space.

## Appliances versus Junk: Technology, Gendered Spaces, and Value

While both male and female itinerant junk traders are called *đồng nát*, local people distinguish between *buôn đồng nát* (trading in junk) as a female occupation and *buôn đồ điện* (trading in electrical appliances) as a male one. Likewise, the women are said to "go to the market" (*đi chợ*), while the men "go electrical appliances" (*đi đồ điện*). After narrating a series of anecdotes about his skills in deciphering the value of electronic waste items, a male trader said: "These junk trader ladies! What do they know about electronic appliances?" Local people attribute male junk traders' specialization in electronic waste to their technical knowledge, which female junk traders are seen as lacking. This explains why the latter mainly focus on seemingly trivial things, such as paper, plastic, and other non-electronic waste—a perception that aligns with the construction of women as inherently backward (Leshkowich 2005). This distinction involves gender stereotypes that, like the Greek nationalist metaphors described by Michael Herzfeld (2005), social groups use to structure their self-representations. Although some contest the stereotypes that pervade such representations, Herzfeld argues, the stereotypes nonetheless play an important role in the meaning making of social actors who consciously deploy them to achieve their own goals.

Stereotypical distinction does more than just carry symbolic meanings, however; in the waste trade, it is directly consequential for the men and women's varying access to urban spaces and their differing sets of urban contacts. The male junk traders tend to deal with the predominantly male staff working in electronic repair, secondhand shops, and increasingly, in the IT sector. The women's contact base is concentrated in the more feminized parts of the service sector, such as restaurants, hotels, and offices. Female junk traders commonly work as cleaners for urban households, whereas male traders rarely do. This gendered distinction is not only linked to the association of men with the public sphere (the outside) and of women with the domestic sphere (the inside), but also rooted in a differential exposure to dirt. Paid cleaning work is considered most unsuitable for men. As male traders often say, "How can men as men (đàn ông đàn ang) clean other people's houses?" Meanwhile, cleaning brings the women into an intimate relationship with urban society. They often invest in cultivating a sort of pseudo-kinship with regular customers in certain neighborhoods, posing as the thankful rural relative who occasionally brings her "sister" or "brother" in the city some rural products as a gift. The more successful female junk traders maintain such personal networks of reciprocity that bind customers to them. These patron-client ties, together with the women's closeness to dirt through cleaning work, render their class status more visible yet allow them access to the urban domestic sphere, a potential source of waste. Their earnings from cleaning counterbalance the irregular income from waste trading, while the cleaning contacts sometimes help them to find lucrative purchases.

The male traders' resistance to cleaning protects them from a combined injury to their gender and class identity, yet it practically excludes them from a sometimes-rich source of waste. Although they might earn greater amounts from the electronic appliances than the women do from the more miscellaneous objects, the women tend to have a more stable income. A number of men have taken up driving taxis, including motorbike taxis, but apart from being competitive, this requires driving skills and significant investments. That's why it is common for men from the district to return and stay home while their wives remain in Hanoi working as itinerant junk traders (see Chapter 1). Although there are many more junk traders now than two decades ago, the proportion of men has fallen significantly, from more than 40 percent in early 1992 to 6.5 percent in 2006 (DiGregorio 1994; Mitchell 2008). The women assume a more ambiguous positioning in their negotiation with waste and dirt, but this positioning affords them greater flexibility. Such gendered access to urban spaces suggests the differing ways in which male and female waste traders participate in the class relations of the capital city through their spatial practices. Speeding away through the city on the back of a motorbike, the men distance themselves from the personalized encounters with their urban and class Other, while through their labor in the urban domestic sphere, the women purposively maintain such encounters. These practices are again embedded in the division between the inside and the outside as mutually exclusive spaces in which men and women can legitimately operate. The spatialization of class, rather than being just a matter of urban architecture and planning, is thus also about how people of different classes and genders access and occupy space, how and where they move about, and the positioning they assume in particular spaces.

Such practices reproduce normative categories of class and gender, yet over time, they also help to reconfigure their meanings and structure. The junk traders' performance of the "miserable junk trader" is so effective that urban people are often surprised to learn how much income they earn from seemingly worthless objects. In the media, rags-to-riches tales of waste traders are common, and they often marvel that people doing such "dirty" work could become rich.[7] While female junk traders do not get rich overnight, they normally make between three and six million đồng (US$150–300) per month (the average monthly salary of a factory worker in 2011 was about more than two million đồng), depending on their skills. Male traders sometimes earn significantly more from the used appliances, but their income is irregular. According to the junk traders, who like to compare their trade to fishing, it depends on their "good fortune" (lộc), which may befall them only in certain months of the year. Nonetheless, such income has made a difference to household economies, consumption, and living standards in Spring District. Over the years, these "miserable junk traders" have earned and saved enough to build houses, set up their children with businesses in the waste trade, and maintain a robust calendar of family and village festivities (see Part II).

The young male traders may sneer at the "junk trader ladies" for their technological ignorance, but they cannot deny that without these "ladies"—possibly their mothers, sisters, or wives—the trading networks that sustain the social and economic lives of Spring District would not have come into existence.

## The Waste Depot: Place Making, Gender, and Class

Compared to itinerant junk trading, running a waste depot is riskier, requiring greater investment, but is ultimately a more lucrative undertaking in which only people with sufficient experience, funds, and social connections can engage. In the urban depot, people rework class and gender in ways that reconstitute the inside/outside division. Men assume a central role in the depot's gendered division of labor, regardless of their spouses' contributions, while hired laborers shift the waste traders' relation to waste and dirt and thus their social positioning. Such dynamics are integral to the creation of urban spaces that are concurrently domestic and public, urban and rural. Figure 2.2 depicts one waste depot

FIGURE 2.2  A waste depot in central Hanoi.
Source: Author's photo, 2015.

FIGURE **2.3 Transaction at a waste depot in central Hanoi.**
Source: Author's photo, 2012.

on a small and unshapely piece of land stuck between two houses, and
Figure 2.3 shows a transaction between a male waste depot owner and a
female itinerant trader.

## Place Making in Ambiguous Spaces

Let us visit the depot (*bãi*) of Phúc, 38, a former appliance dealer, and
Hằng, 34, a former itinerant junk trader. From a beautiful wide, tree-
lined street lit at night with bright lamps, one takes a turn into a
smaller street, then another quick turn into an alley off the righthand
side. About 20 meters farther in is Phúc and Hằng's depot, nested
under a bamboo bush behind some tall buildings. The centrally located plot of over a hundred square meters was priced at about US$7,000
per square meter in 2012. The land belongs to a state organization that
does not yet have any plan for development. With the help of a distant
relative who works for the organization, Hằng and Phúc secured a six-
year lease, paying a monthly rent of 3.5 million *đồng* (US$170) in 2012.

"More than that would be unprofitable for us," Hằng says. The rent is low for its location—it could easily be twice as much from a private landlord. They can keep the plot until the organization needs it, provided that they maintain a good relationship with the relative sponsoring their tenancy.

Their makeshift house is built from recycled material, such as sheets of tin, cement tiles, and wooden bars. It has a common area, a separate bedroom, a kitchen adjacent to the washing area, and a flush toilet. Their furniture is a jumbled set of new and secondhand pieces, yet as Hằng likes to point out, they have "everything" that belongs to an urban household: refrigerator, washing machine, microwave, gas stove, and a huge flat-screen television. Parked beside the entrance is the minivan of a friend who transports their and others' waste to large-scale dealers or recycling villages. They have six-month-old twins, who will live with them for one or two years before being sent to the paternal grandparents in Spring District, where their 10-year-old son is living. They employ Phúc's female cousin and her two teenage sons, all of whom live together with them. The cousin takes care of the babies, while her sons help with manual tasks in the depot. The boys had come together with their mother to work for their uncle after failing their entrance exams for secondary school. Hằng's mother, 63, still works as an itinerant junk trader and lives with her eldest son and the latter's wife in a migrant lodging, occasionally spending a week at the depot to help with the babies. Like Mr. Mạnh in the previous chapter, Hằng's father stays home with several grandchildren and his two elderly parents.

The depot's daily operations involve a wide range of transactions. It requires not just the extremely specific knowledge of waste material and the various trading partners in the waste economy, but also an intimate understanding of the itinerant traders' personality. Hằng says, "You have to know the character of each of them, whether they are honest, greedy, persistent or not in order to have the right mode of transactions. But anyway, the frequent sellers would not dare to cheat very much." Female junk traders, who tend to lodge within a radius of one or two kilometers, come and go, unloading their purchases and weighing them under Hằng's supervision. Each junk trader makes several trips to the depot daily, often lingering for a chat about the success or failure of certain depots, people's land purchases in Hanoi, and the daily life of their children in the village. The women take great interest in the twin boys, often commenting on how precious they are, taking them into their arms and enthusiastically proclaiming: "My little breeder!" Young men from the district sometimes come to watch a soccer game with Phúc and the two teenage boys. Occasionally, a male itinerant trader drops in to check if there are any used appliances he can buy, and a local resident comes in to look for construction material for small repairs. A state sanitation worker, who sells the recyclables she collects while working with the household waste, visits frequently. Street vendors selling fruits, clothes, and vegetables come by to offer their goods. Female workers at a construction site nearby regularly bring iron pieces to sell, which they hide underneath their clothes to slip past the site's security guards. In the depot, village sociality is recreated in a distinct social space for people with diverse connections to the waste economy.

## Inside and Outside, Again

The division of labor in Phúc and Hằng's depot is foregrounded by similar gender categories underlining the labor and trading practices of the itinerant traders. Phúc stays on call for bigger loads of waste to buy at construction sites or factories, keeping track of the waste prices. He goes out to obtain these loads either with his motorbike or with a rental minivan, sometimes accompanied by the two teenagers. Hằng is in charge of housekeeping and the smaller transactions with the female junk traders. While the cousin takes care of the babies, Hằng takes breaks to breastfeed them while giving her orders for cooking the family meal. Here, Phúc deals with the outside world, whereas Hằng operates largely within the depot. Hằng says, "He does more demanding things. I just take care of lighter tasks and the children. Whatever we do, women have to be managers of the home (tề gia nội trợ) so that men can focus on work." With the hired labor at her disposal, however, Hằng focuses less on housekeeping and child care than on money-making activities, and her work is by no means less essential to the depot's operations. Her insistence that she has a marginal role in the household economy points to the same gender norms underlying Ms. Lan's investment in domestic roles during her migration discussed in Chapter 1.

Compared to the household trajectory in which men stay home and women migrate that Ms. Lan and Mr. Mạnh embrace, not only do Phúc and Hằng have a different relationship to the inside/outside realms, but the very definitions of "the inside" and "the outside" have shifted. For them, the urban depot is concurrently inside and outside in varying ways. Now that the two of them are away from their rural household, their ancestral house, and their eldest son, both are in a sense operating outside. Yet the depot is not just a place of work, the mainstay of their livelihoods, but also where they live their lives together with their younger children most of the time. The inside for them is thus extended beyond the ancestral home and the village to include the urban depot; the outside is thereby reconfigured, now encompassing relationships to different actors in the urban waste economy. Even as the boundaries of the inside and the outside shift, their meanings remain important for them in navigating mobility, which is why Phúc and Hằng continue to refer to these spatialized categories of gender. They carry both practical and symbolic significance for people in the rapidly changing conditions of post-reform Vietnam, as other scholars have also argued (Harms 2011, Leshkowich 2011).

## Moving Up: Matters of Dirt and Labor

Another tangible shift in Phúc and Hằng's depot is the changing relation the two former itinerant traders have to dirt, now mediated through the hired labor and the capital they command, which indicates emergent class processes in the waste economy. In most cases, Phúc instructs the cousin's two teenage boys to sort, bind, and load the waste onto trucks. The waste comes in all forms: iron bars from construction sites, used plastic heat-proof sheets, cartons, paper, books, plastic bottles, plastic sandals, cement bags, plastic doors, chopped-off parts of an iron gate, electric wires, and so forth. Waste material has highly differentiated grades of quality. As Table 2.2 shows, for instance, there are 12 grades of plastic, each with significant price differences. An experienced waste trader can tell them apart by looking at the color or the brand name of the used items, by touching them, and even by hearing the sound the items make on the cement floor when dropping (e.g., low-quality plastic produces a dull thudded sound). A discarded ventilator of a certain brand would contain 450 grams of copper, a TV set a little more, a kilogram of wires with a certain size about this much after stripping, and so forth.

With a great miscellany of things and a need to constantly classify the material, work in the depot is continuous from early morning to late evening. Waste traders often state that there is no way around hard work and diligence; waste trading is an occupation of "back-breaking labor and minute attention to detail," said Ms. Lanh, a waste depot owner in HCM City. While everyone seems to be doing something all the time in the depot of Phúc and Hằng, the boys are there to carry out the more physically demanding tasks of putting things together or away, loading and unloading—basically, creating order and clearing space for the purchases to accumulate. Even when the boys are having meals, customers might come by with their loads, in which case either of the two automatically places his chopsticks and bowl onto the table to get on with the tasks. Apart from earning their wage, the teenagers work for their relatives with a view to practicing the trade, so that one day they might be able to open their own depots. Such anticipated mobility notwithstanding, their waste labor and the domestic labor of their mother are relegated to a place in the hierarchy of the depot that is more exposed to dirt and domesticity.

With the hired labor handling menial tasks, Phúc and Hằng can devote more energy to maintaining order in the depot and overseeing transactions with the sellers. Compared with their time working as itinerant traders, Phúc and Hằng's role as depot owners minimizes their exposure to dirt. As the one who negotiates with the itinerant junk traders, Hằng refrains from touching the waste. The junk traders weigh it themselves under her supervision (Figure 2.4 depicts the common scale used by waste depots), sometimes with the help of the two teenagers, as Hằng sits on a chair next to the scale with a notebook, calculator, and pen and records the sums she pays for each purchase. The junk traders can receive payment immediately or keep the note until the sums have accumulated throughout the day. Out of concern for her babies' health, Hằng has a keen eye for the cleanliness of the waste; she refuses to buy anything that appears to have been retrieved from general garbage. Even though Hằng emphasizes her domestic roles, she hardly cleans, washes, or cooks in her urban depot; these tasks are done with the female cousin's paid labor.

Phúc and Hằng's social status has been visibly transformed. Waste continues to be their line of work in the depot, yet they do not perform the "miserable migrant laborer." Their gestures and commands convey that they are in charge. In Hằng's near-constant negotiations with the junk traders, she often justifies the prices she offers by referring to the market fluctuations and their small profit margin. Yet the junk traders said in separate conversations with me that the couple is doing well. Some call them "Master and Madam" (ông chủ, bà chủ) in a half-joking, half-admiring way, referring to the potential wealth they may have accumulated, as evidenced by how much they purchase every day. Although the profit margins on their purchases may be small, they add up significantly. Their depot is midrange—on a good day, they "weighed" (cân; see Figure 2.4) between 5 and 7 million

FIGURE **2.4 A typical scale, the most important tool in a depot.** "To weigh" (*cân*) often refers to the turnover of the depot; for example, depot owners would say, "Today we weighed 13 million [worth of waste]."
Source: Author's photo, Hanoi, 2012.

*đồng* worth of waste (US$250–350), and the depot had an annual turnover of 120 to 150 million *đồng* (US$6,000–7,000). Hằng proudly tells me that they had set aside 400 million *đồng* (US$20,000) in the previous five years and were building a new house in the countryside. Other depot operators have made greater fortunes, being able to purchase transport vehicles and land in Hanoi or to build modern houses in the village, a theme to which I shall return later in the book. As the urban public looks on the waste traders with skepticism and revulsion, these peasant entrepreneurs have been able to significantly transform their relationship to waste. The move from itinerant junk trading to waste depots turns many into business owners who make use of others' paid labor for accumulating wealth and generating value. The further they move up the waste hierarchy, the less exposed they are to dirt—and to its implications for their social status.[8]

TABLE 2.2 Plastic Grading and Pricing at a Waste Depot in Hanoi, March 2015

| TYPE OF PLASTIC | BUYING (VND) | SELLING (VND) |
| --- | --- | --- |
| *Túi bóng dẻo* (soft plastic bags) | 11.000 | 12.000 |
| *Túi bóng kính* (hard plastic bags) | 10.000 | 11.000 |
| *Túi bóng tex* (plastic linings) | 6.000 | 7.000 |
| *Nhựa ghế* (plastic chairs) | 11.000 | 12.000 |
| *Nhựa giống* (plastic chips) | 5.700 | 6.200–6.300 |
| *Yếm xe máy* (plastic from motorbikes) | 4.000 | 5.000 |
| *Nhựa cạch* (hard block plastic) | 3.000 | 3.500 |
| *Nhựa ghi* (water-pipe plastic) | 5.000–5.500 | 6.000 |
| *Dép nhựa tốt, trắng* (white plastic sandals) | 11.000 | 12.000 |
| *Dép nhựa màu* (colored plastic sandals) | 5.000 | 6.000 |
| *Tải rách, dây buộc, túi màu, túi bẩn* (colored, torn, or dirty plastic bags; ropes) | 2.000 | 2.500 |
| *Nhựa chết* (dead plastic) | 1.500 | 2.000 |

Source: Author's compilation.

# Conclusion: Class, Gender, and Urban Space Remaking

The shadows and edges of the city from which the waste traders operate are indeed integral to urban society and economy. Through gendered practices of place making, the men and women of Spring District drive a vibrant urban waste economy, thereby creating distinct social and economic spaces vital to their mobile livelihoods. Their practices of place making are both shaped by and, over time, help to remake Hanoi's urban spatial ordering. Responding to the fluid geography of urban waste, many have effectively captured the waste while fostering social ties in their rural networks and in urban society, a process aptly captured in the metaphor of *mở bãi*—that is, expanding to new frontiers, namely the city and its castaway things. Denied equal participation in the urban space, they accumulate wealth and reclaim particular urban spaces with the help of such spatial practices to "gain control over communal lives and economy" (Zhang 2001: 9). Nevertheless, they also entrench the precariousness of their urban existence as migrants working with waste and the urban perceptions of the spaces they occupy as out of place, not befitting the state-sanctioned notions of beauty and order (Harms 2016). Their practices thus concurrently undermine and consolidate the spatialization of class in Hanoi.

In shaping the value of waste, traders also reconfigure their value as gendered subjects. Contrary to the humble and naive image they project, they are often savvy tradespeople with considerable negotiation skills who build profitable connections to urban people and businesses. The seeming cheapness and dirtiness of the waste they trade in disguises and hence enhances its real value for their livelihoods. If the urban pity for the rural migrants is part of a class-based structure of feeling, then junk traders effectively game the system by performing the "miserable migrant junk trader." Yet these performances are complicated by men and women's differing relation to dirt, which is rooted in the Vietnamese constructions of gender and labor and the differential social value of men and women. The men are dissociated from the implications of waste by working with technology, vehicles, and in the outside world, thus retaining greater value for their labor and personhood, albeit with uncertain outcomes. Remaining closer to household waste and the domestic sphere, the women have a double-layered relationship to dirt, with consequences for the social value of their personhood, which they, however, deftly use.

When purposively highlighting the stereotypes into which they are categorized, waste traders perpetuate them for both practical and symbolic purposes (Herzfeld 2005). Yet over time, they also render them malleable to changes on both terms. What we witness here are not just repeatedly performed roles in the theater of social life (Goffman 1956) or reified effects of social discourses (Butler 1990, 1993), but spatially and socially embedded performative strategies of gendered subjects negotiating with power from a weaker position (Morris 1995, Nelson 1999). As these strategies reproduce the discourse that casts the migrant waste laborer as the rural and class Other—dirty, out of order, and at odds with the civilized urban—they latently produce social mobility and gendered meanings across rural and urban locations, meanings that will be further explored in Part II. Nonetheless, their precarious position, underscored by institutionalized marginalization and the instability of the global waste trade, suffuses a great deal of uncertainty into this spatialized process of value transformation. As the next chapter shows, these conditions are worsened by the commodification of state power and morally ambiguous practices in the waste economy, which a male trader describes as a "half-dark, half-light zone."

## CHAPTER 3

# Uncertainty, Ambiguity, and the Ethic of Risk-Taking

Ms. Thắm, a seasoned waste trader, once said to me, concluding a long conversation in which she had related multiple stories of the risks and dangers in the waste trade:

> This occupation is very precarious (*bấp bênh*), you know. There are all sorts of unexpected dangers. One day you are making good money and the next day you might end up with a great loss, even landing in jail or going bankrupt. We are people with "lowered necks and small voices" (*thấp cổ bé họng* [implying powerlessness and low status]), and we bear the losses if there are any troubles. But what can one do other than taking the risk?

Her statement aptly characterizes the power position of peasant entrepreneurs like her and how it shapes the outcomes of their actions. Simultaneously, it also refers to risk-taking as a mode of action that they take for granted in their mobile lives. This chapter will show that the ambiguity of waste and the transient state of being on the move make waste traders vulnerable to the abuses of both those in power and rogue actors. Apart from the unpredictability of the waste market and urban development, these factors account for the risks and uncertainties in the waste economy that could undermine the viability of their livelihoods. In response, local people have embraced what I term *the ethic of risk-taking*, an everyday ethic that takes such dangers for granted as part of a volatile global economy and patron-client networks centering on the commodification of state power. The ethic of risk-taking refers to people's tendency to take actions despite knowing that there is the risk of undermining a particular value (Boholm 2003: 13) and that the outcomes of their actions are uncertain. Contra the common association of risk-taking with high finance and high-tech start-ups, here it has more to do with peasant entrepreneurs, such as the waste traders, attempting to overcome the perils of having "lowered necks and small voices" in Vietnam's social order today. As we shall see, the ethic of risk-taking at times drives people to embrace morally ambiguous practices that reproduce the very system of power they resent, with consequences for their moral and economic lives. In so doing, however, they also remake the power hierarchy of the city and thus the urban order itself.

The scholarship on risk and uncertainty characterizes risk as instrument of governance and an ideology promoted by powerful institutions. In *Risk Society*, sociologist Ulrich Beck (1992) suggests that modern society carries with it unpredictable disasters, a fact that is disguised by the idea that risks can be avoided if carefully managed via shrewd investments and proper actuarial techniques, such as risk management or insurance. Other authors have written about how risk-based methods of government permeate our lives through medicine, social insurance, public health, public security, and so forth (see, e.g., O'Malley 2004). In these views, risk and uncertainty are defined in relation to statistical probabilities of future outcomes without attention to their social embeddedness (Douglas 1992, Boholm 2003). As this chapter suggests, how people deal with risk and uncertainty depends on their specific understandings of history and culture, social relations, and moral frameworks, as well as on their power position. In the experiences of the waste traders from Spring District, risk and uncertainty are the combined effects of global forces, dynamics of the new urban order, and the commodification of state power under market socialism.

## Economy of Uncertainty: Pricing, Tenure, and Geography of Urban Waste

Following the crash of 2008–2009, waste prices picked up again gradually, but by 2015, they still had not returned to the peak of the preceding period. (Table 3.1 depicts price differences between 2008 and 2015; for a breakdown of price fluctuations for typical wastes over six months in 2006–2007, see Mitchell 2009). Besides the boom-bust cycles of the global waste

TABLE 3.1 Price Changes between 2008 and 2015[1]

| WASTE TYPE | 2008 SELLING PRICE (VND/KG) | BUYING PRICE MARCH 2015 (VND/KG) | SELLING PRICE MARCH 2015 (VND/KG) |
|---|---|---|---|
| Human hair[2] | 2,300,000 | 1,800,000 | 2,000,000 |
| Iron (quality) | 9,000–9,200 | 5,000 | 5,300 |
| Copper (quality) | 170,000 | 85,000–90,000 | 93,000 |
| Aluminium | 30,000–32,000 | 25,000 | 26,500 |
| Lead | 35,000 | 26,000–28,000 | 30,000 |
| Paper (carton) | 3,700 | 2,600 | 2,800 |
| Plastic (quality) | 9,200 | 5,700 | 6,200–6,300 |

[1] The exchange rate in 2008 was approximately 16,500 VND per US$1 and in 2015 was about 21,500 VND per US$1. 2008 was the year in which waste prices peaked before tumbling.

[2] Human hair is only an occasional item traded by Spring District people. There are specialized human hair traders coming from rural areas of the central coast of Vietnam, whose networks extend across the border to Laos and Cambodia. Source: Author's compilation based on traders' remembrance of 2008 prices and actual prices in 2015.

market, prices are also subject to changes in state regulation or other factors affecting demand. For example, the relaxation of restrictions on steel imports from China pushes the price of iron waste down. The political tension between China and Vietnam following the 2014 violent protests in Chinese-invested factories also had a local effect on prices, as Chinese waste dealers who had been bulk buying from recycling villages temporarily refrained from entering the country. Depot owners often deal with price fluctuations by scaling down or hoarding a particular sort of waste when it fetches a low price. One depot I visited in 2012 had been hoarding four tons of copper for years in the hope that the price would rise back to the level they had paid for it around the time of the 2008–2009 crash. As with other commodities, however, external forces are sometimes strong enough to render these strategies ineffective.

Market conditions aside, depot operators' uncertainty originates in their unofficial residential status, which causes difficulties for them in owning property, maintaining long-term land rentals, and formally educating their children (Karis 2013, Nguyen and Locke 2014). Unstable tenure and rental prices mean that depot operators frequently have to move around the city in search of affordable and profitable locations. Phúc and Hằng, the depot owners we met in the previous chapter, have been fortunate with their tenancy thanks to their personal connections, yet newcomers now struggle to find suitable locations in Hanoi and have to look for opportunities in other cities, especially in Hồ Chí Minh City (HMC City) or the Southeast. Existing depots need to be moved around because rent increases make business unprofitable, landowners want the land back, or new municipal developments displace or outlaw them. As such, the social and economic space in which waste traders operate is not locally bounded but produced within trajectories of power that concern both the global economy and the contingencies of socialist control.

Nevertheless, waste traders' high mobility within the city is not always a result of eviction or outpricing; in many cases, it is a strategic response to Hanoi's changing topography, which corresponds to its pattern of waste generation. The central districts generate more consumer waste, while construction waste is more abundant in the outlying districts, where new developments are concentrated (see also Mitchell 2009). Depot owners thus choose to stay close to major construction sites or residential areas. Like in HCM City, numerous New Urban Areas (*Khu đô thị mới*) have been recently developed on the edge of Hanoi, where former farmland has been converted into residential, service, or industrial premises (DiGregorio 2011, Labbé and Boudreau 2011). Together with private housing, these developments have practically turned parts of Hanoi into giant construction sites, which for the traders become ample sources of recyclable waste. A number of operators thus set up shop near a construction site until the building is completed and then move elsewhere.

To capitalize on consumer waste, depot operators settle near residential areas, where itinerant junk traders are concentrated, as Phúc and Hằng in the previous chapter do. Some take advantage of the central plots belonging to organizations and individuals who put them on the rental market until they can be further developed. Private land awaiting development or with unclear tenure rights can still be found in many parts of central Hanoi. Farther out, on the edge of the city, a number of waste traders operate from half-finished villas in new urban zones that are left vacant due to property speculation. The rent there is low, since the owners would rather have any kind of occupants than leave their properties empty. And despite the rental instability, these plots are ideal for waste depots: they are central or accessible, while their "waiting" status means that the local authorities consider the activities taking place there to be temporary and do not strictly monitor them. Similarly, itinerant junk traders are no longer clustered in enclaves of migrant lodgings as before; temporary residences are scattered throughout the city as migrant rental properties, a lucrative business for urban landlords. Such elusiveness and transience in the spatial practices of depot owners and itinerant traders align with their ambiguous social status. Yet they also indicate purposive actions that are inseparable from the performative strategies these traders and depot owners deploy to construct themselves as outcasts, strategies that partly hide the monetary value of waste from the public (see Chapter 2).

## Dangers in the Zones of Ambiguity

I once had a discussion with Thu and Ngoan, former waste depot owners, about the cheats and tricks in their trade. One time, Ngoan bought three million *đồng* worth of copper bars that looked new, with the brand name properly imprinted on them, only to find out later that they were in fact made from lead—the bars had been custom-made to be sold to waste traders. Another time, she bought a significant amount of wire, for the copper inside, which turned out to be filled with much-cheaper aluminum except for the first several meters that she could check. Relating several other incidents of their acquaintances being tricked into buying fake waste, Ngoan said, "There is so much cheating, every possible kinds and ways of cheating. If you are not careful, you'll go bust." Thu nodded in agreement, adding:

> You really need to be vigilant. The problem is that when you find out [about the cheats], there is no way to report the cheater, since it is a clearly undefined legal realm. They could just say that it was a consented transaction (*thuận mua vừa bán*). What count as waste categories is ambiguous, there is no law behind them. It is a half-dark, half-light zone (*tranh tối, tranh sáng*), that's why.

After a pause, he continued: "But then if it were not like that, we wouldn't be able to make our living either. If it were all clear-cut (*cứ đằng thẳng ra*), there would be no doors opening for us to do our trade." Thu's reflections are insightful portrayals of the illicit dealings and dangers commonly confronted by not just the waste traders, but also the waste economy as a whole. The ambiguity of waste as a commodity and legal category indeed underlies the problems that the waste traders have with both rouge actors in the waste economy, such as the counterfeiters of waste or thugs who seek to control waste sources, and state agents.

### Fake Waste

Rather than random incidents, waste faking is widespread. I did not meet anyone who faked waste for sale to depots, but the experiences of Spring District people suggest that it is an organized system with professional producers and a network of distributors targeted at waste traders. Fake waste comes in all varieties, but it often involves items known for containing certain amounts of high-priced metals, such as copper. The items are made to look like the used or leftover material from particular products the waste traders know well—like what Ngoan purchased for example—with the color and brand name of a standard type of wire, the first several meters of which are filled with the right kind of metal. Another female trader once bought a truckload of used car batteries from a particular local brand because she knew how much metal each of these batteries normally contains. After the truck left, however, she discovered that except for the few items she had been given to examine, the whole load had been emptied of the metal and filled instead with cement.

Since waste material has highly differentiated grades of quality and thus fetches varying prices depending on the quality (Chapter 2), fake waste is sometimes made to have the look like or carry the brand name of a product with higher grade material. Waste counterfeiters clearly have intimate knowledge of the waste trade and what traders look for in their purchases. What's more, they seem to be adept performers whose make-believe skills sometimes get the better of even the most experienced waste traders—almost every depot owner has experienced such encounters. The driver of the battery truck mentioned earlier, for example, staged a convincing sale. He put on the most sincere face, saying to the waste trader that he had secured the batteries from somebody working in a factory on an unauthorized deal and would therefore accept a lower price than normal in order to get rid of them quickly. And once money changed hands, he swiftly withdrew from the scene so that she was unable to find any trace of him afterward.

The faking of waste material for sale to waste traders links the waste economy to a huge economy of counterfeiting goods in which every product of market value can find its counterfeited version. Unlike the counterfeiting of a Gucci bag or an item of Burberry clothing, which capitalizes on the conspicuity of these consumer brands, waste counterfeiting benefits from the invisibility of the waste material often hidden in castaway objects. As the waste counterfeiters are on the move and keep changing the range of their faked goods and their selling tactics, this creates a significant terrain of danger for the waste traders. Meanwhile, the profitability of the waste trade depends on traders' access to multiple sources of waste, including unexpected offers from passers-by that could double the monthly turnover of a depot. This makes it difficult to rule out the potential waste counterfeiters completely. In HCM City, the waste traders encountered the counterfeiters more frequently than in the North, where the networks are more close-knit and there are fewer irregular sellers.

## State Agents

Ms. Thắm and Mr. Tình, both in their sixties, are owners of a waste depot on one of the highways leading out of West Hanoi. Having been in the business for years and set up their two sons with their own depots in central districts, they are familiar with the ins and outs of the trade. Because of their advancing old age, they felt unable to deal with the stress of relocating within the urban center, or managing relationships with urban neighbors, landlords, and local officials, and decided to move to a less profitable location away from the central areas and construction sites. Out on the highway, land rentals are cheaper and more long-term, while the distance discourages local officials from frequent visits. "The youngsters [their children] still have their strength, and they are more daring and resourceful than us oldies; they can handle these things. They will continue to work in the inner districts because there is more business there," said Mr. Tình. The couple told me long stories of their children dealing with different kinds of local authorities, something that they also used to do when operating in the city center. For example, the local policeman often asks one of their sons to transport things for him for free, in addition to demanding a monthly payment of 500,000 đồng.

Things are not much different in HCM City. Ms. Lanh, owner of a waste depot in District 12, laughed out loud when I asked if she had any problems in dealing with local authorities. She said, "Oh, they come as frequently as you squeeze the lemon (đều như vắt chanh [something you do every day for drinks and meals]). There are all sorts of them. From the head of the residential group, to the local police, the commune's security groups, the traffic police, the self-governing committee of the residential area, to the environmental officers. All want some money from you, and at the end of the day it amounts to a lot that you have to give to them." While most traders see this as the cost of doing business, having to pay bribes is a source of frustration and resentment. Sometimes, it even provokes resistance. Mr. Mai, another depot owner in HCM City who is a war veteran (cựu chiến binh), tells how he reacted when the demands became excessive:

> You know, all these types [of local authorities], they want some payment from us. The head of the residential area (ấp trưởng) demands 200,000 a month. They can talk really well and convincingly. They would evoke this law, that constitution, every possible legal argument. They try to find fault with everything you do to get you to give them some money. So after several months of paying the ấp trưởng 200,000, I was upset. I told him: "I am not paying anymore. I have to work my back off to earn a living. I have to pay for the rent, the electricity, the water, and for

all sorts of other things. When I came to liberate Saigon, you were not even born. Why would I have to give you 200,000 for nothing?" Later he summoned me to his office to give me a fine or something, where his deputy asked me to write down my case. So I wrote that I am a veteran who is now struggling to make a living and there is nothing in the law of this country that says that I am forbidden to trade waste and so on. Then he looked at what I wrote. Seeming quite taken aback that I am a veteran, he commented that my handwriting was beautiful. But the *ấp trưởng* stopped asking me for money afterward. You know, they just try to test you out, and if you are not strong, you pay.

Mr. Mai's act of defiance indicates that there is some space for negotiation with power in these transactions, but this space is bounded by people's position in the social order. Being a war veteran continues to carry symbolic significance in Vietnam today, since the legitimacy of the party-state rests largely on past and present causes of national defense; people working in the state system are aware of the need for caution in dealing with veterans for fear of backlash. Mr. Mai was aware of his bargaining chip when he put up the fight. Not everyone can afford to do so, however, and most would rather pay the sums to maintain a friendly relationship with the local authorities and the police. The latter have the power to declare waste trading and the material they deal with as out of place and themselves as infringing upon urban order and state regulations. It is particularly so due to the status of migrant waste traders as residents who, without urban household registration, are considered transient in the city, and whose participation in urban economic and social life is seen as questionable. In the ambiguous spaces of the waste economy, state agents keep an avid eye on the likelihood of extracting rents and stand ready to take advantage of the traders' weaker power position. Such rent seeking behavior of state agents is common not only in Vietnam but also in other regional and global contexts (Arnold and Pickles 2011, Sikor and To 2011, Gupta 2012); what is distinct here in how the weaker position of waste traders is compounded by the social ambiguity of waste and their inferior citizen status.

## Stolen Goods and Thugs

Another issue arising from the ambiguity of waste is the traders' exposure to stolen goods. Waste traders are aware that it is illegal to trade in stolen goods, which could cause them trouble with the police. Yet sometimes it is difficult to determine whether the goods had been stolen, and even goods that were not stolen can be easily declared as stolen by a state official (of course, it is also not to be ruled out that some traders might knowingly buy them). As one example, Canh, a depot owner in Hanoi, told me he once bought a hundred kilograms of cables from someone. Soon after the seller had walked out the door, payment in his pocket, a policeman appeared, apparently having been tipped off about the transaction and wanting to fine the trader for dealing in stolen goods. The trader ended up paying the policeman an amount that was worth more than the profit he would have made from the cables. In another example, Ms. Thắm's son bought three hundred kilograms of waste iron from the guards of a bridge under construction. On leaving, he was stopped by the police, who not only imprisoned him for the night, but also beat him into confessing that he had knowingly bought stolen goods. Later, he was brought to court, and the family bribed several persons introduced to them by acquaintances who promised that they would intervene to ensure that he would not go to prison. In the end, Ms. Thắm's son pleaded not guilty, the iron was determined to be waste material by the court, and they just had to pay a small fine. The bribe cost them 41 million đồng (about US$2,000), but they are not able to say if their under-the-table payments were what led to the court outcome or if they had paid the sums for nothing.

The fluidity in the demarcation of waste makes it difficult to categorize it legally while its value can be varyingly interpreted as a commodity, an asset, or worthless objects, and thus it is open to interpretation as a kind of "unregulated free commons" (Alexander and Reno 2011: 20). Such ambiguity creates not just fertile ground for the rent-seeking behavior of state agents, but also a zone in which thugs compete for control, sometimes in a violent manner. The thugs (đầu gấu, literally bear-headed people) operate in places with a high concentration of waste, such as a demolition or construction site. There, they would block the gate of the site, and anyone who entered to buy the waste would be beaten or threatened into leaving. In some places, they ask for a fee on the waste purchase: one informant said he had to pay the thugs 300,000 đồng for every ton of waste iron he bought in a site. In certain parts of Hanoi, a gangster in the name of "Doggy Thanh" (Thanh chó) was notorious for controlling the waste collection and purchases in large construction sites.

All in all, the greatest risks of a waste trader seem rooted in the blurred boundaries between the legal and the illegal. The situation is potentially dangerous in that the traders can be arbitrarily cast as outlaws or become easy targets of criminals. At the same time that the rent seeking behavior of state agents subjects people to the arbitrariness of power, it facilitates the flourishing of the very rogue actors that state power is supposed to contain. Through their encounters with these actors, however, the waste traders do take an active role in reproducing the half-dark, half-light zone that they loathe operating in, as the following vignette suggests.

## Men on the Highway and the Art of Making Law

It was 4 a.m., still dark in the cool early April morning. The van was inching forward at about twenty kilometers an hour on the highway, although the early traffic was flowing. Hân, a thirty-one-year-old driver, operates a waste depot together with his wife on the edge of central Hanoi; the van (of the same kind depicted in Figure 3.1) belongs to them. The couple have access to the waste of a workshop producing iron gates, and Hân could transport a load to a recycling village about thirty kilometers away fifteen to twenty times every month. Sitting in the front seat next to Hân, I could feel the engine working extremely hard, like somebody trying to push a heavy boulder up a steep hill. The van was straining from the overload of cargo. The van itself weighs 2.2 tons and is legally allowed to transport up to 0.8 tons; at maximum, the total weight should not exceed 3 tons. When almost filled up with iron waste, like it was on that day, it weighed 4.6 tons, thus carrying practically three times the cargo limit. Hân mentioned that his truck, like most other waste-transporting vehicles, had been reinforced so that it could withstand a much heavier weight; without the reinforcement, the truck would break under such a load. Despite his reassurance, I was

FIGURE **3.1  A waste-transporting vehicle.**
Source: Author's photo, Hanoi, 2012.

rather concerned about our safety, as it felt like the vehicle could break at any time.

The reason why Hân leaves so early in the morning is not to avoid the traffic police on account of overloading, as I initially assumed, but so that he can "make law" (*làm luật*; i.e., pay a bribe) with the latter more conveniently. He cannot simply drive on the highway with such an overladen vehicle without them noticing, so he chooses to engage rather than avoid them. In 2015, the traffic police had been receiving much public criticism for letting truck drivers operate their overloaded vehicles inside the city, even after a weight limit on the trucks was introduced. Hân's timing therefore also helps the traffic police to "make law" (i.e., collect the bribe) more easily, since there is less attention on the truck, and on the transactions between them, at that time of the day. The trucks can then operate without anyone noticing them and questioning the policemen's integrity.

As soon as he saw the traffic policeman holding out his baton, Hân pulled in and walked over to the man, calmly handing over a passport containing a banknote. The policeman opened the passport, took the banknote, and nonchalantly pocketed it. Hân then quickly turned around to walk back to the vehicle, as if he had just given a pat on a friend's shoulder. He had placed the "law money" (*tiền luật*) inside somebody's expired passport that he had fetched out of waste paper in his depot. The passport looked fine as an official document. It was better for the job than the vehicle's registration book as well, since it is always possible that the policeman might have decided to take it from him. "They are unpredictable, who knows what they might do," Hân said.

Hân hated that he had to "make law" with these greedy policemen, he said, but if he had followed the regulation, transporting the maximum weight of eight hundred kilograms would produce a much smaller profit margin. Waste transport counts as a move up the hierarchy for Spring District traders; many start out as itinerant traders and then, once they have accumulated enough funds, start to operate a depot, buying loads of waste from the itinerant traders. The vehicles are a desirable addition to the waste depot, an indication that the depot has a good turnover, and make the vital connection between the urban waste traded within the city and the places where it will be recycled. At 5,000 *đồng* per kilogram of iron, the load of 2.0 to 2.5 tons that Hân regularly transports is worth around 100 million *đồng*. For each trip, he makes about 1 million, "minus the law and other costs" (*trừ luật với các chi phí khác*); if the official weight limit is to be followed, it would reduce his earnings threefold, making it no longer worth the significant investment in the truck. When I mention other people's complaints about the impact of the new weight regulation on their trucking business, Hân said that the regulation was actually a good thing, because of the lesser damage to the roads and other people's safety and for the safety of the driver and their trucks' durability. But then "one needs to make a living," he says, "[and] we do not have much of a choice. Everything requires money nowadays. If I stopped working a couple of days, we get to know right away the effects on my family's daily life. You know yourself how much it costs to raise the kids nowadays and send them to schools."

Hân's reflection reveals competing legitimacies of acting as a citizen, as a parent, and as a self-interested person—what is morally legitimate here is not necessarily that which is legal and vice versa. He opted for one modality of action to which he accrues most personal value, taking the risk and accepting the fact that the tension between the different moral claims cannot be resolved. This kind of "moral reasoning" is a common feature of people's narratives around the world about situations in which they have to choose between conflicting alternatives of action (Sykes 2009). It indicates the ambiguity of the moral framework that underpins social life in Vietnam today, under which people have to come to terms with moral paradoxes arising from the interplay between market forces and the degeneration of formal law. This ambiguous moral framework in turn shapes how the social order is enacted, not just by those in power, but also by the less powerful actors such as the waste traders or others like them. The "law-making" does not just take place via face-to-face exchanges of bribe such as the ones Hân engages in; it also works more anonymously and in organized manners. The owners of bigger trucks, which are often driven by hired men, would arrange an advanced deal with the police, paying a monthly sum for their whole fleet to cover specific routes in the city, which people refer to as "*bao đường*" (road patronage). Once, while visiting Mr. Tình and Ms. Thắm's depot along the highway in Hanoi, I saw a large waste-transport truck going against the flow of traffic toward the depot, apparently saving the distance they would have to make if they took the proper turn. When the driver and the porters disembarked, Mr. Tình exclaimed, "How dare you drive like that? If only the police saw you. . ." To which one of the men said, "This road is ours. The police are also in our family!" (*Đường này đường của nhà. Cảnh sát thì cũng là người nhà!*) His comment was met with a bout of general laughter. Mr. Tình later explained to me that their employer, a wealthy dealer, has "made law" with the upper echelons of the police and thus would not be fined in the area; otherwise, "these guys would not be so daring."

For more anonymous transactions, truck drivers pay their fees to a middleperson in order to be given a logo to stick on their vehicles' windscreen, making visible to the traffic police that they have paid their dues. According to Long, a waste transporter from Spring District in HCM City, he sometimes had to hide away in an alley for half a day at the sight of a traffic police team until they left when he was still working outside of the road patronage system. This was detrimental to his business, which depended on daily turnaround of the waste that accumulated in his family's depot, so to pay the fees became a reasonable thing to do.

In her work on cross-border trading in northern Vietnam, Kirsten Endres (2014) suggests that the bribes cross-border traders pay to customer officers, similarly termed "making law" by her informants, are part of an endemic system of corruption, something she refers to as "corrupt exception." According to Endres, it is the "only viable way of securing access to economic resources and muddling through the vicissitudes of life" in a system governed by uncertainty (2014: 620). The traders Endres portrays tend to evoke discourses of kinship and compassion to negotiate spaces of action with state agents with whom they are acquainted, much like what depot owners would do to sustain relationships with local authorities in the city. On the highway, a bustling economic space characterized by highly mobile actors and anonymous transactions, however, "law-making" seems almost institutionalized, so that there is hardly any need for the participating actors to engage in relationship building. In both cases, a parallel system to state law and order exists, feeding on the power of state law and order – the latter being enacted in such a way that this second-order system, premised on the very act of violating it, could emerge. Rather than a case of the law being suspended or being broken "in the name of law," as Jakob Rigi (2012: 81) writes of corruption in Russia under Putin, here the law generates a value for the act of breaking it, much in the same way that the market value of certain brands generates value for the faked goods sharing their name. The same can be said about the faking of waste items discussed earlier. This second-order system is partaken in by actors of differential power position, but nonetheless, each enters into the exchange with his or her own agenda, trading in the possibility to create exceptions to the rules of the formal system, such as the weight limit or regulations of cross-border trade (see also Sikor and To 2011). It is no coincidence that to "make law" means both bribing and taking bribes, as both sides are equally charged with sustaining the system.

To participate in "making law" is a precarious act of risk-taking, since the system could break down at any time given the mistrust within it and the arbitrary power of the state agents. As Hân says, "Who knows what they would do?" It is a risk that can only be managed by trying things out, and an incalculable risk given that individual state agents are part of wider webs of power relations in which they in turn are the small guys. Yet it is apparently a risk worth taking. In the waste economy, "making law" is essential to what waste traders, especially depot operators, refer to as their professional skills (nghề). There is a tangible sense of empowerment in the act of "making law." One gains with it the knowledge of how to obtain privileges denied to people who remain within the bounds of state law and order, plus a sense of being able to take things into one's own hands. The risk-taking is highly masculinized, and it is embraced to a greater degree by male traders in their orientation to the dangerous world of the outside. Even though dealing with the dangers of trading waste is not as glamorous as the risks of trading on the stock market or starting up a tech company, to master it is a manifestation of proper manhood in the new economy (see also Nguyen 2018). As such, these male waste traders are remaking the urban power hierarchy at the same time that they enact the ethic of risk-taking through their "making law" practices.

## Conclusion: Ambiguity, Risk-Taking, and Remaking the Urban Order

The "half-dark, half-light zone" that is the urban waste economy of Vietnam represents a space of risk and uncertainty, which emerges from the interplay between global forces and local dynamics of urban development, the fuzziness of categories, and the arbitrariness of state power. For the waste traders from Spring District, this space is filled with the risks of being people "with low necks and small voices," the small persons in the social order of the market economy where socialist values and revolutionary legacies are increasingly losing out to rent-seeking behavior by those in power. The dangers are aggravated by the ambiguity of waste, things that are in a liminal state of being redefined and revaluated, and the waste traders' uncertain status as rural migrants on the move, unregistered and characterized as the dirty Other. As much as the waste counterfeiters, their actions hinge on the ambiguity of waste as material and on fuzzy categories of law and state power. Such ambiguity helps to sustain an economy of counterfeiting that involves not only the faking of waste items to be sold the waste traders, but also the "counterfeiting of legality" (Rigi 2012: 69) through the widespread patronage system of "making law." The different acts of counterfeiting are traceable to a social order in which actors compete for power over others by various means, even the use of brute violence such as in the case of the thugs who take control of waste sources. It is this extra-legal social order, one in which arbitrariness and manipulation are the norm, that links the commodification of state power with the burgeoning of rouge actors. Uncertainty, rather than being a generic feature of the human condition, functions in the system as a means of power (see also Gainsborough 2010). Things are kept undefined and blurry, so that some people can be arbitrarily declared outlaws, certain acts can be capriciously defined as transgression of formal laws, and actual transgression can be given the green light as a privilege that can be bought.

Within this social order, morally ambiguous practices are prevalent in the encounters between actors of different power positions; they are a major source of uncertainty for those with lesser power. Waste traders take the arbitrariness of power and their weaker position as a starting point to navigate the uncertainty, developing an ethic of risk-taking in their dealings with power.[1] This ethic helps them to render unknown places as spaces over which they have some control and makes it possible for them to extend their trading networks to new frontiers. This is ever more important as their mobility trajectories become more complex, with people and families moving farther away from the familiarity of kin and homeplace networks and locations. Risk-taking indeed has become an essential part of how local people "make it in the world," helping them to wrest some control over the urban order and thus remake their power position in that order. Yet what is at stake when risk-taking is normalized is not just safety or livelihoods, but that their actions will become heavily laden with moral ambiguities. Traders who pay the police to get away with their offences, who pay the thugs for access to the waste, or who might half-knowingly purchase stolen goods are aware they are engaged in morally precarious activities that could randomly turn them into legal and moral outcasts. More than taking risks with state law, these actions could endanger the moral life of families and communities.

What are people to do in order to sustain the sense of being a moral person in the midst of such uncertainty? How are they to live the moral life of the person, or carry out the project of *làm người* (doing human), while making a living in a perilous social order over whose rules they have much lesser say? As we shall see in Part II, the moral ambivalence that emerges from the ambiguity of material and social categories spills into family and community relations. It underlines local people's effort at remaking social and moral lives through caring and being cared for, their personal investment in the homeplace, their practices of care and belonging, and their participation in local development.

A beautiful house in the making.
Source: Author's photo, Green Spring, 2015.

# PART II

# Wealth

## CHAPTER 4

# Mobility, Moral Discourses, and the Anxiety of Care

Caring and being cared for in Vietnam today cannot be divorced from processes of class consolidation in which the urban middle class increasingly seeks to distinguish itself from the laboring classes (Nguyen-Marshall 2012, Nguyen 2015b). Urban middle-class practices of care, with an emphasis on social distinction, serve as indicators of civility and human capital—in other words, the "intellectual level" (*dân trí*) of middle-class people. They function as a central trope against which matters of care are measured against, often to insinuate that the inadequate care in other groups reflects their lower moral standing (Nguyen 2015b; see also Chapter 5). In the dominant discourse, middle-class care provides the template for civilized family life, the moral strength of which is ensured by the loving attention of the knowledgeable wife and mother and the authoritative presence of the husband and father. This explains the widespread anxiety around the organization of care in mobile families, and even more so in rural families whose adult members are on the move. Yet although mobility might turn problematic for family life, migrant families are much more flexible and resilient in the face of living between places than is commonly assumed. Class distinction through care practices, meanwhile, is not just articulated in the difference between the urban middle class and rural migrants, but also increasingly in the differentiation within rural communities. Thereby, the moralization of how care is given becomes a major mechanism of distinction.

The gendered and intergenerational negotiations around caring and being cared for described in this chapter are a common feature of translocal households in Vietnam and elsewhere (Jacka 2017). What distinguishes care practices in Spring District is how waste work and the attendant patterns of mobility by local women and men influence household arrangements and entrench the anxiety of mobility. While mobility commonly produces moral anxiety over women's transgression of boundaries and upheaval in caring roles, the social meanings of waste add another dimension to the anxiety. Regional narratives about Spring District contain a mixture of awe at the unlikely wealth generated from waste trading and stories that construct waste traders as somewhat immoral; the exposure to waste is seen as bodily and morally contaminating, making people more vulnerable to vices (see Chapter 2). Such anxiety is projected onto the realm of the inside and is reified in the notion of "social evils (*tệ nạn xã hội*)," the politicized language of a post-reform state campaign that has become vernacularized. Moral discourses around care, waste, and money in Spring District, however, are by no means one-sided—there is often a great deal of mutual exclusion between the waste traders and those who consider themselves as holding up the community's moral standards. In the meantime, how the waste traders engage in these discourses reveals the anxieties and dilemmas in their endeavor to cleanse the degrading connotation of waste work and so remake themselves as moral persons.

## Is It Better to Be Uneducated and Rich? Mutually Exclusionary Discourses

The Trần family house is one of the most impressive in Red Spring, a tall villa covered in emerald green paint with bright red tiles. The family altar is imposing: walking up the stairs through a wide wooden door toward the altar, one can feel solemnity bearing down in the air. It reminds me of the majestic altars in the Temple of Literature in Hanoi: a huge porcelain incense-stick holder painted with blue dragons, and large decorative panels emblazoned with golden characters supported by a red-painted table whose edges are carved and gold-plated. In front of the family altar is an expensive set of antique timber armchairs; on the other side of the room is a massive, flat daybed (*phản*) in matching color. The owner of the house, Old Hoành, a ninety-three-year-old woman, is being taken care of by her youngest daughter, an unmarried and retired secondary school teacher, Ms. Hợi, who is sixty-two. Ms. Hợi is also caring for the two-year-old the grandson of one of her three brothers. One of the brothers is Mr. Hòa, an influential elderly man whose house is on the other side of the village; her other two brothers, who, like Ms. Hợi, are retired government employees, live in other districts of the same province.

Ms. Hợi and Mr. Hòa, who were very friendly and hospitable to Tâm and me, are proud that, unlike peasant families in the village, theirs is a family with discipline and order (*nề nếp*). In one long conversation with the two of them, Mr. Hòa's wife (Ms. Hoài), and a visiting sister who is a nurse in the district hospital, I asked them what "a family with discipline and order" means. Ms. Hợi said that it is one in which there is clear "above" and "below" (*có trên có dưới*). The ones below respect those above and the ones above are kind to those below, the family should be harmonious, and there should be no internal fighting. Further, the children are taught how to behave, do not use bad language, and do not get involved in social evils. "You don't need to be rich, but the family has to preserve certain traditions," she said. Then she looked at me meaningfully, speaking emphatically: "Your host family is a typical uneducated peasant family (*gia đình nông dân thất học điển hình*), one that is chaotic and does not care much about discipline and order. They have never really escaped from their status as uneducated peasants, even if they might be better off now than before." Mr. Hòa and the other two ladies nodded in agreement before contributing stories to prove this conclusion. They related the account of a long-standing feud between our male host's youngest sister and her elder brother over a piece of residential land, which is common knowledge in the neighborhood. Ms. Hoài then told the story of our female host's brother, who once had a tick in his nose for a while until someone pulled it out after hearing his complaints. "Without knowledge, how wretched someone can be," Ms. Hợi chuckled, a little disgusted at the image.

The conversation then shifted to migrant waste trading and its impacts on village life. While the four of them, all of whom have never been involved in the migrant waste trade, understand the need for their fellow villagers to "go outside" in order to cope with limited land and the shortage of employment, their conversations focused on the dark sides of the villagers' exposure to "the outside." The outside for them is the source of social evils such as drug addiction, prostitution, HIV, and gambling. What they find unsettling is how the care of the children and the elderly has been negatively affected by migrant adults' pursuit of money and their lack of attention to moral standards. Mr. Hòa said: "When the parents are away, going after money, the children all become rotten (*hỏng hết*), playing computer games all the time instead of studying. Junk trading earns them money but loses them morals." To illustrate her brother's point, Ms. Hợi told the story of a teenage girl who had gone to Hanoi with a boy, spending all the money her parents had left for her and her siblings. Ms. Hoài then contributed an account of a grandfather who gambled and left the grandson unattended; the grandson has now become a drug addict.

Asking me about my research, and upon finding out that I was interested in issues of care, Ms. Hợi explained to me the difference between *nuôi, chăm*, and *trông*, with *nuôi* being the provision of resources and money, *chăm* literally meaning "looking after, taking care of," and *trông* being "overseeing" or "managing." In their family, she is looking after (*chăm*) her mother while overseeing (*trông*) her grandnephew, whereas her brothers provide for (*nuôi*) her mother, even when they are not living with her on a daily basis. She said that *nuôi* (providing for), the remote act of care being performed by her brothers for their mother, is nowadays the most important because finance decides everything: "Money is political power" (*tiền là chính trị*). In migrant families, according to her, the grandparents do not have much say over the grandchildren because they do not provide for them (in the financial sense of *nuôi*), something that the children are aware of, and as a result, they do not listen to their grandparents. She pointed out that in her family, there is never any bickering over the *nuôi* (provision) for her mother. Her eldest brother simply assumes the responsibility, as is to be expected of an eldest brother, while she, as the younger sister, is there to take daily care of the elder—the care for their mother is thus undertaken in harmony and without any calculation of who gives more or less (*tính toán thiệt hơn*). The others then chipped in with anecdotes of families in the village for which the care of elderly parents is an issue of constant contention between the siblings. They laughed when mentioning the families in which siblings rotate taking care of the parents.

When I came back and told Ms. Lan, our female host, that we had spent the afternoon in the house of Mr. Hòa's mother, she reacted a little cool at first. Later, at dinner, she said while dealing out steaming bowls of rice to us, "Mr. Hòa's family is very orderly (*quy củ*) and archaic (*kim cổ*). They have many rules and family traditions, very uptight and hierarchical. Unlike us. We are a lot more relaxed, down-to-earth, and egalitarian in the family. Their family is not like that; I am not so keen on their ways." Her son Dân, who had come back to prepare for his wedding, chimed in: "They always think they look so grand, but there is not much to it." Then he went on to say that Mr. Hòa's daughter-in-law had obtained her teaching post at the local primary school because they had paid 200 million *đồng* in bribes. If he wanted, Dân said, he could easily buy a graduation certificate for the higher secondary school (he had only finished lower secondary school) as easily as the teacher had bought her post. "As long as one has money, one can have everything. You know, it is better to be uneducated and rich than well-educated and poor (*văn hay chữ tốt không bằng học dốt lắm tiền*)", Dân concluded. Of course, Dân was not ignorant of the fact that at that point, Mr. Hòa's family was wealthy and his was not; his reference point was the future: there are enough examples of people becoming rich from waste work in the district; he just needs to persist and in the long run will achieve it.

In Spring District, such mutually exclusive discourse between the waste traders and the people who consider themselves to be the local elite abounds on many levels. Waste trading/peasant families often emphasize that they have more *tình cảm* (affection) and greater sense of community than the better educated government cadres or employees, who are more egoistic and arrogant. The latter frequently express concerns about moral decay among their fellow villagers who have "gone outside," and the discourse of moral decline is the strongest regarding the Green Spring commune. Green Spring has a longer history and stronger identification with waste trading. Thus, the association of their moral status with waste is common, although nowadays it has slightly lessened due to the spread of waste trading. As much as the "village outsiders" are impressed with the wealth accumulated through Green Spring people's extensive waste depot operations, the counter-narrative is that they are ill-educated; their over-zealous pursuit of money has led to degrading themselves and neglecting their children. Spoiled by money and prone to vices, Green Spring children not only perform badly in school, but also easily take up a whole range of "social evils": drug abuse, internet game addiction, and gang fighting are rampant there. Some informants in Red Spring can go on tirades about the aggressiveness of youngsters in Green Spring. In their description, the village paths are roamed by drug addicts and gangsters who undeservingly live in the villas that their parents built with money earned from waste. This view of Green Spring is also shared by officials and educators, who consider the lower number of children entering higher secondary schools and colleges as an indication of its severe social problems. "They make a lot of money, yes, but a whole generation is lost!" exclaimed the headmaster of a local school, who said that the development of Green Spring is "*rỗng*" (hollowed out), because there are so few people with academic achievements.

After long stays in both Green Spring and Red Spring, I find that Green Spring's social problems are exaggerated. While there might be fewer young adults going on to higher education and incidents of drug addiction are not uncommon (I will return to this issue later), it is difficult to conclude that its young people are more "spoiled" than elsewhere. Young people from peasant households often leave school early to join their parents in the urban waste depot, learn the trade, and become able to set up for themselves at an early age. Not unlike the ways in which Paul Willis's (1977) young English working-class men take up "learning to labor," or become socialized into working-class mentality and values, many are brought up with the perspective of later entering the waste trade. This aptitude clashes with the idea that the ultimate goal of a person ought to be higher education, the ultimate signifier of *dân trí* that reaches back into the Confucian tradition of valuing the literati over other social groups and now embraced as a means of class distinction. The disagreement between these perspectives is captured in the following statement by Mr. Sanh, another educator in a leadership position, who originally comes from Green Spring but now lives in the town center of Spring District:

> They are not poor. They are actually rich, but that's just being rich on economic terms and poor in terms of knowledge. You know, there are students attending college already and dropping out because they see that their friends are making a lot of money and can afford expensive mobile phones and jewelry. They don't see that to get an education one has to work hard and suffer, but at the end what one achieves is much greater than short-term economic benefit.
>
> Many say that nowadays it is better to be uneducated and rich than to be well-educated and poor. They don't see that with my high level of education, I now earn several hundreds of thousand a day in my good job. I go to work well-dressed, wearing clean shirts and polished shoes. They don't see that my children are doing well at school; later they will go to college and have office jobs. My children will have a good life, whereas their children will keep living from hand to mouth like they do.

Like the other people who place themselves in the upper moral echelons of the village, Mr. Sanh's visible contempt for his fellow villagers who are waste traders is based on an assumption of their "low intellectual level" that glosses over a number of issues. First, waste trading is a profession that requires the skills, knowledge, and savviness that are not easily available to anyone, as we have seen. Second, the reason some college students might drop out in favor of trading waste is not necessarily because they are blinded by the promise of easy money with which they can buy fancy consumption goods (although it may be an extra incentive). It is common knowledge that higher education does not automatically lead to white-collar employment and thus to a good life, as used to be expected.[1] The media run regular features regarding how hundreds of thousands of graduates are unable to find employment, and how many need to hide their college degrees while seeking jobs as factory workers.[2] More importantly, the waste traders are well aware that to secure a job even remotely as good as Mr. Sanh's, one either needs money or connection to the right people—or even both.

In the meantime, there is increasing differentiation among the waste trading households that Mr. Sanh dismisses wholesale as a group of people focused on short-sighted goals and unable so see beyond immediate gains. While many waste traders would continue to dispute that higher education is the only respectable goal, quite a few such households also pursue higher education at all costs (see Chapter 5). Despite the declining value of the college degree, it is not uncommon for the same parents who opted for waste trading at a young age to now desire higher education for their children. For many waste traders, it is not easy to distance themselves from the hegemonic desire for higher education arising from the combined effect of cultural values, state governance and global discourses in the market economy, as Andrew Kipnis (2011) has also analyzed in China. In any case, the waste traders would say that their migrant work is precisely for the purpose of building a good life for their children, something that they would have much less chance doing if they stayed in the village. By constructing moral character as that which accounts for people's failure to live up to the middle-class standards he embraces, Mr. Sanh fails to see that what his fellow villagers do in order to care and to be cared for is often a moral choice against the demands of mobile livelihoods and the structural forces shaping their lives.

## Caring and Being Cared for in Translocal Households

In Spring District, household care has become more differentiated. Contested ideas regarding both child and elder care are emerging, while care arrangements entail much negotiation and compromise between generations and genders, even as they continued to be underlined by normative ideas of gendered work. With its members ever more mobile, the household flexibly adapts to changing patterns of migrant livelihoods. Indeed, the idealized "harmonious care" that Ms. Hợi portrays as the way of her "family with discipline and order" would be rather untenable for these translocal households. The tension between idealized care and changing practices results in anxiety over matters of caring and being cared for, especially in cases where the boundaries between the inside and the outside, and the local notion of the appropriate caregiver, are infringed upon.

## Who Cares for the Kids? Grandparenting, Gender, and Never-Ending Worries

I first met thirty-five-year-old Kiên together with his small son at the village's grocery when he came back for a family event; the two were buying cartons of sweetened milk for the boy, who got two days off from kindergarten on the occasion of his daddy coming home. Kiên used to be an itinerant waste trader before shifting to driving motorbike taxi (*xe ôm*); his wife, Minh, was an itinerant trader and cleaner in Hanoi. Their most important goal then was to save up for the house that they had started building some years ago. Living in a small rental room that Minh kept neat and tidy in central Hanoi, they left their two children with Kiên's parents. The grandparents were also in charge of the children of Kiên's siblings; together, six children aged between one and thirteen were under their supervision.

When Tâm and I visited the family in the village, the grandfather had just come back from his multiple trips to the school and the nursery to pick up the children. Every morning, the grandparents first had to give the older children food and take them to school, then came back to feed the smaller ones and bring them to kindergarten, whose gate closes at 8 a.m. The baby was cared for by the grandmother at home. When I asked if they ever felt stressed out, the two said in unison that sometimes they simply did not know what to do. The grandmother told us that she would barely sit down for a mouthful of rice when one of the children would say, "I want to have a poo!" The smaller ones would then want to do the same, and she would have to put her bowl down to tend to them. The grandfather mentioned that the two-year-old boy was violent and often beat up other children in his nursery group. The teacher thus grouped him with the four-year-olds, and the grandfather sometimes had to take the boy on a ride around the village to sooth him. The grandparents occasionally had to cook an extra instant noodle for their own dinner because the grandchildren had finished everything. Big loads of laundry were washed every day, the grandmother said, pointing at the two long lines of clothes hanging across the yard. When I expressed admiration at the efforts they made for their children, Kiên's father said, "Well, you know that they have to go out if they want to be any better-off; it simply doesn't work if they stay at home making no money. Now we live for them, but when we are older and can't do this anymore, they will have to live for us." And the children would grow up, he said; soon, the baby would be old enough to go to kindergarten. The children mostly stay the whole day at school and kindergarten, including on Saturdays, for a small extra fee. "It's much better for them to go to school at home than in the city, where it is expensive and not even as good. Thank goodness there are the schools; otherwise, we would be in great trouble."

As indicated in Chapter 2, married couples tend to migrate together if they set up a waste depot, which requires not only significant start-up investment but also the joint labor of at least two adults. Since they often rent temporarily available land awaiting development or with unclear tenure rights for waste depots, it is normal for the depots to relocate frequently. Therefore, unless a couple has a long-term rental or own the depot, they do not keep their younger children with them in the city; moving around would entail instability for the children. If the children are not able to enter higher secondary school, they tend to join their parents in the urban depot at the age of fourteen or fifteen.[3] If they are able to enter, they have to go to school in the countryside, as it is difficult for migrant children to be accepted at an urban secondary school without the urban household registration (*hộ khẩu*); those who have already joined their parents usually return to the country to complete secondary school. Consequently, depot operators' children usually experience long-term absence of both parents during certain periods and occasionally live on their own, albeit close to relatives.

Although quite a few men opt to stay home with the children when their wives work as itinerant waste traders, it is becoming common for young couples like Kiên and Minh to migrate together during their children's early years. In contrast to the greater emphasis on early childhood of the urban middle class, peasant families tend to regard small children as easier to care for and they can therefore be left with relatives until they are about ten. From this age onward, one parent should be at home to "supervise" (*quản*) them. Grandparents are seen as not disciplined enough and thus unable to shield teenagers from "social evils." Which parent returns depends on the couple's income prospects and negotiations regarding whom the children need the most. Small children need the care of the mother more, whereas older children are supposed to require the father's discipline and authority. Whether the teenager is a boy or a girl sometimes plays a role; it is more appropriate for the father to return if it is the former, and vice versa. (Figure 4.1 is a photo of children from the neighbors playing at our host's in Red Spring; their parents are migrant waste traders.)

Minh and Kiên were planning that he would return when their first daughter became a teenager; they hopefully would have saved up enough for the house by then. Kiên said that there were too many responsibilities at home for his wife to handle, especially with the pending house construction.

FIGURE **4.1** Children playing in Red Spring.
Source: Author's photo, 2011.

Kiên was affectionate toward his wife, a gentle and beautiful woman eight years younger than him, but disapproved of her for not being resourceful enough. She cleaned houses more than she traded waste for this reason, he said, and could continue doing that for the income that they needed, but he could not entrust her with being in charge of these "big matters" (việc lớn). For the time being, counting on the grandparents' help seemed the most sensible for them. "The grandparents are still fit, and they understand the need for us to accumulate some savings for our house and our children's future, as long as we can still make it," Minh said. She was, however, concerned that her daughter was too often scolded by the grandparents for things that were not really her fault, so Minh tried to go back as often as she could.

Although grandparents are considered temporary substitutes for parents, the work of grandparenting in these translocal households is not much different from that of parenting. In Spring District, many people start to become grandparents in their mid-forties, and the emotional dislocation of being separated from the grandchildren that they have been raising for years is similar to that of parents having to leave their children. Ms. Phẩn, for example, is a sixty-eight-year-old widow in Green Spring who is caring for her ninety-one-year-old mother-in-law. Her two sons operate recycling depots with their families in Hanoi, and her last granddaughter had just left to study in Hanoi after living with her for seventeen years. Ms. Phẩn had been the main caregiver for five grandchildren all together since retiring from waste trading in her fifties. She talked to me in her two-story house in Green Spring while cooking a separate meal for her mother-in-law, who could only eat soft food:

> In the past everyone was poor, but there were people around. If something happened or if there was a family event you just needed to shout and the whole village would come. Now there are hardly any young people at home—only old people and children. It's depressing (*chán lắm*).

For elderly women like Ms. Phẩn, empty-nest feelings are prevalent after the departure of grandchildren for whom they have long cared. Although the care responsibilities may make them feel overburdened, life without these children is not easy either. While emphasizing how much they have invested in caring for their grandchildren, grandmothers often speak about their feelings of loss once they have left. "Some nights I just can't fall asleep from missing my granddaughter so much," Ms. Phẩn said.

As with parenting, grandparenting roles are clearly gendered and also structured by the inside/outside division. Male grandparenting is usually directed toward activities outside the home, such as taking the grandchildren to school and picking them up or attending parental meetings. Grandmothers are more concerned with feeding and bodily care for their grandchildren; they are expected to be more attentive to the needs of the children. Below, Quỳnh, a young mother and itinerant waste trader in Hanoi whose two children live with their paternal grandfather in the village considers the absence of her mother-in-law, another itinerant trader, a loss for her children:

> I started leaving when my daughter was one-and-a-half years. My mother-in-law works in Hanoi as a junk trader like me, so I entrusted our little daughter to her grandfather [with whom two other grandchildren are living]. But a grandfather's care cannot compare with that of grandmother's. He would only feed the children and bring them to the nursery. Whenever the children are sick or so, he would call and ask the parents to come back. He cannot wash their hair or give them a bath. As a man, he is interested in his work; he does not pay much attention to the children. They are left dirty and messy. I think if their

grandmother were home, they would be tidier. Grandfather doesn't pay as good attention as grandmother or mother. It makes me cry every time I leave for Hanoi, and it is tough to think about them when being here.

Feeling guilty for her absence, Quỳnh thinks that she should be home for her children, but she cannot, at least not yet. Together with her husband, she has to work to pay off the debt incurred by the construction of their house. More importantly, she has a bigger worry than her children: her husband is prone to gambling and drug abuse. Before they operated a depot together, he had worked as a taxi driver for some years, and then took up taxi driving again after they had closed the depot because he had gambled away their funds. Quỳnh believes that her presence in the city, in addition to that of her co-residing mother-in-law, keeps a check on his vulnerabilities and makes sure that his earnings do not vanish into these habits. These are clearly a concern for the whole extended family. Seeing the need for both women to be there to guard over his son's behavior, the grandfather does not ask his wife or daughter-in-law to come back in spite of his discomfort with caring responsibilities at home; addiction is a serious matter that affects the moral standing of the family as a whole (discussed in more detail later). The care of one's children, Ms. Phẩn once said to me, never ceases; one worries about them until they have long grown up and ventured far beyond the boundaries of their parental home.

## When Grandparents Need Care

Contra the widespread discourse of abandonment in migrant households, elderly people are seldom completely alone—the care of elderly parents remains one of the most important moral obligations. If the parents do not have their own income, the children arrange for their provision, telephone and visit regularly, and usually entrust their care to relatives. The grandchildren often come back during the summer holidays, too. What they have to come to terms with is the waning of a family ideal based on spatial closeness between the generations and daily face-to-face conviviality, an ideal that has been weakened by local people's extensive engagement in the waste economy and the translocality that it entails. As the poem in Table 4.1 suggests, elderly people in Spring District, as in other parts of rural Vietnam, are aware that certain compromises have to be made, even as they are nostalgic for older, idealized forms of sociality and articulate the need to preserve the moral order.

Ms. Phẩn's mother-in-law had been taken care of by her late husband's unmarried sister until the latter died from diabetes. When I first met her in 2012, Ms. Phẩn had been the main caregiver for the bedridden elderly

TABLE **4.1  The Ten Wishes of an Elderly Person** (*Mười Thích Của Người Cao Tuổi*)

| ENGLISH | VIETNAMESE |
| --- | --- |
| The first delight is money in the pocket | *Một thích trong túi có tiền* |
| Not bothering the kids, should social obligations arise | *Ai mời hiếu hỷ khỏi phiền cháu con* |
| Second is a good bowl of soup | *Hai thích được bát canh ngon* |
| Who cares for fine food when the teeth are gone | *Cao lương chẳng thiết bởi còn răng đâu?* |
| Third comes the wish, that one's offspring and in-laws | *Ba thích con cháu rể dâu* |
| Do not stray from the family's ways and filial duties | *Gia phong giữ nếp, hàng đầu hiếu trung* |
| Fourth, the family divides and unites, harmoniously | *Bốn thích thỏa mãn riêng chung* |
| One eats from one's own pot, but enjoys the company of one's children and grandchildren | *Ăn riêng nhưng vẫn vui cùng cháu con* |
| Fifth, village people live together with affection | *Năm thích làng xóm vuông tròn* |
| Are there for each other, in misery, in prosperity | *Đói no sướng khổ, mất còn có nhau* |
| Sixth, one lives long and dies fast | *Sáu thích sống thọ chết mau* |
| Pain and sickness only bring troubles for the children | *Ốm lâu con khổ, lại đau thân mình* |
| Seventh, the graves of the ancestors | *Bảy thích mồ mả ông cha* |
| Are built and made beautiful, looking as good as those of the others | *Xây cất tôn tạo ít ra bằng người* |
| Eighth, people stay away, at home and outside | *Tám thích xã hội gia đình* |
| From gambling and drugs | *Bạc cờ ma túy thực tình tránh xa* |
| The ninth wish is a house full of laughter | *Chín thích đầy ắp tiếng cười* |
| Everyday filled with fresh joy | *Được hưởng không khí vui tươi hằng ngày* |
| Lastly, the moment one departs | *Mười thích phút chót dương nầy* |
| Is marked with decent rituals, but not incurring indebtedness. | *Tùy nghi biện lễ chớ vay mượn nhiều* |
| Such are the wishes of an elderly person | *Tuổi già mong được bấy điều* |
| How many can be fulfilled depends on one's luck | *Mỗi người đạt được bao nhiêu còn tùy* |
| Nothing compares to a life of cheerfulness and good health | *Sống vui sống khỏe khôn bì* |
| When the last Order arrives, one leaves without a burden. | *Nam Tào có lệnh ra đi nhẹ nhàng.* |

Source: Handwritten poem by anonymous poet collected in Spring District, author's translation.

woman for about five years. The last time I saw her in 2015, she felt that she could no longer be fully in charge of caring for her mother-in-law in her own home: Ms. Phấn eyes were getting worse, and she felt weaker. She had asked Mr. Dương, the latter's remaining son, to come back from Yên Bái city, where he had been running a depot with his wife and son, to stay with his mother in the ancestral house. Yet even following his return, Ms. Phấn continued to come over from her house to take daily care of the elderly woman, bathing and dressing her, cleaning up, and sometimes doing the dishes for the mother-in-law and the son, whereas Mr. Dương dispensed her medication and fed her. His most important duty was to be there for her in the last stage of her life, especially at the moment of her passing, for which his presence as a son would be ritually important.

Elderly men are less likely than elderly women to live alone, partly because they are more often survived by their wives and partly because of the assumption that they are less able to deal with living by themselves than elderly women are. Should a man's wife die before him, their children are more likely to arrange for the elderly man to live with someone than if a woman's husband dies before her. If the elderly parent is too fragile, his or her children may arrange for the return of one adult family member, usually one of the sons or an older unmarried daughter, who receives financial contributions from their siblings for taking on the responsibility. I met a number of unmarried older women taking over the care of elderly parents together with children of their migrant siblings; one of them, Ms. Phinh, told me that she was practically "an Ôsin for the whole extended family." (Ôsin is a common term for domestic workers; see Nguyen 2015b.) Occasionally, siblings take turns caring for the elderly parent, moving the latter from home to home, an arrangement that Ms. Hợi scoffed at. For Ms. Hợi and others like her, shuttling elderly parents around undermines their dignity and indicates the family's failure to organize appropriate care for the elders in a harmonious manner; for the migrant waste-trading families, however, it is sometimes the only viable arrangement given their high mobility.

Hiring paid caregivers has become an option for higher income households. While domestic service was common in rural areas in colonial times, since the reforms (đổi mới) its use has primarily been an urban middle-class practice—domestic workers are predominantly female migrants. When I asked if they would consider hiring somebody to care for their parents, local people would say, "There's something weird about letting an outsider care for your own parents." In one case, when an elderly man who had been cared for by a paid caregiver died, the villagers found it scandalous that in his final days he had not been cared for by his children, who had only learned of his death from the caregiver. In the villagers' view, this only confirmed their sense that the children lacked filial devotion. In another case, the children of a ninety-year-old woman, most of whom were operating waste depots in Hanoi, considered hiring someone to look after her, to which she objected, saying that she did not want to live with a stranger. Domestic service is likely to become more accepted, however, especially since some families are able to afford it with their high earnings. In the words of a fifty-seven-year-old man who had returned from Hanoi for the sake of his ailing parents, "We have gone outside and seen urban people employing domestic helpers to care for their parents. Unlike some people who don't go anywhere, we know there's nothing bad about hiring somebody to care for your parents. One should come to see it as a normal thing." Yet even as he has understanding for the others who opt for it, he himself would not consider this option.

Care is often narrowly defined as face-to-face caregiving, and the absence of the appropriate caregiver is moralized as problematic regardless of the different forms of care articulated by people and their social meanings. The practices of caring and being cared for in the translocal households of the waste traders indicate that despite the constant rearrangements and compromises necessitated by mobility, care continues to be underlined by enduring moral norms regarding gendered and generational obligations. Contra the discourse of abandonment and neglect, care remains central to the moral life of persons and families on the move, whether they work with waste or not. Nevertheless, the normative discourse generates a general sense of moral anxiety over mobility and waste work, at times causing a deep sense of moral failure among those families for whom the cycle of care is disrupted.

## "Social Evils" and the Disruption of Care

The term *social evils* (*tệ nạn xã hội*) is on the tip of everyone's tongue whenever they discuss the topic of social change in the district, especially since the days when more people started "going outside." The campaign to combat social evils was waged by the Vietnamese government in the mid-1990s, driven by a widespread concern over the negative cultural impacts of Vietnam's integration into the global economy (note how gambling and drugs are among the biggest worries for elderly people in the poem of Table 4.1). In the early days of the so-called "open-door" period of political and economic reform, the dictum underlying the campaign against social evils was that once the door was opened, toxic winds also entered.

State officials began to identify social phenomena such as premarital sex, prostitution, crime, and drug addiction as social evils to be fought against in order to protect the "fine moral traditions of the nation (*truyền thống đạo đức tốt đẹp của dân tộc*)." According to Helle Rydstrøm (2006), social evils are understood as "dirty" influences of the outside world that endanger the moral order of the nation, much like how globalization has been met with moral panic elsewhere. Since social evils are constructed as the dangers of the outside, it is no wonder that they are associated with the greater mobility of the villagers, while the impurity of waste links it to the "dirtiness" of social evils. Discourses in and about Spring District are replete with tales of social evils among migrant waste traders, the most panic filled of which are stories about drug addiction. The two cases below suggest that the construction of moral panic is undergirded by a concern with disciplining the disruption of care in individual families and framing such disruption as a matter of private responsibility.

Ms. Hải, a retired high school teacher, lives with her husband in a beautiful and large villa surrounded by an ornamental garden and fish pond in Green Spring. Sitting with Tâm and me us on an elegant set of wooden armchairs amidst expensive furniture and home electronic equipment adorning their large living room, she was on the verge of tears when telling about their family. The village head had mentioned to us earlier, in a lowered voice, that their son had died of addiction. She and her husband had never lived outside the village. They became wealthy thanks to a furniture business that her husband jointly runs with his brother who lives in Hanoi. Yet all her children were waste depot operators—she would have liked her two daughters to become teachers, but they had been married into waste-trading families upon finishing school, later also introducing their youngest brother into it. They saw greater opportunities in waste work than in teaching, which they found time constraining and financially unattractive. Her son had died six months earlier from drug overdose. He had taken up the habit after finishing high school, before getting married and starting a waste depot. His waste depot had been doing very well; they managed to buy a truck and were about to purchase a car for use. But his habit had been like a looming disaster over the family. He really had wanted to come clean, and his wife had supported his efforts. They had tried many times to put him through rehabilitation in vain, since one can easily buy drugs in the rehabilitation centers (just for a lot more money than one could outside). The last time he came out, he said that the food there was worse than their dog's food at home, and the conditions of rehabilitation were so harsh that he gave up. At the end of his life, he was weak, and she felt so sorry for his painful withdrawal that she went to buy drugs for him. One had to be careful doing that because they often arrested the drug buyers rather than the sellers, she said. Now that he is gone, life is sad. He had been such a caring son; he had driven her to visit pagodas and places and had always been kind and loving toward her. What is the point of having such a large house and expensive furniture if one cannot look up from having a son dying of addiction?

In another village of Green Spring, Mr. Dương's neighbor told me that he was an "unhappy man" (*bất hạnh*); when someone wanted to be mean to Mr. Dương, they would say that his family was *vô phúc* (without moral blessing of the ancestor, a damning condition that has intergenerational implications). A reflective and gentle man, Mr. Dương was surprisingly open, given that I had just been introduced to him by Ms. Phấn, his sister-in-law, whom I had met a couple of times before. He told me about his life in a sad and matter-of-fact tone, as if confiding in an old friend. His depot has been doing well; now it was under the charge of his wife and their youngest son, who had Down syndrome and "unfortunately has not been able to get married." He had rarely been back to the village, according to Ms. Phấn, not only because of the youngest son's disability, but also on account of the death of his eldest son, who had died of a drug overdose and was survived by his wife and two daughters. The year before, the son's wife had disappeared with a loan from the local Women's Union, leaving her two daughters, ten and twelve, at home. Mr. Dương's only daughter was married to someone who also had a drug problem, and his wife, overcome with unhappiness about her children's problems, had once tried taking her life. At the district hospital, they had used buckets of water to wash out the pesticide she had drunk. His wife had been saved, but as Ms. Phấn told me later, her skin looked very pale and her bones were in bad shape. She did not like the idea of coming back, Mr. Dương said; the shame was too great for her to bear. He also felt a loss of face as the head of a family in which things fell apart. In our conversation, he stressed that he had been responsibly providing for his granddaughters and their mother, yet the mother had left her daughters nonetheless—it was because of the misfortune of his family. Were it not for the importance of showing filial duties to his mother and the need to supervise his two teenage granddaughters (Ms. Phấn also insisted on this factor as being of great importance when convincing him to return), he would rather stay put in Yên Bái working on his depot, where he was only infrequently reminded of his loss of face. For him and his wife, the urban waste depot seemed not just a place to earn their livelihoods, but also a refuge from daily confrontation with the moral scrutiny of the village.

Psychoactive drug addiction has become a global issue that affects a wide spectrum people, and Spring District clearly has not been spared this social problem. It is a "multicausal process influenced by the interplay of many risk and protective factors from different developmental contexts" (Office on Drugs and Crime 2015: 19). These cases alone contradict the assumption that people who work with waste are less concerned about the moral behavior of their children, or that drug addiction is the outcome of parents engaging in migrant waste work. Ms. Hải and her husband have never been waste traders. I know other addicted people in the district who are children of medical doctors, teachers, and local cadres whose families have never experienced any long-term separation. Later in the fieldwork, I also discovered that one village head in Red Spring, who in our conversations had avidly condemned drug addiction as the impact of waste-trading parents' neglect of their children, especially in Green Spring, in fact had two sons who were addicted. This explains the everpresent sadness of his wife that I had wondered about whenever visiting them, and it draws attention to the fact that addiction is not limited to any one group, or linked to the moral deficiency of any one family in particular. The village head's family seems one of those that Ms. Hợi would call "a family with discipline and order." Like Ms. Hải, both parents are retired government employees; the village head is an authoritative figure at home and has decision making power in the village. Both he and his wife were home when their children grew up, and their sons became addicted when working in the city.

It is commonly assumed that mobility causes the disruption of care in the family, with addiction being a clear indicator of such, yet the continued migration by Mr. Dương's family is in fact a way of coping with a situation in which care becomes problematic. What impressed me is how strongly he took the blame for his son's addiction and viewed it as an indication of his family's loss of moral standing, which he believes has caused their other misfortunes. In fact, both his son and his son-in-law had started taking drugs when they were adults, during the time they had worked on a long-distance freight ship. Even without the state campaign listing addiction as a social evil, a drug addict is often considered a moral outcast, some sort of half-human being who has ruined his or her lives and cannot be trusted to have decent human behavior. (Ms. Hải would surely contest this, based on her experiences with her loving son, who remained caring toward her despite his addiction.) The addiction of a family member not only affects the "face" of the parents, but also is a stain that reflects badly on the moral character of whole families. Mr. Hòa in Red Spring, for example, liked to point out to us the addicted people at village events: "*Đấy, thằng ấy nghiện đấy!* (Look at that boy, he is an addict!)" he would say. Such intense moralization of addiction as signifying the moral character of a whole family again thrusts the responsibility of care wholly on the shoulder of individual families. It serves as a stern warning for migrant parents, instilling an imminent sense of anxiety among them, a theme to which I will return in Chapter 6.

## Conclusion: Care, Anxiety, and the Remaking of Moral Obligations

With the household's increased translocal dimensions, obligations between genders and generations are continually reworked as men and women negotiate between caring for others and being cared for over their life course. Conflicting ideas about appropriate care and shifting caring practices emerge as a result; the anxiety of mobility turns into the anxiety of care. For migrant waste traders, the widespread moral anxiety around caring and being cared for is not just the result of transgressing the boundary between inside and outside domains, but also of the social meanings of waste. The causal connection between migrant waste trading and "social evils" is a construction based on the valuation of waste, and of people working with waste, as morally impure. It is an attempt at maintaining the social order and disciplining those who do not conform to it. The wealth generated by the waste traders is viewed with uneasiness, not just because it is supposed to be potentially contaminated with the impurity of waste and thus immorality, but also because it threatens to overturn the social hierarchies that accord people of "high intellectual level" greater prestige and power. In this construction, again, the superiority of care by local elite families towers over the lack, inappropriateness, and disruption of care in peasant/migrant families, not least in those of people working with waste. The dominant discourses of care, sponsored by the party-state, sustain the very power relations that are responsible for the inequalities in caring and being cared for between social groups in the same ways that feminist scholars have written about other contexts (Tronto 1993, Robinson 2011).

In our globalized world today, care "is a central trope around which moral conceptions of personhood, social relationships and societies are anchored" (Nguyen et al. 2017: 209). The construction of care in migrant waste-trading families as morally problematic, I argue, is an effect of a hierarchical social order that depreciates peasants in general and migrant laborers in particular on the terms of "intellectual level" (*dân trí*). This construction has major implications for the waste traders' project of remaking. In Vietnam, caring and being cared for are the foundation of the twin project of *thành người* (becoming human, or becoming a morally and socially responsible person) and *làm người* (doing human, or the work of living the moral life of a person), which makes up the moral framework of a person's life (for a good discussion of *thành người*, see Gammeltoft 2015: 186). In order to become a social person, or *thành người*, one needs to be fed, cared for, educated, and socialized to gradually assume one's responsibilities and obligations for oneself, for one's intimate others, and for society at large. One is recognized as *thành người* the moment one is in a position and ready to reciprocate the care one has received from the others. *Làm người* (doing human), meanwhile, is the art of leading the moral life of the person—it requires the constant work of cultivating moral behaviors, dealing with the moral challenges of life while maintaining a coherent moral orientation as a member of a family, community, and nation, above all, through socially accepted ways of caring. The moralizing discourse around care among migrant waste-trading families thus adds an extra burden on their efforts to shrug off the indignities of migrant waste work in order to refashion their moral self in the village. It casts doubt over the moral framework of their lives. As a result, while the waste traders may contest the discourses—for example, by engaging in mutually exclusive discourses vis-à-vis the other groups—their actions and interpretations are in many cases driven by the anxiety it generates. It is this tension between moral discourses and people's practices that underline the remaking of moral obligations in the mobile community, which preserves as much as it transforms normative ideals of care.

The following chapters indicate that waste traders subscribe to the hegemonic desires and aspirations of today's Vietnam to varying extents. In the same moment they might be arguing for authentic peasant-oriented values prioritizing pragmatism and egalitarianism, many are also striving to live up to the demands of the consumer society or surreptitiously buying land and houses in the city. Others seek to transform their life in the country through adopting urban middle-class consumption practices or gaining recognition through monetary contributions to social causes. Such practices, I will show, are underscored by both the neoliberal notion of private responsibility that permeates the realm of care and locally meaningful moral ideas that the Vietnamese state mobilizes for its development agenda.

## CHAPTER 5

# Rural Entrepreneurship, Local Development, and Social Aspirations

On the veranda of his towering roadside house, Thu was chopping up the last stems of lemon grass next to a pile of about fifty rabbits that had been pre-roasted in rice-straw fire, ready to be made into a variety of dishes for the wedding order the family had received. He said to me affirmatively, "This commune is twenty years ahead of the neighboring commune in terms of infrastructure!" We had been talking about his Green Spring commune and the high standard of its houses, schools and roads. Thu continued:

> It is all because we have gone out to do all these kinds of stuff and exposed ourselves to the outside world and have come to know their ways of living. Now that people can make money, it is easy for the commune [government] to mobilize money from them for these roads and so on. You know, the countryside can only be new if people's pockets are full (*Túi dân có đầy thì nông thôn mới mới được*).

His last sentence refers to the state program of "Building the New Countryside" (*Chương trình Mục tiêu quốc gia xây dựng nông thôn mới*), which aims to improve local infrastructure, productive resources, and social services in rural Vietnam. His commune had done well under the scheme and become one of the few in the province to be selected as examples of the New Countryside in 2013.

For years, post-reform development had been focused on large urban centers at the cost of rural areas. In the last decade, however, the perceived threats to social stability originating from the countryside have led the party-state to pay more attention to the development of rural economy and society. In the same way that the urban renewal agenda is premised on a state-led vision of modernity underlined by civility and social order (Harms 2016), the New Countryside Program represents the state's attempt to modernize the countryside while educating rural people to become certain kinds of citizens. (Figure 5.1 shows a common poster that calls for efforts to build "the new countryside and the civilized city.") And while the program promotes internal strengths (*nội lực*), or locally available resources, as the driving force of development, much of what Green Spring has achieved would not have taken place without migrant waste trading.

Underlying Thu's narrative of local development is a taken-for-granted fact: that the level of investment in local infrastructure, the productive ventures, and the consumption have been largely enabled by local people's long-term engagement in the urban waste trade, what he hints at with "do[ing]

FIGURE **5.1  Poster in a village of Quang Nam province, central Vietnam.** The caption reads "All the people unite to build the new countryside and the civilized city." Source: Author's photo, 2016.

all these kinds of stuff." Despite the precarious conditions of the trade and their social ambiguity as waste traders in the urban society, local people's enterprising capacity and creative use of marginalized urban spaces have turned urban waste into a source of livelihoods and wealth. The waste trade has allowed the commune administration to easily mobilize resources for its various infrastructure projects, even before the New Countryside Program was started in 2009, which explains Thu's statement that the countryside "can only be new if people's pockets are full." Thu and his wife, Ngoan, both in their mid-thirties, had been long operating an urban waste depot before returning three years ago and investing their savings in a mid-sized rabbit farm. They are not the only ones – in contrast to other people from the district who stay in the urban waste trade well into their sixties or seventies, there has been a small trend of younger people returning for similar agricultural productive ventures since the end of the 2000s.

This chapter tells the stories of former waste traders, like Thu and Ngoan, who return to the village and take advantage of opportunities for new productive agricultural enterprises created by the continuing departure of their fellow villagers. These people, often with young families, seek to build a life with aspirations that transcend the rural-urban distinction while still maintaining their translocal outlook. Theirs are class-based aspirations that are framed by a state-sponsored notion of development that promotes internal strength and self-reliance, but without sufficient state responsibility in ensuring sustainable framework conditions. To some extent, their projects of aspirational self-fashioning remake the rural space into one that enables the good life away from the demeaning world of urban waste, thereby changing what it means to be rural. Nevertheless, such projects are viable only for a small number of people, and even for them, the outcome is deeply uncertain. Similar to urban waste trading, there are limits to these rurally based productive ventures and thus to the aspirations of those who pursue them, limits that are inherent in the volatility of market conditions. These stories reveal the self-enterprising nature of local development and how mobility has become entrenched in local livelihoods, even in the event of returning. I shall analyze these narratives in relation to the party-state's changing ideologies of development as manifest in the New Countryside Program to which Thu referred.

## A Shifting Approach to Local Development

The national program of "Building the New Countryside" was initiated in 2009 and modeled after the Chinese program of the New Socialist Countryside. In China, the program was started in 2006[1] to improve the status quo of "rural society, agriculture, and the peasantry," a trio of problem areas that had been provoking anxiety among the political and social elite over a looming crisis resulting from their degeneration (Jacka 2013). Early analysis of the Chinese and Vietnamese programs suggests that while their goals might be similar, the operative logics and local practices are rather different in each country. The Chinese program seems to feature stronger state coordination and provision of resources alongside greater coerciveness in enforcing measures such as concentrated housing, at times reminiscent of the socialist villagization drive in Tanzania during the 1970s (Robin 2009, Ahlers and Schubert 2009, Schneider 2014). Although the Vietnamese program is proclaimed by the state as a more concerted effort than the previous narrowly defined rural development projects, it relies to a great extent on local mobilization of resources while the state assumes a facilitating role. According to the decision by the prime minister approving this program, its goal is to modernize the countryside through comprehensive measures to develop infrastructure, social services, and cultural practices:

> To build a new countryside with a gradually modernized socio-economic infrastructure, appropriate economic and productive structure; linking agriculture with rapidly developing industries and services; linking rural development to planned urbanization, maintaining a rural society that is democratic, stable, and rich in the nation's cultural identity; protecting the environment, maintaining security and social order; steadily improving the people's material and spiritual life under socialist orientation.[2]

The New Countryside Program evaluates rural communes with nineteen criteria, such as proper local planning, built-road coverage, electricity and water supply, sufficient schools, cultural and postal facilities, housing standards, ratio of poor households, ratio of cultured villages,[3] and rate of secondary school graduation or of people buying health insurance. A rural commune is rated as a New Countryside commune if it fulfills at least fourteen criteria, which Green Spring did. Fulfilling these criteria requires not only local people's contributions of money and labor, but also the upholding of moral attitudes such as self-reliance and awareness of law and order. Accordingly, one should lead morally acceptable lives and work hard to earn a good income while preparing for future risks through appropriate forms of insurance.

This program is not entirely new. Fashioning new forms of rurality and rural people has always been on the agenda of the party-state; there have been numerous campaigns and policies with this aim since the advent of socialism (Malarney 2002, Drummond 2004). Yet rather than simply joining disparate projects and programs that existed before, the New Countryside Program signals a new direction in the development approach of the Vietnamese party-state. Until the 1990s, rural development had been alternately focused on collectivization, state-led modernization, and intensification of agriculture. The socialist state had been the main investor and supporter of these agendas; rural populations were supposed to be the recipients and beneficiaries of state programs and services. Thus, the state was largely responsible for their development. Following the reforms (*đổi mới*), however, there has been a shift in rural development ideologies. If state socialist programs were intent on mobilizing collective actions of rural people based on a construction of the need to liberate them from feudal and colonial oppression, the ideological content expressed through the New Countryside Program indicates a concern with unleashing people's innate potentials. In other words, it is about the necessity to liberate them from themselves, from their own inertia and fragmented mode of production. Increasingly, the state supports the fulfillment of development targets by local people and communities by helping them to identity their entrepreneurial strengths rather than by than directing people's economic activities and providing resources for centrally planned goals as before. No longer just promoting local participation, the overriding message of the New Countryside Program is that local communities and people should take ownership of their development and thus be responsible for it while remaining under the political and moral guidance of the state. Put differently, it is a self-help approach to development that largely leaves local communities to their own devices (Berner and Phillips 2005), which, however, continues to be cast in the familiar language of socialist mobilization that highlights the state's guiding role.

Indeed, the Vietnamese state continues to be the mobilizing force that it has always been, one adept at political communication and at maneuvering the workings of the exemplary society that Vietnam is (Malarney 2007). If emulative campaigns (*phong trào thi đua*) among localities were in the party-state's toolkit for promoting socialist production (MacLean 2013), they are now taken to task with responsibilizing people and communities for their development. "Internal strengths" (*nội lực*) and "socialization" (*xã hội hóa*; in the sense of being under the responsibility of the whole society; see also Chapter 7) are the main keywords for local development and welfare provision. The idea is that local communities should strive to develop themselves through mobilizing local resources, and that their efforts will be publicly recognized by the state. Instead of relying on the allocated resources and direction from the state, localities are supposed to compete for the state's recognition of their capacity for development. While the funding for the main infrastructure items partly comes from the provincial government, depending on its resources, a large part is mobilized from local people, organizations, and businesses. The central government rewards the high achievers with funds to build certain items of infrastructure in their development plans. The introduction of financial rewards and grants to high-performers adds a new dimension to the socialist technique of showcasing exemplary individuals and communities to mobilize labor and resources.

Local people like Thu are aware of the underlying dynamics of such agendas, as expressed in his ironic comment that the countryside would not be that new without people's full pockets, an irony that Hans Steinmüller (2011) also identifies in rural people's perception of the namesake Chinese program. Recent media reports suggest that many localities in Vietnam have become heavily indebted in the process.[4] Critics are voicing concerns about local people being unable to meet the mobilization targets, local funds being embezzled and misused, and the local state being overstrained, yet the program continues to be lauded as the best pathway for rural development. Meanwhile, as the case of Green Spring suggests, the program is not merely a "face project" of the government (Steinmüller 2011: 25), for whom the "will to improve" (Li 2007) disguises an anxious intent to maintain its monopoly on power. It is also a "value project" of the local people, in the words of David Graeber (2001: 17), and one that is partly aimed at redeeming the social value of their personhood that has been somewhat sacrificed in the course of working with urban waste. Through local processes, the program comes to constitute a social space for people to locate the meanings of their actions, even though some of the actions might not be that which is valued in the party-state's development framework. What people do and mean sometimes incidentally becomes the very irony they identify in attempted exercises of power by the state.

## Building the New Countryside from Urban Waste

Green Spring has more than seven thousand people in eighteen hamlets (Figures 5.2a and 5.2b depict views of the commune as one turns off the main road). In 2013, Green Spring was rated as a New Countryside commune. According to a commune report that details its accomplishment of formal criteria, more than seventy percent of its population has bought

FIGURE **5.2a   A view of Green Spring.**
Source: Author's photo, 2015.

FIGURE **5.2b   Another view of Green Spring.**
Source: Author's photo, 2015.

the voluntary health insurance, all the local houses meet the national standards, the annual per-capita income is high above the national average, and only three percent of the households are classified as poor. As well, the neighborhoods are safe and cultured, meaning that families are happy, neighborhoods are harmonious, and "social evils" are under control. In line with another criterion, farming land has been consolidated quickly: *dồn điền đổi thửa* (literally "pool land and swap plots") is a major component of the program aimed at reducing land fragmentation for the sake of large-scale farming and infrastructure development.[5] This consolidation has made it possible for some to invest in mechanization and contract farming for a private company that rents hundreds of hectares in the province and elsewhere to farm commercial rice seeds. In comparison to many other communes in the region, Green Spring has high-quality intervillage roads, kindergarten and school facilities, village culture houses, and no temporary houses—not only are most houses here solidly built according to national criteria, as the report states, many of them are in fact impressive villas. Yet much of this superior infrastructure had been in place well before the New Countryside Program was initiated, largely thanks to local people's income from the urban waste trade.

Local officials like to showcase Green Spring's latest public building, an imposing culture house (*nhà văn hóa xã*) that had been built with grant money the commune received when winning the New Countryside title. They like to tell official visitors about how smooth the process of land consolidation has been because of the cooperative spirit of local people, and to take them to visit production models. But when one stays a bit longer and frequents their offices for a while, they will mention, in a somewhat lowered voice, that people in the commune have this particular occupation of trading waste in the cities—as if it were little more than an interesting side fact. One male official said to me: "Green Spring people actually have no profession (*chẳng có nghề ngỗng gì cả*), and that's why they had to take up waste trading." This official's opinion, like that of the monk at the beginning of the Introduction, seems under the purview of the state-sponsored notion of rural development that deems certain kinds of traditional skills and place-based credentials to be the proper path toward greater well-being; there is a nationwide strategy in developing handicraft villages as a way of creating local employment, for example.[6] Accordingly, entrepreneurial spirit is to be unleashed in rural areas, but in an orderly manner and as sanctioned by the state, which relegates the countryside to the realm of traditions, both as a source of nostalgia for the past and as a harbinger of backwardness. Rural people are supposed to develop with their "internal strength" (*nội lực*), and traditional crafts seemingly spring forth as the primary solution. Spring District people's enterprise in the waste trade thus is considered to be a "spontaneous occupation" (*ngành nghề tự phát*), one that strays from the officially recognized development pathways (see also Taylor 2007).

Yet in Green Spring, everyone, including the commune official in the previous paragraph, is well aware of how central migrant waste trading is to local livelihoods and development. The material gain it has generated in the commune has been remarkable, and local people would contest that migrant waste work is anything but a sign of their backwardness. Like Thu, they like to talk about how their migrant work has induced an improved living standard in the commune and more generally its "development." Rather than just focusing on material gains, many point out how their experiences with the outside world have changed their ways of thinking. A female villager said to me that people in her commune were the first in the region to readily embrace cremation after the province had set up a crematory. According to her, this indicates that they have "adopted civilized practices" out of an openness that results from years of "being exposed to the ways of the civilized world." In one of our conversations, Thu made almost the same statement about the changes of his homeplace, adding that one cannot stick to the old ways forever. It is partly on account of this desire for a space in which they could live a "civilized life," and partly because the stigma of waste haunts them as long as they remain in the trade, that Thu and Ngoan and some others have decided to shift from urban waste trading to agricultural production. Theirs, however, is not a simple return to farming, but a reinvention of the entrepreneurship they had exercised in the urban waste trade, which helps them to reimagine rural spaces as an antidote to their marginalization in the city. And while their household strategies and aspirations fit the narratives of the New Countryside to a certain extent, they are fraught with uncertainties and offer limited scope for replicability by others.

## Story of Thu and Ngoan: The Poetry of Rabbit Meat

A fearless and savvy man, Thu is the husband of Ngoan, a strong, hardworking, and quiet woman. They have one son aged five and two daughters aged eleven and thirteen. Both had worked as itinerant junk traders before they started an urban waste depot, which the couple operated for eight years before deciding to return in 2012 (I met them three years after their return). Their three children had been living with Ngoan's mother in the house they built on the land they had bought at auction, when the commune decided to convert the farmland beside the main road leading to the commune center into a residential area. Although the children had always joined their parents in the city during the summer holidays, the grandmother had felt strained by caring for their youngest son, then only two years old, and the two girls, who were becoming "impossible to manage" in the absence of their parents.

Ngoan and Thu often stressed that they reunited the family for the sake of their children. Since the parents came back, the teenage girls had become less rowdy and seemed to do better in school; according to their grandmother, "The girls are very afraid of their father and are now very well-behaved and well-disciplined, unlike when they were living with me." Since their return, Thu said, he no longer had to watch out for the right hour to leave (a wrong hour could bring misfortune). Before, on the monthly occasions he used to drive between their home and their urban depot, he had often feared that he would have an accident on the chaotic highway and that his children would become defenseless without him (bơ vơ). Yet the decision to return was also related to other issues underlying their existence in the city. "Gosh, how they look down on us! With visible contempt," Ngoan said. "They consider us as nothing, calling us mày [derogatory term for "you"], this bitch or that bitch (con này, con kia). They would never say "Hi, sister or niece, please come in; I'd like to sell you something.'" To which Thu added, "Well, this occupation is the lowliest in society. But we had to consider it part of the deal, and brace for the battle (cố mà chiến đấu)." Even so, sometimes he had wondered if it made sense to continue: "One has only one life to live—why would one want to do this forever, being away from children and family, living in the dark corners of the city?"

Thu and Ngoan used the savings left after building their house to invest in a rabbit farm on their former residential land farther away from the commune center. It was the first time that they had raised rabbits, and it took initial losses (the rabbits kept dying in the first year) to learn about their habits, diseases, and growth features. As rabbit meat has become a favored delicacy, they started supplying live rabbits and meat to local weddings and death anniversaries or specialty restaurants in the center of Spring District. My field notes have an entry titled "The poetry of rabbit meat," and this is the text straight from the notes:

> In the afternoon, I came back from an interview to see the whole family sitting together on the veranda preparing the meat to cook for

a large order. The teenage girls were chirping away happily while filling up the huge pot with thin slices of meat and spices; the parents looking obviously pleased with the order, joking around with each other. The specialty dishes they offer to weddings and anniversaries, such as herb-roasted rabbit meat, fetch about US$10 per plate for six—the usual wedding has about 100 tables, and an order could turn around a significant amount. During the popular wedding months (in the autumn), the whole family is busy, and the teenage girls are recruited for whole afternoons for the work. Thu's mother also helps with the slaughter and pre-roasting. In the slow season, they cater more to restaurants farther away or to death anniversaries in the commune. On average, their monthly turnover is more than 30 million *đồng* (about US$1,500). The cooked meat on offer is neatly packaged in white foam boxes. On the boxes, there is a red business card featuring the drawing of a fat rabbit together with their contact details and a line stating that their rabbits are of New Zealand descent, a rare kind with gemstone-like eyes (*thỏ mắt ngọc*). The couple is thinking about setting up a restaurant serving their specialty dishes, taking advantage of their roadside location. (I had tried their galangal roast cuts tossed with sesames, star fruits, and herbs on another occasion: the treat was delicious and would make a star plate on a restaurant table.) All in all, their operation of the farm-to-table food enterprise displays brimming confidence when I last visited; how they conduct their social and business life in the village indicates visible command over their social environment.

Their poorer neighbor, Ms. Mai, however, sees arrogance in their display of confidence. Thu and Ngoan' families were the poorest of the poor in the village until recently, she once said to me, squinting at the sight of the couple passing by on their motorbike as we were chatting at her gate: "There is no need to turn your nose up as soon as you have just emerged out of destitution. These days, one is never sure how things might turn out at the end of the day (*không ai nắm tay đến tối, gối đầu đến sáng*)[7]." While I can detect some jealousy in Ms. Mai's statement, it is quite apt in capturing the uncertainties of Ngoan and Thu's entrepreneurial pursuits, and even the couple's own anxieties over the sustainability of their enterprise. Although Ngoan often contrasted their current life "at home" favorably with the time they had been in the city, she once told me that rabbit keeping was labor-intensive and they had to work even harder than they had in the urban waste depot, where they in fact could make better money.

Asked if they would ever resume urban waste trading, she said if their eldest daughter eventually made it into the university, they would accompany her and set up a waste depot in Hanoi. She did not see any obstacle to that plan:

> We have a profession (*nghề* [she means waste trading])—we know the ins and outs of it. It is not so difficult for us to find a place and make a living with it. The most important thing for us is to accompany the children, that is, if they get into the university at all. Nowadays, the children get to learn about things very early. Without us around them, it is very risky. They would take up bad things very quickly.

Both Thu and Ngoan had a lower secondary education until grade 8 before they went into the waste trade in the mid-1990s, then as itinerant traders. They had left for the city with a single goal: to make enough money as preparation for setting up a family. The aspirations that they have for their children indicate changes not only in their economic conditions, but also, I argue, a classed sense of self that references both the state-sponsored model of personhood centered on modern human capitals and the cultural value placed on formal learning. Interestingly, the fallback position of their aspirations is none other than the recourse to urban waste, something that state officials would dismiss as a sort of non-profession unbecoming of the ideal of employment in the new economy, something people do because they possess no skills. Yet for Green Spring people like Thu and Ngoan, waste work is not a contingent occupation—it has become a profession that requires a depth of knowledge and skills they could deploy when necessary. But even for them, the profession is considered only as a means to a good life, a goal that requires liberating their children from the association with waste. The pitfalls of this aspiration are manifold: to make it to the university alone is not easy, and even if their children do, the likelihood of finding a white-collar job (or "office job," as they say in Vietnam) is becoming smaller. Some adult children of waste traders I met have opened streetside restaurants or taken up factory employment after college, occupations that do not require the long years of higher education. Yet such likely outcomes do not seem to render these aspirations less valid for them.

Thu and Ngoan's decision to go into rabbit farming is part of a microtrend of former waste traders returning to focus on specialty livestock farming, through which they hope to tap into the growing demand for various kinds of specialty meat. In the district, these former waste traders have been investing in farming crocodiles, hedgehogs, quails, snakes, and the like. The idea of creating or participating in niche markets for specialty products in order to gain a quick and large profit margin is attractive, especially to younger people. Their hope is to retain a comparable level of income to what they made in the urban waste trade, but while living in the countryside. The initial investment is often quite significant, and it would not be possible without their savings from urban waste work. Thu and Ngoan have been lucky so far, given that the local preference for rabbit meat has not waned, as is often the case with new specialties. Others have been less successful: the prices of hedgehogs and crocodile meat, for instance, went down significantly sometime after they were introduced, resulting in significant losses for many. People have to find out for themselves about the technical requirements of keeping new livestock, while marketing largely takes place through personal networks. Meanwhile, the market prices for certain products are distorted by temporary surges in demand created by Chinese traders who buy in large quantities at a certain time. It thus remains to be seen how Thu and Ngoan will continue to fare with their rabbits and therewith their entrepreneurial pursuits.

## Story of Xuân and Đại: Love of the Land

"If you love the land, it will love you back!" Xuân said when showing me around her ten-acre farm on the edge of the commune that included a fish pond, grass land, orchids, and rows of sheds where she and her husband Đại kept cattle, pigs, poultry, and dogs for sale. They had rented the land from the commune administration on a long-term contract—few people had wanted to rent it because of the remote location, about several kilometers away from the residential area, making it difficult to supervise. The couple practically lived on the farm, going back to their house in the village only on the weekend or whenever necessary, while their two sons, aged six and eleven, stayed with their paternal grandparents.

I first met Xuân and Đại, in their mid-thirties, in 2012. Both of them are extremely hard-working, their faces and hands dark and wizened from farming. Đại has an instinctive attachment to the land and believes in farming as the way forward for the countryside to develop: "If everyone works in the city, who plants the rice for us to eat?" He keeps plotting to rent more farmland without letting his wife know, which enrages her and creates much tension between them. Xuân speaks about this with open frustration, but she also seems affected by her husband's passion for land and farming.

Although Xuân appears to be the dominant one, talking most of the time and ordering Đại around, he was the one who made the decision to return to farming in 2007, after several years of operating a waste depot in the city of Hải Phòng. At the time, Xuân did not take such a great liking to the land; only her husband had dreamed of coming back. In the mid-1990s, she had followed her mother to work as an itinerant junk trader in Hanoi, and after marrying, the couple had set up a waste depot together. Like many people of her generation, she had never had to do farm work, as the economy of her parents' household had long been focused on urban waste trading. They had been making good money with their waste depot in Hải Phòng, and she had wanted to continue until they had saved a substantial amount. But Đại had been talking incessantly of returning. Xuân told me that he had this "strange" attachment to the land and to the home village; he craved working on the land, always thinking up plans of going back and setting up a flower farm, an orchid garden, a cattle farm. Every day, he commented how great it would be to live in the home village and work the land. "In the end, I gave in. What can one do against such a passion?" Xuân said.

In the beginning, things were not as romantic as Đại had imagined they would be when he was working in their urban depot weighing, sorting, and packing up recyclable waste each day. With their savings, they were able to buy the farmland at an auction and purchase initial inputs, but everything had to be learned anew. The idea of the flower farm was not easy to realize because there was not much of a market for flowers locally, so they settled first on livestock. Lacking market information, they had sold the first herd of cattle at a low price, even though the actual prices had shot up significantly. Without experience, they had not known that the goats they tried keeping would wander around and somehow often end up on the roofs of the neighbors' houses; they discontinued keeping goats after spending too much time gathering the active animals. Then, like for Ngoan and Thu, there were problems with animal diseases that they could not solve. They felt defeated and thought about giving up; at some point in 2010, they almost sold the farm to an interested buyer in order to return to the urban waste trade. Xuân said, "Then we stood on the dike looking down on the farm, looking at the green bushes of bananas bearing fruits, the lush greens and the fertile pond, and we could not bring ourselves to do it. We had worked so much on the land, and it became difficult to leave it." She added that although the income was not as good as waste trading, what they have gained is proximity to their children: if they were in the city, it would be difficult to bring them along because the grandparents could no longer manage them as they were growing older.

Over time, however, things stabilized, and regular income trickled in from the pigs, the cows, and the fish, as well as from the ornamental trees and fruit trees of all sorts that they had planted. During one of my visits to the farm, they sold four hundred kilograms of chicken, which they had kept for more than three months, at eighty thousand *đồng* per kilogram,. The fish fetch them forty to fifty million *đồng* every half year, and the animals up to a hundred million *đồng* a year. Their annual income from the farm amounts to 250 to 300 million *đồng* (US$12,000–15,000)—unless they encounter major problems with animal diseases or price fluctuations, that is. Their farm is considered a "bright point" (*điểm sáng*) by the local government, which often sends visitors there to experience a New Countryside model of agricultural production.

The other part of their story is connected to three other couples, their relatives and village friends, who have also left urban waste trading. During the year that Xuân and Đại were thinking about quitting the farm, these other couples came back and proposed to pool their money for purchasing a tractor and a harvester to work the land that had been left uncultivated by fellow villagers who had temporarily abandoned rice farming to work in the urban waste trade. Per-capita farmland in the commune, as elsewhere in the Red River Delta, is about 360 square meters (one *sào*), and the land is not tradable by law. What they did was to borrow the land from the migrant households, who happily loaned it to them in order to avoid paying the maintenance and irrigation fees. Each couple was thus able to piece together just over one hectare to farm; this was made easier with the land consolidation under the New Countryside Program. The machines make it possible to farm on this scale but require a different method of preparing the field: broadcasting (*gieo sạ*) rather than transplanting by hand as before.

In addition to farming their own land, the group also offer the service of their machines to others who also do large-scale farming but are not yet able to purchase their own. The price for harvesting one acre is about two million *đồng*, which takes a machine operated by three people two hours to finish. The shared venture is similar to that of a small cooperative for which there is detailed and transparent accounting and with clear rules about equal contribution of labor and benefit sharing. For their own harvest, they hire day laborers coming from the neighboring province of Thái Bình. When I visited again in 2015, the group together had three harvesters; the couples operated two of the machines themselves and hired four people to work on the remaining one (Figure 5.3 shows one of the harvesters).[8] By then, more households were doing large-scale farming, and more people were buying machines. Xuân mentioned two households that had been using their machinery service to farm fifteen acres had jointly purchased a harvester that

FIGURE **5.3 Harvester parked in the yard.**
Source: Author's photo, Green Spring, 2015.

year, depriving the group of a significant order. The increased competition has prompted them to look beyond Spring District for customers.

In 2015, however, these couples seemed more settled in their productive ventures. Each ten acres of paddy they farmed fetch sixteen to seventeen tons of rice per crop (with two crops a year). The turnover for each of these households from rice farming alone is about US$7,000–10,000 per year, while that generated from their machines ranges up to US$12,000 per year. When I asked if the combined income from farming and machine hire is comparable to that from operating an urban waste depot, they said that waste trading could be much more profitable—with good connections to businesses and factories, they could make as much as a billion *đồng* a year. Yet none of them had the intention of returning to the urban waste trade just yet. Dương, Đại's sister, a thirty-four-year-old woman with two children, said:

> At home we now make less money, but the air is better and life is lot more relaxing. We also have greater autonomy (*tự chủ*) over what we do, not having to worry about finding a long-term rental place in the city or dealing with the uncertainties (*bấp bênh*) of the waste trade.

Then we can be with the children and have time to educate them, which
is much more difficult to do when operating an urban waste depot.

As the head of the hamlet's Youth Union, Dương had received an award
from the province for being a productive example for rural female youths who
also maintain a harmonious family with children performing well in school.
She is, in the language of emulative campaigns, "the youth's face of the New
Countryside" (gương mặt thanh niên nông thôn mới tiêu biểu). When I last saw
her, Xuân told me that her two sons were also doing well in school. "We have
lacked grey matter (chất xám [she was referring to education]) in our life," she
said, "and our children should try to gain some of it and make it out to be
better than their parents. As long as they have the ability to study, we would do
anything to support them, however hard we have to live." Like Thu and Ngoan,
they seem to be keeping faith in the progressive trajectory of human development pictured in the state's vision of development. In the new-countryside
Green Spring, many younger parents today articulate a stronger desire for
their children to obtain higher education than their parents' generation did.
The declining value of the college degree notwithstanding, higher education
represents that which many see as an essential part of the good life that is
worth striving for. The headmaster in Chapter 4 might be wrong to state that
higher education will inevitably lead to the good life, but his assumption
points to a powerful notion of higher education as something intrinsically
good, especially for improving one's "intellectual level" (dân trí) – the benchmark of good citizenship. This notion is not just prevalent in Vietnam: across
East Asian societies, the hegemonic desire for education is being produced by
the interplay between cultural ideas and governing techniques focused on the
accumulation of human capitals (Kipnis 2011). In Spring District, it has
become one of the strongest driving forces in local people's project of remaking, an aspiration that paradoxically would require the very abandonment of
waste as a source of livelihoods and as a craft trade with which they identify.
Even as the waste traders might continue to put forward counter-arguments
based on alternative ways of valuing social achievements, as Chapter 4 suggests, they do so precisely on account of the hegemonic power of this desire.

# Conclusion: Value, Entrepreneurship,
# and the Remaking of the Countryside

Constructing the countryside as a counter-space to the dislocations of migrant
lives, a small number of people in Spring District have turned their waste-
generated earnings and attachment to the land into thriving agricultural

enterprises in the homeplace. Through such meanings and actions, they set in motion a process of remaking the countryside, which is still commonly viewed as the harbinger of backwardness and underdevelopment. Indeed, their enterprises entail the very modes of production that are being promoted under the New Countryside Program, which entail large-scale farming, intensification, and mechanization. The government might celebrate this as a success of the New Countryside Program, but such revaluation is in the first place the outcome of people's disenchantment with migrant lives in the cities, where they are discriminated against both socially and institutionally. Contra the official rhetoric of internal strengths, their experiences with and earnings from urban waste trading are instrumental for their local productive ventures and their contribution to local development. In the meantime, the small group of returning waste traders has already amassed the opportunities opened up by the absence of land owners and the land consolidation effected through the New Countryside Program; others will find it more difficult to acquire sufficient land for profitable ventures. Further, prices of agricultural products are no less fluctuating than those of the waste they traded in the city—and they have little control over these. As such, their productive ventures, praised by the local government as models of how a new countryside should turn out, might over the long term be curtailed by limited resources and uncertain market outcomes.

In *The Will to Improve,* Tanya Li (2007) suggests that the intention of the state and other development actors to improve lives masks the structural inequalities they themselves help to create through their institutional practices, especially via the construction of peasants as backward. Working from within these inequalities, the Green Spring peasant entrepreneurs' actions defy the categorization of them as passive actors waiting to be developed by external powers. They have taken advantage of available opportunities to proactively improve their lives and remake their positioning vis-à-vis the state agenda, and in so doing recast themselves as agents of change in the countryside. In the meantime, their practices and aspirations facilitate the development approach that promotes self-enterprise and self-help development. Yet their cases also indicate the limits of this development approach, given the unequal structures of opportunities they find themselves in, structures that are immersed in uncertain market conditions and their institutionalized marginalization. Likewise, the heavy indebtedness resulting from overzealous New Countryside construction elsewhere reveals the shortcomings of self-reliance and self-development. Although it is less coercive than in other similar contexts, both past and present (Robin 2009, Schneider 2014), the Vietnamese party-state's will to improve does not seem to match a readiness to *take responsibility for* what needs to be done. As this chapter suggests, and as Chapter 7 will suggest, this responsibility is conveniently placed on the shoulders of local people by means of moral mobilization.

In a study of rural economy and globalization in Borneo, Michael Dove (2011) shows that small-holding farmers commonly practice a combination of capitalist cash-crop and subsistence farming; the former is more prone to market fluctuations, and the latter more protected. The migration literature holds a common assumption that the village and subsistence farming represent havens of security on which people can fall back in case migrant livelihoods fail. Yet in the political economy of Vietnam today, which is more and more connected to the global economy and its seemingly perpetual crisis, nothing is secure. For Green Spring households, it is the migrant waste trade more than agriculture that has become their fallback position, although this is to a greater extent due to their anxiety over the potential for failure in their agricultural enterprises than because waste trading is inherently more secure. Uncertainties indeed reverberate across the city and the countryside as spaces of livelihoods and social mobility. In telling the stories of the few people who have temporarily succeeded, I do not want to romanticize. For anyone who succeeds, there are others who do not, and for those who do succeed, the fear of failing is always present. What I wish to show is the interplay between a vision of development that centers on self-enterprise and self-reliance and local people's aspirations for social recognition and belonging. Here, we have a glimpse of the politics of value in which the state not only seeks to appropriate the value created by the people's actions, but also to define what value actually is for its developmental agenda. Yet we also see that self-enterprise and self-reliance can only achieve as much under conditions of uncertainty.

These savvy villagers are well aware that the state approach to local development can only go so far as their individualized strategies can— in Thu's words, only when "people's pockets are full" on their own accords. In the same state agenda, however, they find a social space for meaning making. Their own value projects, while building on specific ideas of the good life, social aspirations, and idiosyncratic personal attachments, also draw on state visions of modernity and civility (see also High 2014, Harms 2016), visions that are articulated through programs such as the New Countryside or ideas around "the intellectual level of the people" (*dân trí*). Villagers like Thu do not question the "new countryside" as a desirable goal, despite their awareness that they are being made accountable for sustaining it. Yet even those who have made it back through the few locally available opportunities are constrained by the uncertainties of the wider market that they experienced as waste traders, which emerges from political-economic processes that are beyond their control. The next chapter further suggests that most people keep on pursuing their goals notwithstanding, being driven by expectations about future possibilities for making money and consumption (Berlant 2011, Beckert 2016) that are increasingly articulated as part of emerging class relations.

## CHAPTER 6

# Money and Consumption: Gendered Desires, Class Matters

Every other day, on his way transporting iron waste to the steel-making village of Đa Hội on the outskirt of Hanoi, Hân drives by Vincom Village, a luxury, gated residential development that features European-style villas lining artificial lakes dotted with private, manicured gardens. During a trip on which I joined him, he told me that he had once followed a taxi-driving friend into the complex to take a look around. "It's the dream of a place to live, you know, so modern and beautiful. The apartments in there are already six to seven billion đồng (about US$300,000), and one doesn't even need to think how much one of those villas costs," he said, eyes fixed on the road. When I commented that at the rate of his current earning, he could one day save up enough to buy an apartment there, he laughed: "One can always dream, but it's not for us. The place is for the super-rich (đại gia); we can never make enough to afford to live in such a place." After some minutes, he added, "And anyway, you know, we need to live in places where it is possible to store the waste."

Like other waste transporters, Hân cultivates a long-term relationship to one furnace owner in the steel-making village, Ms. Thảo, and only sells his waste iron to her. He said Ms. Thảo's family owned an impressive villa in the town center, with luxury furniture and beautiful design. Her adult children were operating thriving businesses selling iron products manufactured in the village (from waste iron). Hân had been invited to three of her children's weddings. He was impressed with grandness (*hoành tráng*) of these weddings, which featured popular folk music bands (*quan họ*) and sumptuous banquets for hundreds of guests. "They are extremely wealthy; [even rich] people from our village are nothing compared to them (*Họ giàu lắm, người làng mình không là cái gì cả chị ạ*)," he said.[1]

Hân was interested in my experiences living abroad; he said it must be nice to live in Europe, with all its grandeur and civility, and asked many questions about life in Germany. It occurred to me later that Hân's urban encounters, like those of his fellow villagers, are not just about surviving the dangers of the city and managing the precarious conditions of making a living—or in Thu's words, "bracing the battle." They are also about dreams: dreams of money and of the good life, of not just being the one stuck on the outside looking in at the life of the urban middle class but of having such a life. In this chapter, I will show that such desires drive Spring District men and women to action as much as their struggles for livelihoods and care do. In the face of all their struggles, people carry on doing what they are doing because they expect that life will somehow be better as a result. After all, Hân's extended family has already grown more prosperous after being dirt poor only two decades earlier (at least if one doesn't count one of his uncles, who has suffered one big loss after the other in the wake of his adult son's death in an accident). Hân's two siblings are doing well; both are depot operators in profitable locations of Hanoi. So are his parents, who have a large, modern house in Green Spring. Indeed, the wealth generated in Green Spring and the consumption it enables have become exemplary forces that draw people from the district and beyond into the waste economy, the setbacks and downfalls for many notwithstanding. Their desires and aspirations are discernably underscored by Jens Beckert's (2016) idea of "fictional expectations"—namely people's anticipation of a progressive trajectory of better lives and greater likelihood of gain in riches over time, even when confronted with evidence of otherwise. As important components of the political economy of remaking, they are pursued in ways that are congruent with both the translocal life that the waste traders lead and their mode of production.

As the previous chapter suggests, aspiring to the good life is seen as a mark of desirable personhood, and "common sense" holds that a region can only develop if local people themselves aspire to development. Yet the social implications of waste work often hinder their efforts in realizing these aspirations. The obscurity and humility expected of waste traders require that they refrain from displaying wealth in urban spaces in order for wealth to be generated; even people who have been able to purchase urban properties or engage in urban consumption have to manage their appearance carefully. This reminds one of what Ann Marie Leshkowich (2014) terms "the political economy of appearance" with which southern Vietnamese market traders engage following the reforms (đổi mới). As Leshkowich notes, "[T]rade was an act of speculation requiring entrepreneurs to perform as if they believed market-oriented economic development would continue, while also displaying themselves in ways that could afford protection should the recently opened door slammed shut" (2014: 21).

By now, it is clear that marketization continues to advance, yet the waste traders have also come to experience first-hand its debilitating uncertainties and trade-offs, as well as the anxiety it produces. Driven by this anxiety and by the need to remain inconspicuous in the city, the waste traders' practices of "displaying themselves" are geared toward the home village, or the inside realm. How local people strategically reveal and disguise their wealth depending on the context also recalls Erik Harms's (2013) characterization of elite urban men's practices of "conspicuous invisibility." Yet the ways in which they traverse between the city and the countryside in acts of consumption that are visible in the home village but relatively hidden in the city is better captured by what one might call *contingent conspicuousness*. Thereby, the village continues to be the place in which they seek social recognition for money making and spending, even as they might be living away from it or, in some cases, may not return. In these practices, men and women again negotiate between the inside and the outside in differing ways, infusing these spaces with fresh meanings as sites of consumption, remaking it at the same time as they are reconfirming its significance for their actions.

## Money, the Gods, and the Anxiety of Mobility

The head monk in charge of the pagoda in Green Spring[2] joked in one of our meetings: "In this commune, five percent of the population are party members; the other ninety-five percent are under my control." The Venerable, as he is known, has a good local standing on account of his monastic rank and his official role in the central Buddhist order. People see him for all important life matters, such as children's school performance, business, birth, sickness, marriage, death, or the drug addiction of a family member. Most of my informants return to visit the pagoda regularly. People come to the pagoda carrying trays loaded with offerings of wine, beer, sweets and cakes, as well as rice and chicken to pray for protection and luck for their newly opened waste depots or newly purchased transport vehicles. As people say their prayers openly in front of the main altar, sitting among them for some hours on a busy day allows a sense of a whole realm of fears, wants, and wishes. People pray for good fortune (*lộc*) in "working away from home" (*đi làm ăn xa*); for money to flow; for their waste transport vehicles to run smoothly, without accidents or legal troubles; for a land purchase to go through; and for their children to stay away from drugs and other social evils. Here, the dream for money mingles with the dread of its undoing, both of which invite the intervention of the gods.

The procurement of a transport vehicle is a significant event for a waste-trading household. Once purchased, it becomes a living member that needs care (the work of maintaining and servicing a vehicle is often referred to as *nuôi xe*, literally "raising a vehicle"), and it has the potential to enable the household's rise through quick and lucrative earnings or to destabilize the households through all sorts of unknown dangers on the highway. A blessing ritual for the vehicle is offered by the monk at a price: people would bring their newly purchased vehicle to the pagoda together with an offering of boiled chicken and sticky rice placed on its hood, upon which the Venerable performs the blessing. The monk said to Tâm and me that since they "started to go out," local people have had greater demand for such rituals—there are thousands of such vehicles in the commune, and private cars are also not rare. The vehicle's alternate roles as generator of wealth or misfortune makes the alliance of the gods necessary, even if it comes at a cost. Meanwhile, the blessing ritual for a newly purchased vehicle signals the legitimacy of their purchase, the wisdom of the money spent, and the resultant increase in the prestige of its (male) owner in the village.

The head monk seems adept at capitalizing on the anxiety of mobility for the wealth of his pagoda. Besides one-off ceremonies such as the vehicle blessing or a land purchase, he offers a standard ritual for each life-cycle event at a price. Life-cycle services include a ritual to "bring the soul of the deceased to the pagoda" (*đưa vào chùa*) to seek protection, which takes place forty-nine days after the person dies, or a marriage ceremony (*lễ hằng thuận*), which has recently become popular in urban areas. A popular ritual is the *bán khoán* ceremony, literally the "handing over" of a child, often a baby boy, to the gods. *Bán khoán* is a folklorist practice incorporated into Buddhist pagodas, where deified personas are worshipped alongside Buddhist figures as protectors of children, having the power to rectify the ills caused by supernatural forces. It is commonly believed that young children's problems with health, behavior, and even school performance arise from their exposure to evil spirits or offended gods due to the timing of their birth. Such children are considered "difficult to raise" (*khó nuôi*) and should be ritually "handed over" to the pagoda through the ceremony so that they receive protection. In the district, many consider doing this even when the children do not display any obvious problems. Fifty-seven-year-old Ms. Vân, who has had the ceremony arranged for her three-year old grandson, says to me, "Sacredness arises when one worships; peacefulness is assured when one observes the ritual" (*có thờ có thiêng, có kiêng có lành*). She believes that once the boy is "handed over" to the pagoda, the protection will also be extended to his family's waste-trading activities:

> My children are trading people (*người làm ăn*) and they rely on luck to have a smooth business. If the age of the children does not match the age of the parents, all sorts of bad fortunes and ill health will befall us. Since my grandson's age is not in harmony with his parents', I told my children that it was necessary to do the ritual to obtain the protection of the deities (*cầu các ngài che chở*).

While such services are not entirely new, their monetary costs are. Donations for the ceremonies used to be voluntary (*tùy tâm*); nowadays, there is a price tag for each, which increases according to the prices of market goods and services (*theo thời giá*). For example, a full *bán khoán* ceremony is priced at seven million *đồng* (about US$350), including offerings of food, drinks, and cash donation. Given the increasing popularity of these rituals, the pagoda's revenues are significant, even without the irregular donations by successful migrant traders. Apart from individualized services, there are annual Buddhist festivities that draw large numbers of people. Migrants tend to return for such events, and spending on these is a major household expenditure category, referred to as "festivities, gatherings, and anniversaries" (*hội hè đình đám*), an omnipresent category that consumes a significant chunk of their earnings. Regular gatherings, often on the first and the fifteenth day of the lunar month, in which people pool money and rice for a festive meal, are well attended by the local elders, especially elderly women, for whom they are an important source of sociality. People often complain about the costs of pagoda services; some are critical of the monk's business-mindedness (and his rumored personal indulgence in sumptuous food). Yet the pagoda as a social institution represents part of their inside realm in relation to the world beyond, and thus an important social space for the migrant waste traders. It constitutes a public sphere in which not only their dreams and wishes, but also their anxieties and worries, their yearning for recognition and belonging, can be seen and heard.

## "Civilized" Living and Vacant Houses

Green Spring commune stands out in comparison to other rural places in the Red River Delta not just because of its public works and productive assets; lifestyle and consumption here are visibly urbanized. Unlike in the city, where they need to keep a low profile to trade waste, the command over the social space of their home village allows those who can to display middle-class consumption and lifestyles. Thu and Ngoan may look shabby in their work clothes on their rabbit farm, but the couple has a three-story house, with individual rooms, modern kitchen and bathroom, running hot water, and timber furniture, including a set of armchairs costing more than US$1,000. Like many others in the commune, they drive one of those gas-operated motorbikes that are popular in the city, costing about US$1,500. When the couple are on their motorbike with their son in the middle, dressed in their better clothes and Ngoan's long hair let down, they look rather similar to urban middle-class couples on the streets of Hanoi or Hồ Chí Minh City. It is common to see young people occupied by expensive smartphones at public events; many have computers or laptops at home with internet connections. Despite the concern over addiction to computer games, many parents view it as necessary for their children to be updated with technologies.

In our conversations, local people like to tell about going on a beach trip or a tour to scenic sights, showing photos of families in bathing suits or posing together in front of these sights. During a joint meal, Xuân and Dương, the agricultural producers in the previous chapter, told us about their recent trip to the Bái Đính pagoda, a resort-pagoda complex in the neighboring province. They had hired a bus together with twenty other people from the village to visit the pagoda. These sight-seeing tours have become a normal part of their life, they said. When Dương's mother commented that they had to go to the pagodas to pray for the smooth operation of their farming business, Dương turned to me and said, "Actually, now that we are still young and in good health and are able to enjoy it, we need to travel to know about places (*biết đó biết đây*). Otherwise, we'll not be able to do anything when we get older and become weaker." (Dương is tall, good-looking, and fashionable; one can never help noticing her from a distance, elegantly dressed on her red scooter, with her neat little daughter in the back). It struck me then how middle class the aspirations of this group of rural entrepreneurs are: higher education for their children, leisure, fashion, and modern technologies—aspirations that a generation ago were not associated with Green Spring people, who were said to live from hand to mouth, pursuing money at the cost of morality and dignity. Such articulations must, however, be understood in relation to the experiences they have as waste traders, experiences of being seen as dirty outsiders who upset urban order and civility through their occupation with waste, something that earns them money but not the respect of urban people.

At the time of my visit in 2015, Xuân and Đại were building their house, a dream home that suited their attachment to farming and Đại's romantic imagination of rural life. It was to be built in the traditional style with a tiled roof, open plan, and wooden pillars, yet with all the modern amenities, such as an en-suite toilet and fitted kitchen. Xuân proudly showed me around the construction site, explaining what they were going to do with the new house, pointing to where the children and their friends could sit and play and where they were planning to display a set of antique wooden furniture (*sập gụ, tủ chè*), the style favored in the past by wealthy rural people. She mentioned that her children had felt embarrassed living in their tiny house. They therefore found that it was the right time to build a new one, although it was only for the children to occupy most of the time, as Xuân and Đại would continue to spend their days on the farm. While their house boasts a rural idyll in its design, it has the features of modern housing that have become standard in Green Spring, where newly built villas are a common sight—some clearly built to impress with their spacious surroundings.

Nevertheless, many local houses are left vacant much of the year, until the owners come back for the lunar New Year holiday (*Tết*) or when there are family events. During *Tết*, Green Spring comes alive with the bustling of people and motorbikes, with cars and waste transporters parked side by side in the yards or on the village paths. Many families return from the city in vehicles loaded with stereos, fridges, foodstuffs and whatever are necessary for the festivities and the sojourn "at home" that may last up to a month. The houses then are vacated when people leave again for the cities, starting another year of urban work with shorter visits to the village during the year. Taking walks around the village with my Green Spring neighbors during those summer nights (many local people have taken to strolling together in the evening, for the benefit of health, they said), I kept wondering about the sense of the eerily quiet and dark houses that lined the village paths. Why would people invest so much of their money and effort in grand houses that they do not live in everyday, or have to wait for years until they can? Later, I realized that there is no such thing as a vacant house in this place. The house belongs to people wherever they are, the inside realm that houses their ancestors, their past and their dreams of the future, their place within the world; it is a haven away from the outside realm laden with the dangers being people with "low necks and small voices."

Their dilemma is, with few exceptions, that to live in these houses means having to quit the waste trade and thus facing difficulties in sustaining the lifestyle that befits such houses. It is much like after having bought an expensive suit: one feels compelled to acquire a whole range of other items that together can produce the matching appearance. In the same vein, higher earnings make it imperative to give greater gifts of money on important events or bigger donations to local causes than otherwise. In other words, the upkeep of the dream for the good life, for "civilized" living in the autonomous space of the home village, depends on the continuation of a precarious existence as migrant waste traders in the cities; few people can start a rabbit farm or mechanized farming, as the villagers in Chapter 5 did. Meanwhile, I am not suggesting that the life local people lead in the city is all work and no pleasure. Even as their practices might be invisible to the urban public, men and women from Spring District consume in ways that correspond to both the inside/outside framework and globalized forms of desires. Yet the consumption must be managed so that it is displayed or hidden depending on location and social context, practices that I shall use the term *contingent conspicuousness* to characterize.

## Consuming the City and the Gender of Desire

In a paper on masculinity and market trading (Nguyen 2018), I show how young male waste traders, using the occasional windfalls they earn in the waste trade, engage in practices of consumption that are popular among urban middle-class men. Congruent with the association of men's actions with the realm of the outside, these young men feel emboldened not only to travel far from home, away from the purview of their parents, and to take risks, but also to experiment with things and embrace adventures beyond the village. They do not shy away from sensual pleasures deemed to be exclusive to urban middle-class men, such as consuming expensive alcohol and food in fancy places or visiting women who are paid to entertain men; such experiences mark an important measure of being male in the new economy (see also Hoang 2015). Spending money and playing become part of a desirable manhood that they associate with city life, a hegemonic form of masculinity that breaks free from the moral mold of the previous era to embrace worldly pleasures and global consumption as worthy male pursuits. In the city, where the spatialization of class is spawning spaces of consumption exclusively catering to the urban middle class (Harms 2009), they represent both a masculinized way of appropriating space and an act of emulating middle-class practices. Their parents might be displeased with what they consider excessive spending habits, but tend to shrug it off as things that "boys do." One of these days, "the boys" will settle down in marriage and become more prudent, as the common expectations of them go and which later in their lives do materialize to certain degrees.

Since young female waste traders tend to remain within the guardianship of their mothers, sisters, or other senior females when in the city, their consumption is more oriented toward the inside. Their personal investment, however, is more directed at the inside realm that concerns their future spouses rather than their parental home, which will become the outside (*bên ngoại*) once they get married. While ruling out the explicit pleasure seeking embraced by young men, young women take care to dress themselves in fashion when not working and are encouraged to tend to their bodies in ways that produce presentable outward appearances. Whereas the young men are given much greater leeway in spending the money they make, the young women's earnings are more likely to be controlled by their mothers, who often say that they save these earnings on their daughters' behalf. In many cases, the money is spent on gold jewelry, worthy additions to their dowry when married. It seems that at a young age, women are already familiarized with their anticipated work of producing the inside realm of their future conjugal families, even when their spouses are yet to be identified. Their consumption as such prepares them for their inside-oriented gender roles, even as they are on the move. Whereas the young men pride themselves on spending money on fleeting pleasures as an indication of their worldliness, not to spend money unless necessary, or to spend it on socially accepted objects, seems a moral obligation to which the young women are inclined to adhere, at least performatively.

The following vignette reveals the traces of these different spatial orientations in the consumption practices of male and female waste traders in the city:

Đăng lives with his wife, Liên, in a migrant lodging shared with other waste traders from Spring District. Both of them are itinerant traders, and their two teenage children live with their grandparents in the village. Once, somebody wanted to sell a huge block of metal that used to be the core of an engine and demanded three million *đồng* for the object (US$150), which was suspiciously covered in moss, so that the first person who was approached declined to buy it. Đăng then discussed with two young men living close by, Danh and Hưng, who proposed that the three of them buy it together, hire a truck, and take it to a depot; whatever the outcomes, they would just split the difference. Đăng was insecure about the possibility of losing a large sum from the purchase, but he agreed after some convincing by the other two, who are usually more daring than him. They pooled their money to buy the block, which they later sold for nine million *đồng*. That night, they went together for a beer-drinking session during which Danh and Hưng, who already had mobile phones, told him that he too needed to have one, so that they could exchange information [mobile phones were becoming more available but remained a luxury for many at the time]. The next day, Đăng asked his wife to give him back the money he had given her for saving. Liên was at first reluctant but gave in when Đăng said he would spend the money on buying more waste. When he returned with a new mobile phone, Liên broke into tears—the phone cost almost a month's savings of one person. Another time, after purchasing an antique standing fan of the Marelli brand that earned them an even a greater sum than the other purchase [these are one-off events rather than daily occurrences], the three men went together to an upmarket restaurant. They ordered goat meat and a bottle of imported cognac; the meal cost them one million *đồng* (about US$70). When Liên learned about it, she complained about their wastefulness in the presence of the other two. Under influence of the alcohol, Đăng, who normally is quite gentle, shouted at his wife: "What do you want? You have gotten hold of so much money within one day. Of course I get to spend some money if I make so much. If you continue to be cheeky, I will show you who is in charge!" Danh and Hưng then cheered him on, being tipsy themselves: "You are right, you are a man, you've got to show who is in charge, who the head of the family is!" And to Liên, they said, "You are being very unreasonable. He did not do anything out of proportion." At that point, Liên broke out crying again.

The power relations between genders aside, the vignette reveals quotidian frictions between the differing spatial orientations of consumption by men and women. The men feel entitled to have a taste of the urban consumption that often eludes them; it seems important for them to experience the power of being "men with money" in the urban landscape of consumption and reclaim what they are excluded from at other times. The women, meanwhile, would claim that they stay away from any consumption in the city for the sake of the family's more important needs; as one female itinerant trader explains:

> My husband used to "go out," but he had to come home to "keep the goal" because men can't save. They would make some money, but has to spend on [bought] breakfast, on tea and cigarettes and other things and in the end there is not much left. We women do not spend much; we cook rice for breakfast; we live in cheap places and do not have these other expenses. Only by living frugally do we set aside a little to build and buy (*kiến thiết sắm sửa*) for the family at home.

In the women's narratives, money is not to be spent on ephemeral pleasures of the outside world, but for the worthy pursuits of consolidating and building the inside, and they disapprove of their husbands' tendency to stray from these pursuits—although at times also grudgingly accepting it. Both Đăng and Liên feel justified to state their conflicting claims (obviously boosted by tears in her case and alcohol in his) on how money should be spent. Thereby, they draw on the gender norms and expectations foregrounded by the differing spatial orientations to which people subscribe, not least in regard to money and consumption.

Of course, I am not suggesting that the women do not consume: they simply rule out certain ways of consuming while emphasizing others as appropriate. My earlier research on domestic service shows that the consumption of migrant domestic workers in Hanoi, predominantly married women, is geared toward the domestic sphere of their rural home (Nguyen 2015b, Chapter 5). In particular, their urban income is often invested in helping the male members of their family, their husband and sons, to fulfill their most important life goals, including, apart from getting a wife, building a house and purchasing a motorbike (in place of a buffalo as before[3]; see Box 6.1). The organization of feasts on important events for the patrilineal family, such as death anniversaries or the renovation of the ancestral tombs, represents a significant item on their list of yearly expenditures. Married female migrant waste traders act in the same vein, being focused on the production of gendered prestige for their household and thus reproducing the patrilineage. Rather than just aiming to "produce familiarity" within the inside realm (Brandstädter 2009), however, many are beginning to emulate practices of consumption by urban middle-class women in order to produce distinction for their rural home. Figure 6.1 shows the living room in the rural home of a female itinerant waste trader, and Figure 6.2 depicts the kind of furniture coveted in Spring District.

---

**BOX 6.1    A MOTORBIKE FOR LOVE**

I met Ms Nga, a forty-year-old itinerant trader, and her son, Nam, who was turning 17 and about to enter the waste trade, when they came back in preparation for a relative's wedding. In one of our after-dinner tea sessions, Nga brought up the topic of them buying a motorbike for Nam. Nga said it should not be more than nineteen million đồng (US$900). She liked a black motorbike because the color looks good for a long time, but Nam preferred a red one of a particular brand. Mr. Mạnh, my male host (Nga and Nam were his neighbors), joked that they should buy one of those Honda Cub 81s that he owned (an out-of-fashion model) and save the money for other things, adding that in the past it was coveted by many people. Nga said, "Times are different now; if he "goes to love" (đi yêu) on such a motorbike, the girls would be terrified by the noise it makes. No, you cannot take a girl on such an outmoded motorbike."

Locally, đi yêu means to court or date someone; love, rather than an emotion, evokes a young man's active deed of going out to seek the woman of his life and cultivate affection in her with a view toward marriage. Finding the suitable marriage partner is a serious matter that concerns the whole family; therefore, Nga did not think twice about equipping her son with the motorbike, an object of prestige that will help him in the search, even though this would mean a dent in her savings. I was struck by how she gently created pressure on Nam about "going to love." She would crack jokes about the possibility of a certain girl being the likely object of his attention, and then one suddenly realized that she actually meant it, dead seriously. She expected him to get married quickly and start setting himself up: "Since my sons do not pursue higher education, it is best for them to have their own families early to straighten up and keep them in order." The investment in a motorbike is thus nothing less than reasonable: "If the girl's family sees that we can afford a decent motorbike, they would think that we are hard-working and decent people and that our family is a promising place for their daughter," she told me.[1]

1. In my book Vietnam's Socialist Servants (2015b), I also discuss how the motorbike features in the consumption practices of the migrant domestic workers. Like Nga, a cleaner-junk-trader (page 124) articulated the same reason why her family wanted to purchase a Honda Dream motorbike, in addition to it being a ready means of livelihood should a male member of her family wants to take up motorbike taxi driving. The difference between the two accounts is the brand of the motorbike. In 2007, the Honda Dream was no longer fashionable but still seen as a solid investment because of its classic build and durability. When I talked to Nga five years later, the Honda Dream was out of the question as a family investment, and they were talking about a more contemporary model from the same company.

FIGURE 6.1 Living room of an itinerant waste trader in Red Spring.
Source: Author's photo, 2012.

FIGURE **6.2  Living room furniture coveted in Spring District.** This set cost about US$2,000 in 2012.
Source: Author's photo, 2012.

On a bus trip to Spring District, I sat next to a middle-aged woman from a commune neighboring Green Spring. She was visibly pleased to have secured a good seat for the journey. Lightly made up and in elevated heels, she wore an eye-catching imitation mink coat and carried a brand-new, red, faux leather handbag with sparkling silver chains. We struck up a friendly conversation, and it turned out that she was an itinerant junk trader and mother of two teenagers living at home with their father. She also cleaned for a number of urban families in Hanoi by the hour. I asked what the occasion was for which she looked so chic (*diện thế*), and she responded that she was coming home for the tomb-changing ceremony[4] for her husband's brother—but that in any case, one had to look decent when coming home. "Nowadays it is different from the past, when one could not afford to dress well. Anyway, how I dress is nothing compared with the city people I work for," she said. Then she told me about one of the families she cleaned for, a very wealthy couple who were apparently higher-up cadres in the army: "I have no idea what they do that earns them so much money. They can just spend and spend without thinking about it! You can't imagine the kind of expensive clothes the lady buys for herself and her children. She has a big cabinet full of expensive shoes and she keeps buying more and more, just like that." She marveled at how well their children dressed for school and at home; their son always went to school in an outfit of well-fitting jeans, checkered shirt, and a woolen beret, she said. (Clothing was also a topic that the domestic workers in my previous research frequently brought up to highlight the difference between them and their employers.)

At some point, our conversation shifted to life as a migrant in the city. She said that it was tough; one must work very hard and should not appear as too demanding. She had been charging people the same hourly rate of cleaning for years without asking for a raise for fear of being seen as greedy (she got the recyclables they wanted disposed of, though). In any case, she said:

> You cannot just stay at home [i.e., in the village]; one needs money to buy so many things to make the house a decent place. The kids would not put on a piece of new clothing if they do not find it fashionable enough these days. And their schooling requires so much money. It is no longer a matter of having enough to eat like before; one has to strive to do as well as the others (*phải cố gắng sao cho bằng người ta*).

My companion's encounters with the domestic sphere of the urban middle class seem to engender in her dreams and desires for some measure of middle-class women's consumption, much in the same ways that Hân's urban encounters do. Her outward appearance and her statements indicate that they are consequential for her consuming behavior, which prioritizes displaying her home, her children, and her body for social distinction. However, the distinction she seeks is to be located "at home" in the village, the realm of the inside vis-à-vis the world beyond it.

Before coming to Spring District, I had often seen female waste traders in their work clothes in the city: functional and gender-neutral outfits that are likely accentuated by a conical hat tied by a handkerchief, which also serves as a facial mask when necessary. That's why the contrast in how they appear in the village became instantly noticeable to me when I first met them in their rural home. Many take care to dress themselves in fashion, and their everyday clothing at home looks more sensual and feminine than when they are in the city. Most invest in a number of outfits for special occasions: not everyone owns an imitation mink coat, but the possession of "decent-looking" items has become important for even the most modest female waste trader. Ms. Thắm, longtime waste depot owner in

Hanoi with a flamboyant character, once proudly listed for me the better clothing items she possessed, including four sets of *áo dài* (traditional Vietnamese tunic) in different styles and two dress suits (*bộ giuýp*, as she called them) that she wore to events in the village. In the month before we had the conversation, she had been back to Green Spring to attend one death anniversary, one wedding, one funeral, and one lineage gathering. She showed me a gold ring inlaid with gemstones that her two daughters-in-law had jointly given her on the last International Women's Day (March 8th) and mentioned that she was saving up until the end of the year to purchase a "genuine" pearl necklace (*ngọc trai xịn*). "It will be a good finish for my outfits and make me look more presentable," she said.

As elsewhere in Vietnam, the construction of a house in Spring District represents the first important goal for married couples. Once their house is built, the women often seek to gradually acquire household items that are popular in the city; gas cookers, refrigerators, microwaves, and washing machines are no longer a rarity in the district. Such items not only signal "civilized" living, but also allow their owners to accentuate their embrace of new practices of domesticity. "All these years of going out, how can one not improve things a little bit? I have bought all that is necessary; our kitchen lacks nothing (*chẳng thiếu thứ gì*)," Hằng, the depot owner we met in Chapter 2, said when showing me smartphone photographs of her new house in Spring District, whose living room is adorned with imposing wooden furniture, a new fridge, a large fish tank, and a cuckoo clock on the wall. As much as they differ in spatial orientation, it seems, men and women's practices are underlined by concurrent references to globalized desires for middle-class consumption.

## Becoming Urban? Class Matters

When I first visited Hân and his wife, Thanh, on the edge of central Hanoi, having been given the address of their "house" by their relatives, I did not expect to find a shed similar to those that have been set up on the numerous depots of Hanoi for their owners. Later, I realized that the relatives had referred to it as their "house" because Hân and Thanh are the owners of the land; the expectation is that a house will eventually emerge from that land. Their recent purchase of the land counts as a major achievement for the couple, a sign that they are earning and saving well. Fifty square-meters in size, the land is situated outside the dike that protects central Hanoi from the Red River—not the best place to be when flooding occurs). It cost 1.5 billion *đồng* in cash (about US$70,000). The couple had savings of 500 million *đồng*, and the rest was borrowed from their siblings and parents on both sides. "It was a little bit too daring (*hơi liều mạng*), but if one is not daring, one will never get to own a place in this city. You know, here an ounce of land is an ounce of gold (*tấc đất tấc vàng*). Besides, this plot is very suitable for our occupation; it is close to the main road and not far from the city center," Thanh said to me. Their residence might look unkempt, and it might be a long time until they can pay off the debts and start building a solid house, but the fact that they own the land makes them wealthier than many middle-class Hanoians.

Their three children, all in primary school, live with the couple. The children go to a local school nearby, and Thanh spends much time caring for them and taking them to extra classes. Since Hân has a stable source of iron waste from a workshop, she can take it easy with their depot, sometimes closing early in order to devote herself to their children. She is praised in the extended family as an extremely resourceful wife, managing both their household and their depot while still taking good care of three children—Hân works hard on his truck but does little else in the family. Thanh (like their three children) has a Hanoi household registration (*hộ khẩu*), while Hân's remains in the village. Hân explained to me that they had needed Thanh to shift her *hộ khẩu* to Hanoi so that they could legally own the land and because it made it easier for the children to be accepted into schools in the city, especially the higher secondary schools they will attend later. He kept his household registration in the village because they one day might return. If the children acquire a good education and can leave waste trading, then their mission would be complete (*hết nghĩa vụ*), and Hân and Thanh could come home and live a better life there than in Hanoi, which, in his words, has "too little land for too many people" (*đất chật người đông*).[5]

I later visited Hân's parental house in Green Spring (of which he will have a share of the inheritance when his parents pass away). Since his parents were still operating a waste depot in Hanoi, the house was then being looked after by his unmarried aunt, one of my close informants. The house is spacious, airy, and well-designed, and the kitchen is modern, clean, and well-equipped. It would pass as a respectable suburban house in Hanoi, except that it is located in a village surrounded by rice fields. When I commented on the contrast between their comfortable house in Green Spring and the kind of residences in which Hân and his parents live in the city, the aunt said, "You know, one has to live in such city places in order to make some profit. In clean spaces, they will not be allowed to trade waste. The junk is dirty and messy and nobody wants to live close to a junk trading family." Her nephews and nieces, including Hân and his family, would eventually come back to the village, she said, because "even if it is more beautiful and modern in the city, it's their [urban people's] houses, their streets (*nhà của người ta, phố của người ta*)."

Hân's aunt did not take into account the fact that he and his brother indeed have acquired urban properties and can well say that these are "our houses," although they choose not to become official residents of Hanoi in order to keep their return to the village open. Yet her statement points to the limits of the desires that Hân articulates at the beginning of this chapter, desires to have an urban middle-class lifestyles. Hân is aware that such social mobility in the city depends on the ability to viably disentangle himself from waste work and the association with waste. To be able to join the urban middle class would mean finding an alternative to what has been for decades the source of livelihoods and wealth for his family—indeed, what they excel at doing. In the meantime, it is not possible for the family, at least not yet, to just go back and live in the beautiful house that his parents built. That's why their household remains split between the city and the countryside, even when they live together with their children in one place. In some ways, they are caught between the city and the countryside by the very hegemonic vision of the good life that spawns the kind of class-based desires we can detect in most places of our globalized world today.

## Conclusion: Fictional Expectations and the Remaking of Gendered Desires

Underlying local people's practices of consumption and spending money are the anxiety of mobility and hegemonic desires that are premised on enduring gendered notions and emerging class-based ideas of the good life. As described in the previous chapter, a number of migrant waste traders return to the village with entrepreneurial pursuits; their personal and economic investments have helped to reinvent the countryside, hitherto deemed to be backward and uncivilized, as a space for new kinds of social aspirations. This chapter shows that the reinvention is also occurring through consumption practices and lifestyles that go beyond the traditional gendered goals of acquiring prestige to take on class connotations. The dream of "civilized" living, leisure and consumption—the mainstays of the middle-class lifestyle—is, however, within reach only for a few. For many, this dream continues to be a fantasy that they struggle to maintain in their translocal lives, the "fictional expectations" about which

Beckert (2016) writes. These expectations keep local people continuing their pursuit of a better life while suffusing a great deal of anxiety into local lives, anxiety that manifests itself in their readiness to pay large sums for ritual services aimed at protecting their mobile livelihoods. For the time being, waste-generated income allows them to realize some aspects of "civilized" living in the village, but at the cost of their social positioning in the city, even for people who have built modern rural houses or acquired urban properties.

*Contingent conspicuousness* arises out of this social positioning, not only for the waste traders but also for many other migrant laborers whose livelihoods are shaped by the political economy of appearance that Ann Marie Leshkowich (2014) highlights. Yet whereas Leshkowich's southern market traders stealthily practice middle-class consumption out of fear for the social and political reprisals they had previously experienced before the reforms (*đổi mới*), the waste traders of Spring District engage in contingent conspicuousness for other reasons. First, the viability of their mode of production, which is premised more on inconspicuousness and humility (or a performance of these), would be hampered should they seek to display wealth to the general urban public. Second, such efforts might fail to achieve the intended effect of gaining prestige in a social order that classifies them as the dirty Other vis-à-vis an urban middle class priding itself on cultural distinction and the kind of human capital the traders might not possess. Thus, it is more effective for waste traders to "display themselves" to the village community, where alternative understandings of their value are possible as a shared evaluative framework.

Thornstein Veblen's (1979) notion of "conspicuous consumption" refers to the display of wealth through the consumption of valuable goods and personal services to bolster social status by what he terms "the leisure class," or the property-owning class in early industrial societies. This consumption, especially the use of servants and the wifely labor of women, is a means through which this class distances itself from productive labor, according Veblen. The waste traders' contingent conspicuousness resembles Veblen's portrayal in their underlying anxiety to gain prestige through displaying wealth. Yet it differs on account of consumption practices that are intimately connected to their world of labor and positioned toward the social space of their rural homeplace. Given the high moral value placed on the ability to rise out of poverty (see Chapter 7), this consumption is also meant to signify moral strength rather than just to display wealth. Shaped by hegemonic desires for middle-class consumption, contingent conspicuousness nonetheless indicates the strategies of consuming subjects with their own agenda, who consciously manage to be seen by selected audiences on account of their social position.

Meanwhile, the waste traders' consumption is equally influenced by the same gendered orientations toward the inside and the outside (*nội/ ngoại*) that also structure their mobility and access to urban spaces. Men and women consume differently, with goals and meanings that differ yet complement each other. The male traders' practices appear driven by an attempt to appropriate the urban space as an outside realm; underlying them are apparent efforts to somewhat rectify the spatialization of class in the city that produces exclusive spaces for the middle class (Harms 2009; Zhang 2010). The women's consumption is more oriented toward their home and their bodies, the realm of the inside, even as they are earning money and living away from their rural home. As such, not only are the boundaries between the inside and the outside malleable, but also the gendered practices of reproducing them. In Spring District, the changes have to do with the emergence of desires for consumption and leisure, for property ownership and "civilized" living, desires that are partly prompted by the men and the women's differing encounters with the urban middle class. As much as class-based desires have remade the inside/outside binary, local men and women's gendered practices of consumption have also rendered class boundaries porous.

Desire, therefore, does not just concern what it means to be men and women in the new economy; it is also part of the complex class relations emerging across the city and the country. What happens when desire becomes treacherous, when the expectations for continued improvements do not materialize? What happens when some people are not able to pursue, or not interested in the collective pursuit of the dream for the middle-class version of the good life? The next chapter discusses how the production of success and failure is moralized through the glorification of those who "make it" and the chastisement of those who fail or do not conform. I suggest that the production of success and failure in moral terms defines the responsibilities for losing and winning as private matters in the same way that livelihoods and care are framed as individualized responsibilities.

## CHAPTER 7

# An Exemplary Person, the Poor, and the Limits of Remaking

Since the beginning of my fieldwork, I had heard about Madam Q. Whenever I told local people that I was researching the waste trade, they would invariably mention her, in deferential tones, as the pioneer, the pathbreaker, the patron of the trade. Stories about her assume an almost mythical quality; they depict her as an extremely wealthy waste trader from the district who started out as a trash picker in Hanoi during the colonial period, then operated one of the few waste depots there throughout the subsidy period (*thời bao cấp*) and raised her sons to be successful entrepreneurs in the steel sector after the reforms. Beside her mythical rags-to-riches life, she appears saintly on account of her well-known good deeds for her natal village, which is now Green Spring commune. Apart from the worshipping temple of her lineage, she apparently financed the construction of the commune's graveyard for war martyrs and the former nursery of the commune. People told me she also made major contributions to the reconstruction of the local Buddhist pagoda. The giving seems strategically aimed at public works that have strong emotional relevance to local people, including works that are under the direct responsibility of the local government.

In this narrative, Madam Q., who is often mentioned in association with her successful sons, is depicted as an exemplary person of the new economy, somebody who masters the odds of the market with entrepreneurial skills and contributes to the well-being of others. This chapter contrasts the local construction of Madam Q. as an exemplary person with the narrative of the poor households as the beneficiaries of state care and others' compassion. Based on income, the "poor household" is a formal welfare category that channels limited state provision and charity to a small number of people in need. It has, however, also become a social category embedded in local relations and power structures. In contrast to Madam Q., poor people are depicted as lacking in enterprise and striving; unable to make proper living, they deserve such support and sympathy only if they fulfill certain criteria of deservingness. What connects the seemingly separate constructions of the exemplary person and the poor is the production of success and failure that is embedded in local histories and market socialist ideas of moral personhood.

In this chapter, I show the link between the production of success and failure and the state project of socialization (*xã hội hóa*), a policy that seeks to galvanize local resources and diverse social actors for local development and welfare provision. While it is closely related to the New Countryside program and other state development projects, socialization is broader in scope and has a greater emphasis on public goods and social care. Localized practices of socialization help give a public face to the act of giving, especially if the giving is targeted at the homeplace. Poverty relief and charity have always been important for social and political life since precolonial times, arenas in which both the state and the social elites have been competing for influence and moral authority (Nguyen-Marshall 2008). For people from Spring District, as for others in Vietnam, belonging to the homeplace also constitutes a defining feature of the moral person, and gaining recognition there is a moral incentive (Schlecker 2005). These values are now actively promoted by local institutions and governments through societal processes that glorify the generous givers who come from the locality. By default, they are successful entrepreneurs whose economic success and demonstrated concerns for others embody moral strength. As with the New Countryside Program, socialization becomes meaningful to local people as a social space in which to locate the value of their actions and to remake themselves as moral persons, even as many might resent the burdens it generates. As a policy aimed at moral mobilization, it is invariably connected to the ethic of striving, an ethic that predominates social life under market socialism.

## Socialization and the Ethic of Striving

Under state socialism, the term *xã hội hóa* (literally "socialization") used to refer to "the process of being made into collective property,"[1] a process that nationalized property, natural resources, and other means of production for collective goals. Following the reforms, however, the term has taken on different, if not opposite, connotations. Sometimes it refers to the reverse process of collective property becoming partially or fully privatized, as in "socialization of the railway," "socialization of the traffic infrastructure," or "socialization of the public hospital." In other cases, it implies being under the responsibility of the whole society, as shown in a statement by the prime minister between 2006 and 2016, Nguyễn Tấn Dũng, that stresses "the involvement of all social actors in welfare" as the cornerstone of the state's strategy for socioeconomic development:

> Social security and welfare must be deeply socialized, with an organic linkage between the rights and responsibilities of each individual vis-à-vis work units, the community and the whole society. Alongside recognizing the role of the state, we must pursue the "socialized implementation of social policies."[2]

While they evoke different aspects of post-reform restructuring, these statements point to the devolution of state responsibilities that occurs hand-in-hand with market and third-sector expansion into what used to be public sectors, similar to other post-socialist contexts (Wong 2005, Read and Thelen 2007). The turn away from the ideal of the socialist state being responsible for the welfare of all citizens signifies what governmentality scholars view as the move from a social to a post-social state (Rose 1999, O'Malley 2004). According to these authors, *the social* emerged in the nineteenth century as an arena of collective actions on the societal level aimed at rectifying social problems. During the twentieth century, the state acted on such rationalities of the social through welfare systems targeted at improving the lives of all social groups and protecting them from poverty, unemployment, and other social problems. Thereby, citizens were constructed as subjects of rights and needs, to be governed through collective responsibility, social justice, and social solidarity (Inda 2006). Later in the last century, however, the social went under fierce critiques, especially regarding the social state's tendency to foster dependence on welfare and its interventionist and cumbersome bureaucracies (Offe 1982). Consequently, the idea of public provision of welfare as central to government lost its sway—according to the new logic, the state should step back from taking responsibilities for social problems that are better addressed by a range of social and market actors.

While the writings on the social mainly refer to post-industrial Euro-American contexts, those transformations parallel what has been happening in post/late-socialist settings such as Vietnam. Especially pertinent are the delegation of welfare responsibilities that had been assumed primarily by the socialist state to other actors and the minimization of the direct welfare relationship between the state and citizens. In contrast to post-industrial contexts, there has been in the last decade a re-expansion of universal health insurance and old-age pension programs besides other forms of social protection. Unlike state socialist welfare, which was of uneven and low quality but aimed at a broad base of provision, however, welfare programs today operate on principles of user fees, minimal protection and strict means-testing (Nguyen and Chen 2017). The highly publicized emphasis on the poor household as a target of policy intervention serves to signal state care for (and its burden with) those who are not capable of self-care, at the same time with emphasizing everybody else's responsibility for their own wellbeing. In the country that bears the name The Socialist Republic of Vietnam, the social has been reinvented through a mix of neoliberal techniques of self-governance with socialist mechanisms of mobilization, which often ingeniously draw on moral-economic values. To contribute to the socializing project is framed not just as a citizen's duty, but also as a moral obligation rooted in the Vietnamese tradition of mutual support and compassion. Official letters sent to garner contributions to socialization causes often begin with the following phrase:

> In the spirit of "intact leaves covering torn ones" (*lá lành đùm lá rách* [Vietnamese idiom on mutual help]), sharing the burden of the households and regions that are still in difficulty, assisting in the improvement of the material and spiritual life of these households and providing the conditions for them to overcome the difficulties in order to have a stable life, . . .[3]

Nationwide, the Fatherland Front, the state organ that coordinates mass associations, issues yearly calls for donations to various funds under its patronage, the most well-known of which are the "Fund for the Poor" (*Quỹ vì người nghèo*) and the "Fund for Child Protection" (*Quỹ bảo vệ trẻ em*). Often, the Fatherland Front sends an official letter down the administrative hierarchy to rural villages or urban residential units, whose leaders then collect donations from individual households. The minimum amount to be donated is fixed locally, often ten thousand to twenty thousand *đồng* in the country and fifty thousand *đồng* in the city. Emulative campaigns (*phong trào thi đua*) are staged among sectors, administrative levels, residential units, and mass associations, producing titles and prizes for those who best carry out their socializing spirit. Lists of household donations are publicly displayed in village cultural houses or the bulletin board of urban residential units; the lists I came across reveal that quite a few people donate more than the recommended sum. In addition, mass associations such as the Youth Union, the Veterans' Association, and the Elderly Association also collect donations from their members. Companies, government offices, or private donors request contributions from their employees or sets aside a fund from their operating budget to be targeted at poor households in particular localities, as the private bank in the second vignette below does. The contributions are announced in the local media as an indication of how successfully a locality or sector has implemented the campaign, and those with the best results are given awards, commendations, or titles. As an indication of the effectiveness of the mobilization, the total cash contributions to the Fund for the Poor in the first nine months of 2016 were 945 billion *đồng* (about 41 million US dollars) while direct donations into local social protection programs in the same period amounted to 2.751 billion *đồng*[4].

Again, these practices are reminiscent of the emulative campaigns at the height of state socialism, in which moral incentives were the main instrument to encourage mass actions aimed at boosting productivity (MacLean 2013). Like for the New Countryside Program, exemplarity and the cultural values placed on charity and compassion continue to be integrated into the state machinery of social and political mobilization, although they are adapted to suit the new logic of welfare provision. If state socialism fostered a citizenship geared toward optimizing one's labor for collective goals in return for the promise of state care, the moral foundation of citizenship today is an ability to care for one's family through private means and a heightened sense of compassion for the disadvantaged Other. The discourses around socialization divide people into contributors, who are cast as responsible, capable, and morally superior citizens, and receivers, who are constructed as incapable, lacking in *dân trí* (intellectual level), and morally inferior[5]. Ironically, these dynamics invoke similar discourses around poverty and charity and the underlying rationale of privatized welfare provision under French colonialism (Nguyen-Marshall 2008).

The logics of exemplarity and Othering that underline the socialization project are underscored by a predominant ethic of the post-reform economy: the ethic of striving, which is akin to Yunxiang Yan's notion of "the ethics of the striving individuals" in contemporary China (2013: 263–288). Similar to Yan's China, to be a moral person in Vietnam nowadays means to relentlessly strive to work hard and develop oneself in order to access wealth and power, to rise out of poverty, and to gain social recognition. People are driven at once by a desire for success and by a fear of failure or falling from where they are: "the two work together to push the individual to strive, with or even without the chance to succeed" (Yan 2013: 272). As the story of Lãng in Box 7.1 shows, those who go against the tide of striving are reprimanded, marginalized, and disrespected, even within the family and kinship; there is indeed little dignified space for people who fail to conform to this dominant ethic of the new economy. Lãng's aptitude for non-striving perhaps would be perfectly acceptable in another time, when the social pressure on gaining access to wealth and power is not as intense. The tension and anxiety resulting from the striving spirit in the new economy, however, give rise to an enhanced desire for cultural belonging and, at times, also recourse to the collectivist values of state socialism, values and desires that the party-state capitalizes on for the sake of socialization. The ethic of striving thus helps to turn socialization into a moral project, for to be able to give—and thus to participate in socialization, thereby obtaining public recognition for the giving—not only indicates one's success, but also creates a sense of belonging to a place, a community. Striving as an ethic is sustained on the juxtaposition between successful people, such as Madam Q., and those who fall through the cracks, such as the poor households discussed in this chapter. To be able to help the latter confirms the former's moral authority and their power to define the needs of the disadvantaged Other.

---

**BOX 7.1   LÃNG, THE DRIFTER IN A WORLD OF GOAL-GETTERS**

"Ah, the addict comes back!" said Ms. Mai in a gentle, mocking tone when her eldest son, Lãng, walked in through the gate after two months of migrant work in Hồ Chí Minh City. As I quickly learned, however, he was by no means addicted to drugs; his mother calling him an addict had less to do with his unkempt look than with people's opinion of him as a good-for-nothing, a total loser whom nobody takes seriously.

I came to know Lãng as somebody with a child-like mind, curious and rather guileless. His mother loves him but has given up on her expectations for him. Unlike the many characters of Green Spring I met, who are zealous goal-getters determined to succeed in the waste trade, Lãng is a drifter. He does not stick to any occupation for long, always prioritizing his need for personal autonomy, safety, and health. Among others, he has tried migrant work on demolition teams, been a casual laborer in Hanoi, and was even employed as a milk taster for a well-known milk company. The demolition work was too dangerous; many of his co-workers were killed by falling walls. As a casual laborer in Hanoi, it was too undignified for him to be at the beck and call of other people. To trade waste would require the savviness (*khôn khéo*) that he thinks he lacks. His most favorite job ever was as a milk taster: "You know, I got to drink so much milk, even washing my face and hand with milk. There were these cartons of fortified milk that sell fifteen thousand each in the market, and at work I would drink four of those every day." Then the company moved to a district in Nghệ An, which was too far from home for him, and he was afraid to be seduced by the ethnic Thai women there: "The women there are notorious for their seductiveness. It's true," he said, while looking at me earnestly.

With a family of four, including his wife and two children, aged six and four, he would perhaps be happiest staying home, working in their paddy field and spending time with his children. Lăng's family is not poor; his wife earns a good income from providing injections and medicine for local cattle, and they have built a good-sized house on the land his parents gave them after marriage. But the pressure is high that he does something "proper"; his siblings are all running profitable waste depots in Hanoi. His wife often complains that he "does not do anything", but her complaint is rather an evaluation of his lack of striving given the high level of economic activities by his siblings and others in the village. In fact, Tâm and I often saw him working diligently on their paddy and vegetables or looking after his children, activities that apparently do not count as "to do something" as expected of a young man in Spring District according to the framework of striving.

## Vignette 1: The Queen of Waste and the Spirit of Giving

Thanks to the help of Ms. Thao, a seasoned waste trader from Green Spring, I finally had the opportunity to meet the legendary Madam Q. during my second stretch of fieldwork. On that day, we meandered in Ô Chợ Dừa area in central Hanoi, the former center of the waste trade, first visiting Ms. Thao's relatives from Spring District who have long settled down there. Ms. Thao introduced me to people as her niece, a student who was doing a research project on the waste trade; my stated wish to meet Madam Q. for an interview triggered some excited discussions about her family. Madam Q.'s close neighbours were informed of down-sides in her story that the myth circulated in Spring District left out: things had not been going so well for the family for years.

Madam Q.'s house was on a main road, where Hanoi's first waste depots used to be. The elderly woman, in her mid-eighties, lived at the back of a shop front with a sizable garden, together with her maid from rural Thái Bình – the shop is a part of her house that is rented out. She looked like a queen, dressed in shiny silk attire and looking pale-skinned and well-nourished amidst her antique wooden furniture. On the wall were photos of her imperious appearances, whether by herself in different poses and with her large family (Ms. Thao whispered to me that the el-derly woman has many adopted children, which indicates her influence).

In a rather patronizing tone, Madam Q. answered my questions briefly, hinting that her career and reputation were so well-known there was no need to ask about them. Her two sons were operating major iron-producing factories in Hải Phòng City, she said, and her family had per-formed innumerable deeds of public virtues (công đức) about which everybody knew. The part of the story she did not tell me was that one of her sons' companies was on the verge of bankruptcy, and that her young-est son had died of drug addiction. The decline in her sons' business, according to some local cadres in Spring District whom I talked to later, explained why she no longer donated to Green Spring. Madam Q., how-ever, told me that having sufficiently performed her giving duties, she now needed to focus on her family's important internal affairs, such as that of building a family graveyard on land that her sons had bought on the outskirt of Hanoi.

Somewhere in the middle of our conversation, I learned that she had in fact been born in Hanoi rather than in Spring District, as I had been often told, although her parents, who worked in the colonial Hanoi Sanitation Company, had originated from Green Spring. It later occurred to me that she is an inspiring myth for Spring District people, a kind of patron saint for the waste trade, an ideal they look to without knowing (or needing to know) exactly who she really is. Madam Q. said that she had never had to work hard in her life, but always had other people do things for her; she spoke of her family's political connections during the central planning period that had allowed them to thrive in the waste trade even then. She had been successful because of her ability to "think big," she said, rather than laboring away as most people from Spring District do. All the same, local people's belief that she has persisted and become so wealthy against all odds inspires them to follow her example in the hope of eventually achieving similar success. The myth about Madam Q. seems a plausible account of how they could transform the value of waste and remake themselves as people working with waste through accumulating wealth and contributing to the development of their homeplace. Her life and deeds exemplify the place and its moral essence of having the will to rise up from poverty and low social status through one's enterprising spirit and self-reliance. The myth seems so powerful that her aura of affluence and entrepreneurial distinction persist even in the face of downturns in her family's fortunes.

In a discussion of life on the urban edge of Hồ Chí Minh City (HCM City), Erik Harms (2011) suggests that myth making—like the myth of Madam Q.— carves out a social space for people's actions. In this case, it also constitutes a moral resource through which people working with waste give meanings to their actions, meanings that are useful for the socialization project. Ms. Thao, my enthusiastic guide on that day, is an avid admirer of Madam Q.; she had heard about the elderly woman from her own mother, one of the first itinerant junk traders from Green Spring. During our visit, she deferentially listened to the latter's words as if they had come from a superior being, despite Madam Q.'s rather condescending evaluation of people from the district. "How wonderful her stories are!" Ms. Thao kept exclaiming, repeating the tales I had already heard from others about Madam Q.'s past donations to Green Spring from the back of the motorbike on our way back to her depot out on the highway.

At sixty, Ms. Thao herself has been operating a waste depot together with her husband in Hanoi for fifteen years; her two sons and daughter, all married, are operating their own depots in different parts of Hanoi. The whole extended family practically live in Hanoi: her grandchildren go to school there, and one of her two sons has managed to buy a piece of land on the edge of the city. Yet a large part of their social and public life takes place in the village, where, in Ms. Thao's words, "our ancestors and grandparents are." The family members regularly return for communal and family events, and local leaders can then easily collect their contributions to various local causes, such as building a waste treatment facility or a setting up a local fund for rewarding high-performing school children in their village. Once, we discussed the reconstruction of Green Spring commune's Buddhist pagoda, which, as the head monk had told me in an earlier conversation, cost 21 billion đồng altogether. Ms. Thao proudly announced to Tâm and me that her family, including her three children, had donated one of the impressive timber pillars on the upper floor of the pagoda's new pavilion (see Figure 7.1).

The readiness of Ms. Thao's family to make these contributions is clearly inspired by the exemplary giving of people like Madam Q., and it is likely to have an exemplary effect in itself. Such dynamics of the exemplary society are neither particular to the present time nor limited to Spring District. "Public giving for virtue" (*công đức*) is a tradition that extends far back into the pre-colonial past (Nguyen-Marshall 2008). People's motivations for giving are varied, either to gain prestige for their family, to accumulate virtues for their offspring, or to showcase their success. Often these motives are all present, as Binh Nguyen (2016) shows in her poignant account of giving by a wealthy female migrant in Ho Chi Minh City seeking to build a patronage network in her northern native village. Even though she did not quite succeed in the end, her acts of giving, like those of Madam Q., are actively promoted by the local government. In these cases, we could see how community and administrative processes work together to glorify the generous givers, by default successful self-enterprising individuals. Such local practices of socialization appeal to migrants in particular

FIGURE 7.1  The newly built prayer pavilion of the pagoda in Green Spring.
Source: Author's photo, 2015.

because they give a public face to the act of giving targeted at the home place. Most waste traders I know, including those who have migrated more than a thousand kilometers to HCM City, respond positively to the appeal of local institutions and authorities for donations to social causes or the construction of local public works. Their contributions are publicly announced, while larger donations—like those of Madam Q.—are lauded as gifts from the "the sons and daughters of the homeland" (*những người con quê hương*), exemplary acts of giving for others to emulate.

And like Thu in Chapter 5, local people often emphasize their generous giving as something that distinguishes them from people in places where making ends meet remains a daily struggle: "As we can make pretty good money with this occupation, people are more generous (*rộng rãi hơn*) when it comes to contributions [to local projects and events]; some tens of thousands or even a hundred thousand are not something one needs to mull over," said Ms. Thao. The socialization project appears meaningful for the migrant waste traders through mechanisms that appeal to a moral personhood premised on belonging to the home place and moral-economic ties to that place and its people. Meanwhile, being able to cleanse themselves of the connotations of waste through such public acts of virtues is an additional incentive for them. They signify their achievements within the framework of the striving individual and their ability to remake themselves as moral persons notwithstanding the adversity of migrant waste work.

The next vignette reveals how the same processes construct the anti-heroes of socialization through the category of "the poor" (*người nghèo*), which singles out those who are failing through a morally laden evaluative framework. We shall see that such moralization of failure masks the structural limits of remaking.

## Vignette 2: In Support of the Poor Households

The poor household has become a major policy category that defines the direction of post-reform welfare: state provision is conditional on the most essential incapacities, except for those on state payroll or having exceptional merits, such as war invalids or heroes. A small number of households in each village are deemed as poor or near-poor following an annual formal assessment of their income and possessions. In 2017, poor households were those with per-capita monthly income of less than seven hundred thousand *đồng* VND (about US$32), and the benchmark for near-poor households was one million *đồng*. In Spring District, three to five percent of the local households were categorized as poor in that year.

Poor households are entitled to benefits such as free health insurance, a monthly allowance to cover electricity costs, low-interest loans or housing support, or school fee reduction, similar to the recipients of the Five Guarantees Program (*dibao*) in China (Nguyen and Chen 2017). Near-poor households receive some token support while representing a pool of potential poor households for the following annual assessment. The formal list is to be approved by local people through village meetings, and eligible households must fulfill certain criteria of deservingness, based on the intensity of their economic difficulties and shared understanding of needs. Formally categorized poor households have also become a category at which charity and philanthropic giving are targeted. Through the work of targeting, a community of the poor is invoked for the demonstration of compassion and moral integrity by corporations, celebrities, or spontaneous groups, dynamics that remind one of poverty-relief movements by the intellectual elites in the colonial time (Nguyen-Marshall 2008, Nguyen 2016).

## Ten Signatures and One Candidate for a Housing Grant

One evening, Giang, a commune Women's Union cadre in Green Spring, asked me to accompany her by motorbike on an assignment that she was supposed to fulfill quickly. The Women's Union is one of the most active among Vietnam's mass associations, state-sponsored institutions created during state socialism for political mobilization and education but that are now assuming certain features of non-governmental organizations (Rydstrøm 2016). With a vertical structure from the national leadership level reaching down to the villages, these organizations remain important instruments for the party-state to implement policies and communicate political messages. The provincial Women's Union had recently received a housing grant from a bank for twenty-five poor households in the province (each was to receive forty million *đồng*), and Green Spring was eligible to nominate one household for the grant. A list of five households had been drawn from the commune's official records of poor households, and one household out of this list was to be chosen for funding. Giang had gone to take a look at their houses before. On the day she asked me to join her, however, she had received orders that the list needed to be handed in the next day, countersigned by all the village heads and Women's Union leaders of the candidates, so that the district union could further assess their eligibility. This meant that Giang had to visit the houses of ten people to collect their signatures.

When Giang and I came to the first village, Duy, the village head, a man in his late twenties, and his mother received us. Previously urban waste traders, they were now relatively large agricultural producers who worked fifteen acres of paddy, owned a harvester, and hired five laborers to work for them during busy periods. Giang explained the selection process, and the village head signed the list as his mother confirmed that the household proposed from their village was "very miserable" (khổ lắm).[6] They went on to describe that the wife was almost paralyzed and the husband was chronically ill. The couple could not do anything for their own livelihoods, while their children could not help much, being poor themselves. Duy's mother, who spoke with a tone of pity, said that the house of this family was one of the worst in the village, and it was therefore worth helping them to get the grant.

After getting a prompt signature from the Women's Union leader of that same village, we arrived at the house of Ms. Mai, the only female village head in the commune. Our conversation with her was more extensive, and her husband, who used to be in charge of the commune's irrigation, joined in as well. Ms. Mai asked Giang why the household of the man she had recommended earlier to the commune social protection officer for any available support was not included in the list. The man's two children were disabled, she said, and he had an Agent Orange allowance (soldiers or combatants who were potentially exposed to the defoliant called Agent Orange sprayed by the US forces during the war are a state welfare category). Giang responded that the officer had mentioned his name, but the other commune leaders had said that he did not deserve the support because he had left his wife for another woman. But, Ms. Mai said, it was his brother who had left his wife, the man himself was in dire circumstances, and his house needed upgrading urgently. Ms. Mai's husband added that the man and his wife are "mentally slow" (đờ đờ) and that their children were "pretty doomed" (hỏng cả) with their own disabilities; "they are not up to much by way of making a living," he said. Giang assured them that she would try to add this household to the list in consultation with the commune leaders. She then asked Ms. Mai whether the household already had a red book certificate (land use right document) for their residential land; if they did not, it could be a complication for the program.

The two women also talked about the possibility of the household's siblings and relatives helping out with the construction of the house. Forty million đồng would not be enough: building a small house costs at least a hundred million đồng, so it would be pointless to secure the housing grant for somebody who could not mobilize additional resources from their relatives. Ms. Mai asked if the number of beneficiaries could be increased since there were more people in her village who needed support for building a house. For instance, there was a woman who had been living with her son's family for a long time, caring for the grandchildren, but recently had been thrown out by the daughter-in-law after her son had died of cancer. Now she had returned to her former house, "which is as small as our kitchen, both leaking and deteriorating," Ms. Mai said while shaking her head, as her husband nodded in agreement. And so it went—even the mere collection of the signatures seems to set in motion community processes through which people are sorted into categories while local networks of patronage become visible. One striking feature of the conversations between Ms. Giang and the village leaders was the latter's quasi-competition for "speaking suffering" (kể khổ) on behalf of the proposed poor households, namely to demonstrate that each of them was the poorest, the most pitiful and the most incapacitated. It seems that their sufferings must be made into a kind of spectacle in order for them to be rendered worth helping. The subtext of this strange competition was a comparative evaluation of the ability to enterprise (biết làm ăn) between the poor households and others.

The housing grant from the private bank that Giang administers is not a regular program. As one of its main activities, the local Women's Union works with the Bank for Social Policy to dispense credits for poor and near-poor households (the housing grant discussed here came from the "socialization" contribution of a large joint-stock bank). The credit amounts to fifteen million đồng for near-poor, and thirty million đồng for poor households, at 0.6 percent annual interest over three years (starting from the fourth year, it was to be paid back in installments). Giang said that most poor households are rather "desperate" (bần cùng), and that some do not dare to take the credit, not knowing what to do with it. As I commented that thirty million would help if one wants to open a waste depot, which would cost fifty million to eighty million đồng, Giang smiled and said: "People who dare thinking about opening a waste depot would by no means be in such a situation as to be classified as a poor household." Of course, I should have understood the logics myself—she was evoking the ethic of striving that local people take for granted as guidance in their life. If one is enterprising enough (biết làm ăn) to "go outside" and trade waste, as many others here do, then one would not end up being poor. In fact, one would be a contributor to the welfare of others rather than a receiver of others' support.

## Who Deserves to Be Poor?

Giang herself probably knows very well that not everyone who trades waste becomes rich or is exempt from becoming poor. The booms and busts in the trade generate losers as well as winners, and the precariousness of migrant livelihoods translates into insecurity in household reproduction. Sickness, accidents, legal problems, and the like can also bring down the fortune of a whole family overnight. During a meeting to assess the annual list of poor households in a Red Spring village, two households that had experienced just such circumstances were put forward as candidates. First was the household of Thanh, an itinerant waste trader who had died falling off the staircase of a house under construction in Hanoi that she had entered in order to buy waste. A severe head injury had led to her death four days later, ending her emergency treatment at a daily cost of ten million đồng. Strong arguments were made for her surviving husband and children by the village head and Mr. Hòa, a wealthy elderly man, that hard times awaited the family now that the father had to raise his children singlehandedly and with mounting debts from the hospital and funeral costs. The other case concerned the household of Ms. Miện, whose husband had been hospitalized for weeks with a severe liver problem that everybody attributed to his excessive drinking. Ms. Miện had had to disrupt her junk-trading work in Hanoi in order to return and take care of her husband, who had been living at home with her teenage son. Without health insurance, his treatment had cost them a significant amount, and as Ms. Miện feared, it was likely to exhaust their savings. Poor household status, among other benefits, would help cover a large part of their formal medical expenses through the free health insurance. At the end of the meeting, and after a heated debate, Thanh's surviving household made it into the list, whereas Ms. Miện's did not.

Whenever I met Ms. Miện during those days, she would complain about how depressing it was that she was stuck at home without earning any income, and that her husband's conditions would never be back to normal, hinting that she found the decision of the village meeting unfair. In the other villagers' opinions, however, her household's circumstances were not comparable to Thanh's: Ms. Miện could still carry on her migrant work, while her husband's eldest son was "doing good business" (làm ăn được) in Hanoi and should be able to support his parents. More importantly, her husband's health problem was self-inflicted, caused by alcohol consumption rather than misfortune, and thus deserved less sympathy. In short, the situation of Ms. Miện household was not perceived as deserving, despite her personal disagreement with the evaluation. Thanh's household, meanwhile, had the backing both of relatives who were local leaders and of other villagers because its circumstances had been induced by her migrant work, whose precarious nature was highlighted through her accident. Village conversations for days had been focused on the event, unanimously constructing Thanh as a female martyr who had sacrificed her life for her children and family. People had even been circulating stories about her not having breakfast to save money (that's why she was too dizzy to keep her balance, they said), and how she had long desired to buy herself an *áo dài* (the traditional tunic) to wear at weddings but never did. All these elements struck a chord with the villagers—especially the women, many of whom used to be or are migrant waste traders themselves.

At Thanh's funeral, Mr. Hòa, the respected elderly pensioner who spoke up in support of Thanh's family at the village meeting, said to me emphatically, and somewhat pleased with his pithy statement, "You are witnessing a prime example of the negative impacts of migration." According to him, Thanh's death represented the price that his village has to pay for his fellow villagers' ventures into risky frontiers. In his opinion, Thanh had not only sacrificed for her family, but her sacrifices exemplified those of the whole village, which therefore should help her surviving family. Yet behind his expressed compassion for the unfortunate family was an admonition that the peasant families in his village are reckless with their lives, and that their occupation in the waste trade has left moral consequences on village life, a view that he frequently put forward in our conversations.

A discourse of "the deserving poor" emerges in such local deliberations of the poor household category. The poor household status is thereby no longer merely a means-tested state benefit; it is transformed into a token of care by the village toward its needy members, yet for which the latter have to prove their deservingness. Those who receive the benefit thus are not only beneficiaries of the state, but also indebted to others in the village. Thus, rather than appearing to be imposed from the top down, the conditionality becomes imbued with the meanings of reciprocal relationships. For the migrant waste traders, whose urban citizen status is marginal, their participation in such negotiations is a confirmation of their rural citizenship, which is embedded in kinship and neighborhood relations. The symbolic meanings of such state transfers as the poor-household benefit are as important as their financial benefits. They simultaneously reconfirms the moral authority of the state as being caring and responsive, despite its turn away from the socialist promises of ensuring a broad base of wellbeing, and helps to strengthen moral-economic ties within the village.

For vocal villagers such as Mr. Hòa or local cadres like Giang or Ms. Mai, it is a chance to solidify their social status through their patronage of the needy. Mr. Hòa's influence derives largely from the fact that his three sons are successful businessmen and academics who hold prestigious jobs in Hanoi and HCM City; they have built him and his wife a comfortable house and provide them with a sizable monthly fund. The elderly man also has a say in the village because he is articulate and often comes up with convincing ideas about how things should go in village affairs. His demonstrated sympathy for poorer families is much like that of Giang and Ms. Mai. When we once sat down for a cup of tea, Giang told me that working as a mass association cadre, she felt satisfied whenever she had a chance to help poor villagers with some practical improvements of their life. If opportunities arose for such help, she did not mind working even in the evenings. Similarly, Ms. Mai emphasized in our many conversations that she tried to support poor people whenever she could. "We are not rich," she said, "but we are healthy and our children are still doing okay with their depots. These people are way more unfortunate in their life, and the more we can help them, the better." As the head of the village (*xóm trưởng*), Ms. Mai receives a small allowance for her work with a range of administrative and bookkeeping duties of state projects at local level; her husband has a pension as a former state employee. Being a commune cadre, Giang has a state salary, and her husband earns five times her salary as the captain of a freight ship, allowing them to maintain a lifestyle comparable to that of an urban middle-class family. Although the monetary gains of their work are not significant for the two women, their engagement in local affairs rewards them with prestige in the local community and connections to the local government.

People like Giang, Ms. Mai, and Mr. Hòa are indeed significant for the socialization project. Not only do they play crucial roles in mobilizing local contributions on account of their personal prestige, they are also instrumental in the classification between capable and incapable community members, between the undeserving and deserving poor, as a basis for targeted welfare provision. More importantly, they represent the desirable moral subject necessary for the project: citizens who are able to care for themselves and help people in need with demonstrable moral conviction. In other words, they represent another kind of the exemplary person, different from people such as Madam Q. but no less instrumental for the production of success and failure as moral matters.

## Conclusion: The Production of Success and Failure and the Limits of Remaking

In the logics of socialization, the responsibilization of individuals and communities goes hand in hand with sensitizing their moral orientation toward the task of benevolently helping other people, akin to the ethical citizen Andrea Muehlebach (2012) identifies in post-industrial Italy.

What differs in Vietnam is how socialization simultaneously draws on moral impetuses of the new economy, socialist ideals, and a reinvention of traditional values (see also Jellema 2005). As the first vignette indicates, the exemplary person nowadays is not only enterprising, capable of and responsible for taking care of themselves and their families, but is also ready to contribute to social causes. "Doing charity" (*làm từ thiện*) has become a social movement in urban Vietnam that involves numerous groups of people collecting donations for the poor and the disadvantaged. Individuals with some level of stardom or media attention vie to demonstrate their charitable acts, not unlike the way Madam Q. publicizes her good deeds in the homeplace. By extension, companies and businesses cannot ignore the need to showcase charitable activities in order to build social prestige, political connections, and the moral authority needed to succeed in the market. Amidst widespread moral anxiety in a fast-changing society, the moral impetus of giving has taken on a hitherto unknown urgency, and this partly explains Ms. Mai and Giang's insistence on their motivation to help the poor when carrying out their work.

Whereas local governments of poorer localities struggle to mobilize funds, socialization in Spring District has benefited from local people's viable income through the urban waste trade. It has also been driven by people's aspiration for recognition in the homeplace, an aspiration that for many arises from the very social stigma they experience as waste traders in the city. Exemplary acts of giving by wealthy people like Madam Q., acts that are publicly lauded and go down in local history, further boost the spirit of giving. Since quite a few local people do well economically, they tend to make generous donations in response to the local government's calls. For less well-to-do households, or those that are barely making it over their subsistence requirements, the frequent collection for various social causes can sometimes be onerous. Yet the pressure of living up to the social expectations escalated by the wealth generated from the waste trade is high. In the same vein that local people are compelled to make contributions to family events and festivities in the village, donating to social causes becomes a moral obligation that can only be ignored at the cost of one's social standing in the community.

Couched in the terms of helping the disadvantaged and developing the homeplace or building the nation, the moral logic communicated through socialization resonates with local people, helping to embed it within local social dynamics and relations. As such, socialization inhabits actual practices of mobilizing resources from a diverse range of social actors, including individuals, households, communities, and the private sector, for the provision of public goods and welfare. Above all, it is a project aimed at producing the moral personhood suitable for the developmental agenda of market socialism. This moral project weaves together neoliberal ideas of self-reliance, local moral-economic values, and socialist ethos to produce a moral subject who is at once enterprising and giving— a striving individual.

Yet as the two vignettes in this chapter reveal, there are limits to the ethic of striving, and thus to local people's project of remaking. However hard they try to secure their livelihoods and meet the demands of sustaining social life, the likelihood of falling through the cracks is just around the corner; they have little sway over the uncertainties of the post-reform economy. Although many have been able to capitalize on the opportunities of the waste economy, there is no guarantee that they will continue to do so, given market fluctuations and the precariousness of migrant lives. Even the seemingly indomitable Madam Q., who epitomizes the local dream of success, does not appear to be able to stem these forces. For many people, the fruits of remaking can be unmade overnight by the vagaries and dangers of working in the shadowy places of the urban economy. Some limited help might be available in the case of extreme misfortune, such as the poor household benefits, yet it comes at the cost of having one's moral behavior openly scrutinized by others, and sometimes even being pitted against that of one's fellow villagers. The moralization of success and failure disguises the debilitating effects of political-economic forces and institutional constraints on people's mobility and livelihoods. At the same time that the merits of remaking in the instance of success are galvanized for state agendas, the blame is put squarely on the shoulder of individual families and local communities in the case of failure. As such, Spring District people's goal of remaking themselves as moral and social persons has limitations that are rooted in the very political-economic conditions that give rise to their project and continue to structure its unfolding.

# CONCLUSION: THE POLITICAL ECONOMY
## OF REMAKING
........................

The title *Waste and Wealth* is intended to convey that uneven and uncertain process in which waste, an emblem of valuelessness and low social status, is transformed into wealth, not just as an economic outcome but also as aspirations for the good life and social recognition. It is a process of value creation that occurs in the face of uncertainties within the global economy and the unpredictable trajectories of power under market socialism, which I refer to as "the political economy of remaking." Remaking involves not just turning waste into a commodity, a productive resource, or money, but also how migrant waste work has come to reconfigure the social relations within families and communities, between the city and the countryside, and between people and the state. It is part of people's quest to continue living the moral life of the person in a changing and uncertain world. This process is immersed in the interrelated politics of value and politics of morality that are rooted in exemplary forms and imagined futures (Bakken 2000, Graeber 2001, Beckert 2016), forces that drive people in their actions while rendering success and failure as moral matters. These politics result in uneven outcomes and anxiety while engendering a form of moral personhood that plays into the Vietnamese party-state's governing approach, which cultivates private consumer choice hand-in-hand with authoritarianism.

The political economy of remaking becomes visible through ethnographic inquiries into how people's economic life is embedded in social formations that link the city with the countryside, both of which are under the purview of the state's twin projects of privatization and modernization. It is a framework that structures not merely the waste traders' actions, but also the outcomes of their everyday engagement with the global market, the urban society, and the state. In this way, local people's actions—and the moral meanings of their actions—become consequential for how the political economy of Vietnam today unfolds (see also Leshkowich 2014). Concurrently, the experiences of Spring District people reveal the limits of remaking that hark back to the workings of this political economy, which casts peasant entrepreneurs like them aside as obstacles to development even as the fruits of their labor are optimized for the sake of that development. The lens of remaking, following Alexander and Reno, allows us to see waste recycling as "an economically productive enterprise no less lucrative and no less morally complex [and, I would add, no less politically implicated] than other modes of material transaction" (2012: 15).

Globally, privatization and neoliberal restructuring have been dispossessing many people of their land, their employment, and their social entitlements, producing marginalized classes of people. This dispossession has been eloquently portrayed by authors writing on industrial decline, land closure, rural-urban migration, and urban renewal in different world regions (Harvey 2005, Wacquant 2008, Ferguson 2015, Pun 2016, Li 2017). Dispossession does not always take spectacular forms; equally often, it occurs through the gradual emergence of privatizing logic and capitalist relations in local life that stealthily strips away people's access to former communal resources and destabilize older ways of care (Li 2014). In highlighting the political economy of remaking in my account of the migrant waste traders from Spring District, I do not dispute the damaging effects of privatization and restructuring. The story of remaking, however, is just as important to tell; it reminds us of the human capacity for resilience, adaptation, and transformation *despite* dispossession and exclusion. Like everybody else, the people who are conceptualized as the outcast, the surplus population, or wasted humans also have dreams, hopes, and aspirations that we need to take seriously. While in many cases these might end up being stymied, squashed, or taken away by the same forces, their goals of remaking are nonetheless valid. Without taking pains to understand them, the narrative of superfluous life "can lead us to imagine that these really are disposable people" (Denning 2010: 80) instead of showing people as being cast aside by structural forces, thus defeating the very purpose of critiquing the global order.

The political economy of remaking, I argue, speaks to the diverse ways in which many people with "low necks and small voice" quietly act on the market and localized systems of power to pursue their aspirations and sustain their moral life. The limits of remaking notwithstanding, the people of Spring District have in this manner produced values that matter for family and communal lives, values that help to remake their place in the global order and eventually the order itself.

## The Waste Economy, Mobility, and Globalization

The Vietnamese waste economy is but one part in the global economy of recycling, an economy that is subjected to forces of speculation, precaritization, and labor devaluation. Yet it also constitutes a site of material and social regeneration. How peasants from Spring District have been incorporated into the underbelly of Vietnam's expanding urban centers as migrant waste traders is not unlike what has been happening in many places the world over (Alexander and Reno 2012, Gregson and Crang 2015). Through their labor and entrepreneurship in the economy of recycling, waste traders from Spring District are connected to world-wide circuits of material flows and global cycles of production and consumption. Such connectivity allows them some access to the global economy from their marginalized positioning. Yet it also exposes the traders to its crises and vagaries, to events and processes beyond their control, thus spawning dangers that could potentially destabilize livelihoods, families, and communities and ultimately unmake the values that they have created.

Meanwhile, the case of Spring District suggests that people's mobility is equally motivated by localized ideas regarding how to sustain and continuously remake social and moral life in the face the market economy's demands. Central to local trajectories of mobility are the gendered categories of the inside (*nội*) and the outside (*ngoại*) that do not just structure the spatial orientation of men and women, but also serve as evaluative frameworks for their mobility. In turn, their mobility has significantly remade these categories. The inside and outside realms have taken on new configurations as people adjust the norms defining what is socially acceptable for men and women—for example, when the women "go outside" to work as itinerant traders and the men stay home to "keep the goal." These practices have formed translocal waste networks that are simultaneously inside and outside. At once permeable and enduring, the inside/outside binary continues to serve as a social space for men and women to seek meanings for their actions, and it offers them a degree of stability amidst the uncertainty and precariousness of their mobile lives.

Global economic instabilities aside, these conditions are created by the trajectory of power under market socialism that keeps rural people and rural labor on the move. In this book, we have seen contradictions in how the Vietnamese state scapegoats migrant laborers in the cities as polluters of the urban order and urban life, even as they are providing the labor necessary to service the expanding urban societies. We have also seen how socialist instruments of control such as the household administration (*hộ khẩu*) not only tie rural people to the countryside, but also relegate them to a subordinate place when they are on the move. And we have seen that while demonizing the mobility of rural people as an emblem of unruliness and incivility, state institutions surreptitiously capitalize on the very mobility for their agenda. The greatest uncertainties for the waste traders, however, are generated by their subjection to widespread rent-seeking behavior of state agents. Such behavior helps to create a system in which things are intentionally kept uncertain by those in power for the purpose of extracting rent from those with lesser power. As far as the waste economy is concerned, this system thrives on the ambiguity of waste as a social and legal category, which sustains all sorts of morally ambiguous practices by different actors, practices that generate risks and dangers for the waste traders. As such, the precariousness of migrant waste trading is co-produced by the instabilities of the global market and the increasing commodification of state power.

The hypermobility of people, materials, and ideas has become one of the most pervasive conditions of our globalized world today, driven by what Zigmunt Bauman (1998) describes as the compression of time and space for the sake of capital accumulation. In *Overheating*, Thomas Hylland Eriksen (2016) sketches a globalized world in which runaway processes such as unprecedented mobility and waste generation are drastically redefining the local and stripping away local agency. The mobility of Spring District waste traders is indeed internal to these global processes. Nevertheless, local people take an active part in fashioning how these global processes unfold. When turning waste into a commodity with their labor and mobility, they are in fact helping to decelerate waste generation.[1] When referring to localized systems of meanings and moral-economic principles in their engagement with the market and power, they recast economic activities as moral undertakings, and as such pose implicit challenges to the logics of market and power hierarchies. The precarious conditions of migrant livelihoods thus are sometimes experienced as enabling by local people, who view these conditions as allowing them some room to maneuver in negotiating power and the freedom to fulfill their social obligations. Together with those of millions of others who are working in recycling worldwide, the daily practices of making a living and leading the moral life of the person by the people of Spring District reconfigure these very global processes that frame their actions. In Vietnam, as in other East and Southeast Asian countries, the labor and mobility of peasant entrepreneurs have indeed been important drivers for the rise of the region in the global order.

## Labor, Gender, and Class

On an abstract level, waste is neither subject nor object, but is instead what Julia Kristeva (1982: 4) terms the abject, "what disturbs identity, system, order. What does not respect borders, positions, rules. The in-betweens, the ambiguous, the composite." According to her, it is not necessarily low hygiene standards or lack of order but the confusion of categories that breeds abjection. Following Mary Douglas (1966), the presence of waste endangers the boundaries between the pure and the impure, which are essential to the maintenance of social and moral order. In the city, migrants who work with waste are perceived to be absorbing the lowliness and dirtiness of waste labor and to be transgressing the divide between the civilized urban and its uncivilized rural Other; their bodies of disorder cannot be separated from the labor that removes dirt and waste to establish order. The labor of waste is the labor of abjection, which turns its subject into an abject, a liminal entity that does not belong to any fixed category, that which is feared and disgusted at the same time. The abjection underlines the stigmatization of waste work and people working with waste, manifesting the workings of wider power relations in the social order of Vietnam today—namely the devaluation of labor and the rural-urban distinction. It is indeed central to local people's class experiences across the city and the countryside. As the contours of class remain blurred on economic and occupational terms, distinction in the new economy primarily occurs through moral and cultural idioms. The abjectification of people working with waste, and by extension of migrant labor and rural migrants, serves as an important mechanism for the dominant class to assert their primacy, as has been observed in other social and historical contexts (Cohen and Johnson 2005, Campkin and Cox 2012).

Yet "what is socially peripheral is so frequently symbolically central," according to Peter Stallybrass and Allon White (1986: 5). Even as the urban middle class constructs its dirty and backward rural Other as the basis of its cultural supremacy, it comes to realize that the lowly Other is essential to its very existence; after all, no High can ever exist without its Low.

The waste trader—the rural Other—is well aware of this "power of the Low" and strategically deploys it for his or her own purposes, notably by performatively evoking moral-economic ethics of subsistence and reciprocity to appeal to the urban customers. If waste traders have been relegated to a subordinate position through the abjectification of their work, it is also this work that enables them to remake themselves as a moral and social person, and in doing so remake the place of their community. The labor of salvaging urban waste and giving it a market value may be demeaning, but it provides the very material conditions necessary for them to cleanse the demeaning connotations of waste in order to remake themselves. Although local people resent the abjection of their labor and personhood and wish for their children to be liberated from it, they have also taken advantage of it to generate value. Thanks to their labor and mobility, spaces of abjection over time become spaces of livelihoods, entrepreneurship, and communal life that are vital to the urban economy and the development of their homeplace.

As such, local people have been able to reclaim value for the labor that has been devalued via actions that at once draw on and remake multiple moral frameworks, past and future. One such framework is again the inside/outside binary, which accounts for the gendering of the labor process and the gendered valuation of work in the waste economy. While defining appropriate work and labor for men and women, it also guides them in navigating their translocal lives and relationships. Even as translocality is recasting the boundaries between the inside and the outside, men and women from Spring District continue referring to them as domains of gendered labor. As we have seen, the male waste traders establish distance from domesticity and dirt via association with work in the outside realm, the work of dealing with technologies, with dangers and risks, and with masculinized urban spaces. The women stay closer to dirt and the domestic spaces of the urban middle class, working out of an assumption that it is women's job to deal with trivial things not worthy of attention. From their abject positioning, the male and female waste traders appropriate urban spaces in their own ways, for their own purposes, by deploying the very normative categories of inside and outside that structure their mobility and labor. In performing different kinds of gendered labor, they play into the abjectification of their labor and personhood, yet the outcomes of their actions eventually defy that abjectification. As such, the labor processes within the waste economy are foregrounded by how gender and class intersect to produce differential valuation of labor for men and women, even as both operate from a position of abjection.

## Value and Morality

Central to the political economy of remaking is how people "recycle" waste into values that they consider essential to their moral and social life under the precarious conditions of the economy and politics. These conditions force them at times to transgress certain moral boundaries and at times to switch between differing value frameworks in evaluating their actions. Such acts of "moral reasoning" are common responses to the dilemmas of our world today, "where need shades into greed, gift into bribe, and the public into the private as people struggle for both autonomy and relatedness in historical circumstances where the existence (or nonexistence) of prevailing ethical standards provides rules to be avoided rather than obeyed" (Gregory 2009: 199). In Vietnam, the "recycling" of waste into values not only takes place between differential "regimes of value" (Appadurai 1986), but also across the inside and outside domains as spaces of value creation. As we have seen, this is an uneven process that is fraught with compromises, contradictions, and trade-offs for men and women. Yet it is equally a transformative process whose outcomes simultaneously unite and divide the local community. A common identity as migrant waste traders has emerged, along with the division of local people into losers and winners. This division creeps into local lives as taken-for-granted facts via discourses that cast losing and winning as matters of moral strength while masking the insidious effects of marketization. The moralization of success and failure instills deep anxiety into local society, an anxiety that reflects on the conduct of moral and social life across the city and the countryside.

Chapter 3 discussed the ethic of risk-taking and Chapter 7 the ethic of striving, which are everyday ethics that have emerged out of people's daily engagement with the social and political framework of their lives. If the ethic of risk-taking underscores local people's familiarization with the unpredictability of the waste economy and their readiness to accept the likelihood of negative outcomes, the ethic of striving emphasizes the tireless pursuits of money, wealth, and power in Vietnam today. Clearly, these ethics are mutually constituted: striving leads to risk-taking, while risk-taking promises a possibility that the goals of the striving person can be realized. These ethics also result from the emphasis on self-responsibility and self-enterprise under market socialism. People are to succeed in acquiring wealth, power, and the good life through their own efforts; should they fail, it is because they are not enterprising enough, not daring enough, and not responsible enough. As in other privatizing contexts, these neoliberal ideas are becoming more salient in Vietnam today. They in fact resonate with people's decades of resentment against the rigid control of state socialism over their lives (see Hsu 2007 for a discussion of similar dynamics in China) and their increasing mistrust in the integrity of state institutions. The experiences of the peasant entrepreneurs from Spring District, however, suggest the need to distinguish between the striving of the middle class or risk-taking in the world of high finance and the striving of people with "lowered necks and small voices." Their lesser power and inferior citizenship status result in a greater likelihood of negative outcomes, of falling from where they are, and of becoming outcasts even in the homeplace, within the family and kinship. Likewise, in the case of success, they are more often confronted with trade-offs, compromises, and even sacrifices than are those higher up in the social hierarchy.

Visible tension exists between these everyday ethics and the moral framework of *làm người* (doing human), or that of leading the moral life of the person. Nowadays, *làm người* simultaneously references cultural ideas of reciprocity and care, state-sponsored notions of civility or citizen responsibility (Gammeltoft 2014, Harms 2016), and exemplary behavior shaped by various currents of globalization, even pop culture (Bayly 2013).[2] Risk-taking and striving at times lead waste traders to break away from the mold of moral categories and engage in activities such as "making law," which ironically are often aimed at fulfilling the goals of *làm người*. One of the greatest compromises that local people make in their translocal life is to adopt arrangements of care that allow adult members to engage in migrant work, which induces a great deal of anxiety. This anxiety around care arises against a normative middle-class framework for caring and being cared for that do not correspond with the reality of making a living and leading family lives on the move. But even more so for the waste traders, the social implications of waste problematize translocal care arrangements as reflecting on the moral standing of families on the move. Any disruption of care is thereby attributable to the supposed "immorality" that results from exposure to waste, which is deemed to be morally polluting and socially questionable, as seen in the easy association of waste traders with "social evils." While the waste traders contest such dismissal by pointing out their own values vis-à-vis the local elite, the anxiety prompts them to constantly shift care arrangements within their families—and to blame themselves when their own families are affected by social problems such as drug addiction.

This same anxiety underlines local practices of spending money and consumption. If local people's encounters with urban society have spawned gendered desires for middle-class consumption and lifestyles, they have also made local people painfully aware of the gap between themselves and the middle class. And of the fact that in seeking to fulfill the dream of a middle-class lifestyle, they are caught in a double bind, for living a middle-class life would mean abandoning their mode of production and with it their source of income and wealth. The practice of *contingent conspicuousness* that emphasizes displaying themselves to the home village community is thus an outcome of people having to juggle the irreconcilable demands of work and life in the waste economy. They are indeed burdens incurred by the ethic of striving that predominates Vietnamese society today.

The vacant villas in Green Spring stand tall as reminders of the contradictions between local people's marginalization as migrant waste traders in the city and the wealth they have accumulated. They remind one of the enduring unequal power relations between the city and the countryside, between the laboring class and the middle class; rural migrants continue to be the ones with "lowered neck and small voices" in the social order of Vietnam today. The villas, meanwhile, are not just objects of consumption. Through people's personal investment, over time they become social beings, similar to the waste-transporting vehicles that are ritually blessed in the local pagoda or the motorbikes on which young men ride to "go to love." They attest to local people's capacity to remake waste into objects of prestige that make up the pillars of local social and economic life, thereby transforming it. The value creation, however, is inseparable from the moral anxiety arising from the trade-offs and compromises of their translocal lives and their status as migrants working with waste. Political-economic questions of value, labor, and production are as such invariably connected to the construction of the moral person and acts of "moral reasoning" by actors who are confronted with the demands of leading the moral life of the person in mobility and uncertainty.

## The Moral Personhood of Market Socialism

Chapter 7 suggested that rather than just a state rhetoric, *socialization* inhabits actual practices of mobilizing resources from a diverse range of social actors, including individuals, households, communities, and the private sector, for the provision of public goods and welfare. Above all, it is a project aimed at producing the moral personhood suitable for the developmental agenda of market socialism. This project weaves together neoliberal ideas of the self-enterprising and self-responsible person, local moral-economic values, and socialist ethos to produce the striving individual, a moral subject driven at once by the dream of success and the fear of failure (Yan 2013). To be moral thereby is to be able to ensure one's livelihood and well-being through one's own efforts and private resources while being willing to help people in need and contribute to the development of the homeplace and the nation. In this logic, local people are held accountable for the development of their community at the same time that they are made responsible—or even punished—for any failure to live up to the benchmarks of the new economy. Leaving the question of their definitions aside, success and failure thereby have nothing to do with the crushing uncertainties and highly unequal power relations in the global and national economies. They are entirely a matter of the moral strength and the will to develop of a person, a family, and a community. In this way, moral strength is internal to people's "intellectual level" (*trình độ dân trí*), the all-explanatory means and end of development in the eye of the party-state whose "will to improve" (Li 2007) is not matched by adequate responsibility for the social consequences of marketization.

The interlocking mechanisms of the exemplary society (Bakken 2000) and imagined futures (Beckert 2016) make possible the realization of such a demanding moral project. The people of Spring District are both influenced by exemplary norms of the new economy and fueled by fictional expectations of ever-continuing improvements. Exemplary persons such as Madam Q. provide a moral anchor for local people, giving them the belief in their community's resilience against all odds and its ability to rise up from poverty and destitution to become wealthy and able to help others. Exemplary behavior as promoted through the New Countryside Program instills aspirations for civilized living in a harmonious and tradition-preserving countryside. The exemplary society locates people's actions and meanings as part of a common history that flows continuously from the past to the future. Meanwhile, the imagined futures of global capitalism infuse social life with certain imaginaries of the good life, which drive people in their striving, their risk-taking, and their strategies to generate wealth. The waste traders carry on in the face of being the ones with "lowered necks and small voices" in the social order with a certain confidence in the progressive trajectory of betterment, even if at times this requires the helping hand of the ancestors and the gods. The exemplary society and imagined futures thus work together into a promise that as long as one works hard, is savvy enough, and stays away from "social evils," then one has the prospect of "doing as well as the others do," as the lady in the imitation mink coat told me on the bus (see Chapter 6).

Despite the booms and the busts, the unfulfilled dreams, the falling into disgrace on loss of livelihood, accidents, legal troubles, or the likelihood of becoming the receivers of others' charity, the waste traders move on with their lives and therewith sustain the waste economy. It is through people's daily struggles with living the moral life of the person under such treacherous circumstances that the moral becomes a force that gives direction to the political-economic frame of their lives. The waste traders of Spring District, like other Vietnamese and even the Vietnamese nation, are caught between the controlling gaze of the past and the unruly pull of the future. As in many other places of the world, these forces drive people to action, producing uneven results that, when evaluated in this contradictory framework, are at once exhilarating and unsettling, rewarding for some and anxiety-producing for others. In the political economy of remaking, the value creation is uncertain and double-faced, encompassing the paradoxes and politics of moral, social, and economic life in a globalizing world.

# NOTES

................

## Preface

1. I use pseudonyms for all people and localities, except the larger cities and regions.

2. In my first book, *Vietnam's Socialist Servants* (2015b), the group of female itinerant waste traders who provide cleaning service to urban households was treated as one among several types of domestic workers. In fact, my earlier acquaintance with them led me to Spring District for the field research of this book. The main focus in the previous book was the domestic workers' relationship to the domestic sphere of urban families, although I also touched briefly on how they manage their own family matters from afar. What set the cleaner-junk-traders apart from other types of domestic workers are their greater autonomy and lesser dependency; it will become clear in this book that these are largely due to how they operate as itinerant waste traders.

3. The sanitation company then made three monthly contracts with them: they all had registration cards, received health checks, and the women would get pregnancy benefits. According to the elderly couple, the sanitation company then was "full of people from Spring District"; many from the district also worked at the Đại La brick factory, the chimney of which still stands in front of the now Pullman Hanoi hotel. The brick factory was owned by Mr. Năm Diệm, also the director of the Sanitation Company; elderly people in Green Spring remember it as the Năm Diệm brick factory.

4. According to Cohen and Johnson (2005: xxiii), "As European empires increasingly came to dominate other parts of the world, filth was also a

powerful marker of racial and national distinctions, which were overlaid [...] on those of sanitary policy affecting conceptions of class and gender." The organization of urban sanitation in Hanoi was part of a hygienic mission by the French colonial government; it was not surprising that mostly rural migrants were recruited into this sector, given the rural-urban cultural distinction that continues to this day and the lack of waged work for the migrant population then.

5. Farm land, managed by the agricultural cooperative until it was redistributed to households following the reforms (đổi mới), remains under state ownership and the state ultimately has discretion over its usage. According to the 2013 Land Law, households have transferable use rights to farmland for fifty years, while residential land is subject to longer-term use right and is inheritable. In Spring District, each of the household's sons normally gets a share of the family residential land, while the one taking care of the parents is likely to inherit the parental house. When women get married, they tend to move in with her husband's parents before their own house is built. Unmarried women continue to live in their parental house but may or may not inherit it, depending on whether the sons (if any) exercise their inheritance claims to it. Whether the unmarried daughter takes the main responsibility for care of the parents might be a factor in favor of her inheriting the parental house.

6. Ms. Tạ is a researcher based at the Institute of Anthropology, Vietnam Academy of Social Science.

7. We once interviewed the head of the local Elderly Association in the township. This man, who was unimpressed when the village head introduced me as somebody with a doctorate, said that the list of people from the township gaining doctoral titles that he was in charge of keeping had become overcrowded; he almost ran out of space in the log book. People originating from the township who gain a doctoral title can have their names inscribed on a stone stele in the communal house, and according to him, the number of doctorate holders originating from the township has increased manyfold since the mid-2000s: "They keep flooding us with announcements of their doctoral titles. One perhaps needs to reconsider how these titles are awarded these days," he said. As a result of a national program to train tens of thousands of PhDs between 2010 and 2020, there is indeed an inflation of doctoral title holders, yet the locality seems to record a higher incidence than the average.

8. In my opinion, local people are not strictly against being in the news; their reticence to be interviewed, photographed, or filmed is more an issue of power. Feeling that they do not have control over what is to be done with the information about themselves or the narratives of their life when these

become public, people tend to do what is within their reach to prevent the likelihood of misrepresentation—namely to decline access until they are convinced otherwise. If the informants keep a distance from the researcher or decline access, therefore, they do so for good reasons.

## Introduction

1. In October 2017, the Vietnamese government announced that the household registration booklet will be abandoned, leading many to think that the household registration system was about to end. The announcement created momentary euphoria among people, especially rural migrants, whose multiple aspects of life have been governed through the household registration system. This was quickly dampened by the revelation that the system was instead to be digitalized. If successfully implemented, the move toward digitalization, which reflects the current government's occupation with joining the Digital Revolution ("the 4.0 revolution" is a buzzword these days among policy circles and the media), is likely to consolidate the system. In fact, this points in the direction of the digitalized surveillance that the Chinese government is putting in place. Meanwhile, the announcement also produced effects that the policy makers had probably not anticipated: people's ensuing disappointment on finding out that the booklet would only be replaced with a digitalized version triggered much media and social network discussion regarding the extent of misery the system has been inflicting on people's life, especially for migrants. (See, for example, *39 thủ tục hành chính* ăn *theo sổ hộ khẩu* (39 administrative procedures that require the household registration booklet) at https://vnexpress.net/infographics/phap-luat/39-thu-tuc-hanh-chinh-an-theo-so-ho-khau-3667800.html accessed on 24.11.2017.) Public articulation of the problems people have with the system might over time pose a serious challenge to it.

2. Some readers might wonder if this statement is related to Bruno Latour's (2005) idea of objects as autonomous and reflexive agents capable of shaping social and political life. While I accept that the interactions between human actors and objects might produce certain outcomes, I think that to treat objects as autonomous makes it difficult to tend to power relations between people, especially the ways in which humans seek to dominate and exploit others when hiding behind objects that are perceived as autonomous. Here, I only make the case that waste becomes a social category through a system of categorization that deems exposure to dirt as morally impure, which then has implications for the people who work with it.

3. In 2014, a brief tension was created by the violent protest of Vietnamese workers in Chinese factories of central Vietnam, and the many guest houses

serving Chinese waste dealers in a number of recycling villages in northern Vietnam had to close because of the temporary halt in arrivals of the Chinese customers.

4. Scott defines reciprocity as "a reciprocal obligation to return a gift or service of at least comparable value at some future date" (in reference to Marcel Mauss's idea of the gift) and the right to subsistence as a norm governing "the minimal needs that must be met for members of the community within the context of reciprocity" (1977: 167).

5. Bakken distinguishes the exemplary society from Foucault's notion of a disciplinary society, arguing that the former offers more room for individual reflexivity. Nevertheless, the process of moral learning that he emphasizes does not differ greatly from Foucault's notion of governmentality. Governmentality refers to attempts to govern through cultivating desires, aspirations, and beliefs in the population, so that people willingly act according to intended courses of action without need for coercion or persuasion. As such, Foucault characterizes similar mechanisms of making people willingly consent to what is demanded of them through social and moral means on which Bakken elaborates.

6. According to Susan Greenhalgh (2010), the Chinese term *suzhi* was originally used in its eugenic sense of reducing birth defects in the population. Later, it came to incorporate broader meanings of human capital development as the Chinese state started to invest in a range of policies aimed at building a citizenry fit for a knowledge-based economy and global competition. The interplay between these "human quality"–centered population policies and market forces, Greenhalgh argues, has led to the emergence of the self-governing and self-optimizing citizen-subject in China today. More research would be needed to conclude whether the same dynamics have also occurred in Vietnam, but the resonance between *suzhi* and *dân trí* clearly suggests similar interest in the development of human capital by the state in both countries.

7. Tine Gammeltoft refers to the more formal term of *population quality* (*chất lượng dân số*) and Erik Harms uses the term *consciousness* (*ý thức*) in their discussions of similar dynamics. While these terms are sometimes used interchangeably, in my opinion *dân trí* has wider relevance than the others as a policy term that has been vernacularized, reflecting the level at which a state-sponsored ideology feeds into everyday discourses.

8. *Quan điểm của Đảng về phát triển nguồn nhân lực trong thời kỳ công nghiệp hóa, hiện đại hóa* (The Party's views on the development of the country's human resource during the times of rapid industrialization and modernization), *Tạp chí Cộng Sản* (*The Communist Review*),

September 10, 2012, http://www.tapchicongsan.org.vn/Home/
Nghiencuu-Traodoi/2012/17716/Quan-diem-cua-Dang-ve-phat-trien-
nguon-nhan-luc-trong-thoi.aspx (accessed January 5, 2016).

## Chapter 1

1. It has been argued that Bourdieu's portrayal of the Kabyle house, deriving
   from his interviews with Algerian peasants who had been resettled away
   from their native homes, is a form of self-essentialization by informants
   who were nostalgic about a more pure past untainted by capitalist influences
   (Goodman 2003; Silverstein 2004). Keeping in mind that Bourdieu's
   portrayal might be problematic in regard to the link between his data and
   his theoretical development, I think that insofar as the inside/outside
   binaries are also essentialized ideas, the parallels can still be drawn for the
   sake of comparison.
2. *Dạy con từ thuở còn thơ*
   *Dạy vợ từ thuở bơ vơ mới về.*
3. I owe the articulation of this point to Erik Harms.
4. Ms. Lan, like many other traders from her village, insists on eating the rice
   from their own field, even though they can easily buy good-quality rice in
   the city at a lower price than what they can get for their home-grown rice.
   I several times received gifts of rice from their home field as a token of
   reciprocity for the gifts that I brought my hosts. The symbolic value of
   home-grown rice is quite significant; thus, the work of growing rice at
   home has other meanings than mere food production.
5. How Ms. Lan managed the housework division whenever Tâm (my research
   partner) and I stayed in their house is fascinating. If we were around when
   she was home, Ms. Lan would categorically refuse to let either of us do the
   cooking, cleaning up, and the dishes. Should she be away in Hanoi when
   we were there, she always talked to us in advance, often repeating the same
   message in an apologetic tone: "Please help me to do these tasks when I am
   not around. It is not an issue for us women to do them, but it would be
   complicated for him as a man. You would understand." Yet whenever her
   son, who is much younger than both of us, came home, the son would do
   the dishes without Ms. Lan saying anything; he would even cook for all of
   us if his mother were away, clearly having received instructions from her
   not to let us do housework.
6. Like other market traders, people in the district often compare junk trading
   to fishing. It is believed that good fortune (*lộc*) is essential for the trade; those
   who are not successful are said to "go to the market without a lucky streak."

## Chapter 2

1. From 2002 to 2006, according to official figures, selected appliances among Vietnam's electronic waste increased, in tons, as follows: discarded televisions, 190,445 to 364,684; computers, 62,771 to 131,536; mobile phones, 80,912 to 505,268; refrigerators, 112,402 to 230,856; air-conditioners, 17,778 to 49,782; washing machines, 184,140 to 327,649 (MONRE 2011: 25).

2. As with other kinds of migrant laborers, media portrayal of waste traders tends to use the archetypal motive of the pitiable rural migrant, sometimes conveying a combination of disgust and pity, especially through images of filth and disorder in their living spaces. Such attitudes are exemplified in articles about junk traders such as the following (all accessed on February 20, 2013): Dương Đình Tường, *"Lao xao tiếng ai đồng nát"* ["The voices of the junk traders"], http://nongnghiep.vn/lao-xao-tieng-ai-dong-nat-post79659.html, *Nông nghiệp Việt nam online*, June 13, 2011; Minh Yến, *"Xóm ổ chuột với xú uế giữa đất vàng thủ đô"* ["The slum full of filth in the golden land of the capital city"], *Khampha*, August 8, 2012, http://khampha.vn/tin-nhanh/chuyen-ve-nhung-nguoi-nhoc-nhan-bam-rac-c4a14955.html; Truong Phong, *"Nát ơi"* ["Hey, Junks!"], *Tien Phong*, July 9, 2012, http://www.tienphong.vn/xa-hoi/phong-su/583987/Nat-oi-tpp.html.

3. In his wonderful book on the history of environmental racism in the United States, Carl Zimring (2017) provides a fascinating account of how the scrap trade was first dominated by migrant Jews from Europe in the early twentieth century who had few other employment opportunities (similar to the early Chinese male immigrants who went into laundry service). The Jews left the trade as they became more upwardly mobile in a less anti-Semitist society of the mid-twentieth century; the trade was then transferred to African Americans alongside a greater emphasis on the moral superiority of whiteness over people of color. By that time, according to Zimring, the Jews and other southern Europeans, via their greater economic and educational advantages, had become incorporated into a changing notion of whiteness. The social mobility meant that they could free themselves from the stigma of waste; even those who stayed in the trade did so as managers of large companies in which the work of direct waste handling was carried out largely by non-white people in ghettoes far from the suburbs where they lived.

4. *Quy định về quản lý hoạt động bán hàng rong trên địa bàn Thành phố Hà Nội* [Regulation on street vending activities within the city of Hanoi] 46/2009/QĐ-UBND. Hanoi People's Committee (January 15, 2009).

5. *Nghị định về sửa đổi, bổ sung một số điều của Nghị định số 80/2006/NĐ-CP ngày 09 tháng 8 năm 2006 của Chính phủ về việc quy định chi tiết và hướng*

*dẫn thi hành một số điều của Luật Bảo vệ môi trường* [Decree on amendments to a number of articles under government decree 80/2006/ NĐ-CP dated August 9, 2006, on guidelines for implementing some articles of the law on environmental protection]. The Government of Vietnam (February 20, 2008).

6. See coverage at http://vietnamnet.vn/vn/thoi-su/kinh-hai-bom-no-cham-phe-lieu-giua-thu-do-295102.html (Accessed on July 17, 2017). As I was finishing the manuscript at the beginning of 2018, media reports appeared about a major explosion at a warehouse in the recycling village of Quan Độ on the outskirts of Hanoi. The explosion was caused by an undetonated bomb in the warehouse of a large-scale dealer who seemed to trade in significant quantities of bullet and bombshells (the trade in military vehicles and discarded wares has been practiced by many in this village for decades). In any case, this incident is likely to have repercussions for the much smaller-scale activities of Spring District waste traders in terms of public antipathy toward waste traders.

7. Van Hai and Ha Ngoc, *"Giàu bên bãi rác"* ["Becoming rich next to the waste dumps"], *Laodong,* July 20, 2013, http://laodong.com.vn/lao-dong-doi-song/ giau-ben-bai-rac-128579.bld; Xuan Ngoc, "Thu mua đồng nát, tậu nhà Hà Nội" ["Trading in waste, buying a house in Hanoi"], *Vnexpress*, March 22, 2011, http://kinhdoanh.vnexpress.net/tin-tuc/vi-mo/thu-mua-dong-nat-tau-nha-ha-noi-2711235.html. All accessed October 25, 2013.

8. The dynamic reminds of Carl Zimring's account: when the once-ostracized Jewish scrap traders had become successful in the trade, they either left it for other white-collar professions or become managers and owners of waste businesses; the work of actual waste handling, along with the stigma, was transferred to other marginal groups, namely African and Hispanic Americans. Nevertheless, scrap traders from these latter groups do not have the same mobility trajectory as the early Jewish scrap traders did. On account of their different positions in America's racialized structure of opportunities, few are able to move up the social ladder through waste work (see note 3).

## Chapter 3

1. Negotiations with legal ambiguity concern not only low-status and marginal groups, but also in many cases the global elites participating what Carolyn Nordstrom (2004) terms *non-formal economies*. Her book on war-zone shadow economies, in which the transactions of huge quantities of global commodities into and across war zones take place, suggests that the invisibility of these transactions is indeed a mechanism of profit making by powerful players.

## Chapter 4

1. See Kuan (2013) for an account of similar devaluation of the college degree that sets the context for competitive parenting among urban middle-class families in China.

2. See, for examples, *225,000 cử nhân thất nghiệp và cái giá phải trả của một nền giáo dục ì ạch* [225,000 unemployed university graduates and the price to pay for a sluggish education system], *Giáo dục*, http://giaoduc.net.vn/Giao-duc-24h/225000-cu-nhan-that-nghiep-va-cai-gia-phai-tra-cua-mot-nen-giao-duc-i-ach-post165246.gd; *Thêm 200,000 cử nhân thất nghiệp trong năm 2017* [200000 additional unemployed graduates in 2017], *Vietnam.net*, http://vietnamnet.vn/vn/kinh-doanh/thi-truong/them-200-000-cu-nhan-that-nghiep-trong-nam-2017-356094.html; *Thật bất hạnh khi tốt nghiệp đại học rồi lại đi làm công nhân* [How unhappy it is to become a factory worker with a university degree], *Giáo dục*, http://giaoduc.net.vn/Giao-duc-24h/That-bat-hanh-khi-tot-nghiep-dai-hoc-roi-di-lam-cong-nhan-post168098.gd (assessed on June 25, 2017).

3. The educational system in Vietnam is divided into three levels: primary level includes grades 1 to 6, lower secondary level includes grades 6 to 9, and higher secondary level includes grades 10 to 12. Education up to the lower secondary level is universal by law. The higher secondary level is more selective, and entry is highly competitive.

## Chapter 5

1. Detailed information is available online at http://www.chinadaily.com.cn/china/2010-10/20/content_11436582.htm (accessed on August 24, 2016).

2. Prime Minister Decision No. 800/QĐ-TTg, dated June 4, 2010, on *Approving the National Target Program of Building the New Countryside between 2010–2020*, available online at http://www.chinhphu.vn/ (accessed on August 26, 2016).

3. An elaborate set of criteria defines a "cultured village" (see *Regulation on the criteria and procedures for recognizing cultured families, villages and urban residential units*, available online at http://www.moj.gov.vn/vbpq/lists/vn%20bn%20php%20lut/view_detail.aspx?itemid=27229 accessed on July 8, 2017). A village is recognized as a "cultured village" if it has (1) a stable and viable local economy, (2) healthy and diversified cultural and spiritual life, (3) clean and beautiful environment and landscape, (4) compliance with the guidance and direction of the Party as well as the law and policies of the state, and (5) solidarity and a spirit of mutual help within the community. Under each of these points are subsets of criteria, some of which overlap with the criteria of the New Countryside Program.

4. See *Con nợ nông thôn mới và những giá trị bị bắt nhốt* (The debtors of the New Countryside and values that are taken hostage), *Vietnam.net*, http://vietnamnet.vn/vn/tuanvietnam/tieudiem/con-no-nong-thon-moi-va-nhung-gia-tri-bi-bat-nhot-340545.html; *Xây dựng nông thôn mới, hơn 40 số xã chìm trong nợ* (Building the new countryside: 40 per cent of the communes drowned in debts), *Hanoimoi*, http://hanoimoi.com.vn/Tin-tuc/Kinh-te/851085/xay-dung-nong-thon-moi-hon-40-so-xa-chim-trong-no; *Chương trình nông thôn mới bộ mặt thay đổi nhưng nợ 15 ngàn tỉ đồng* (Building the New Countryside: a new face but indebted with 15,000 billion), *Vietnam.net*, http://vietnamnet.vn/vn/tuanvietnam/doithoai/chuong-trinh-nong-thon-moi-bo-mat-thay-doi-nhung-no-15-ngan-ty-dong-340582.html, accessed on 30 November 2016.

5. The consolidation involves rezoning of the fields, building intra-field roads, and taking out a small proportion of farmland for public works, industrial development, and residential land. Among others, this puts the scattered plots of a household together.

6. See, for example, *Chương trình mỗi xã một sản phẩm tiếp sức cho nông thôn mới* [The one commune-one product program as a driver of the New Countryside), *Hanoimoi*, http://hanoimoi.com.vn/Tin-tuc/Kinh-te/869739/chuong-trinh-moi-xa-mot-san-pham-tiep-suc-cho-nong-thon-moi (Accessed on July 4, 2017).

7. Vietnamese saying, literally "No one can keep their fists tight throughout the day and their head on a pillow throughout the night," referring to the inherent unpredictability of life.

8. The government subsidizes farmers who purchase harvesters for large-scale farming. However, the subsidies only go to those who purchase harvesters approved by the state, which according to the informants are of low quality and often quickly end up needing significant repairs. They therefore prefer to invest their own funds in purchasing second-hand Japanese machines, which they find more durable and efficient, even though it means foregoing the subsidies altogether.

## Chapter 6

1. I was very pleased that he included me in his village when talking about it; he seemed to think of me momentarily as "one of us."

2. Unlike Green Spring, Red Spring commune has a sizeable Catholic population. In an earlier publication (Nguyen 2015a), I touch on how mobility plays out in the relationship between Catholic migrants and their churches. There is similar anxiety over the moral behavior of the migrants, although the local churches seem to have stronger authority over them than

the Buddhist pagodas do over the other migrants. I leave this discussion
out in the book since my focus here is on the anxiety of mobility rather
than religion.

3. The adage *Tậu trâu, cưới vợ, làm nhà* (Buying a buffalo, marrying a woman,
building a house) sets out the primary life goals that peasant men are
traditionally supposed to fulfil.

4. Some years after the first burial, the bones of the dead are transferred to a
more permanent coffin and grave.

5. The same thing is said of most rural places in the Red River Delta, including
Spring District.

## Chapter 7

1. Thị Bình Thuận Phan, "Hiểu thế nào về xã hội hóa?" ["How to understand
the term socialization?"]), *The Saigon Times*, March 21, 2005. www.
thesaigontimes.vn/127757/Hieu-the-nao-ve-xa-hoi-hoa.html.

2. Department of Cooperatives and Rural Development, "Bảo đảm ngày càng
tốt hơn an sinh xã hội và phúc lợi xã hội là một nội dung chủ yếu của chiến
lược phát triển kinh tế xã hội 2011–2020" ["Ensuring better social security
and welfare is a major component of the 2011–2020 socio-economic
development strategy"], http://nguyentandung.chinhphu.vn/Home/Bao-
dam-ngay-cang-tot-hon-an-sinh-xa-hoi-va-phuc-loi-xa-hoi-la-mot-noi-
dung-chu-yeu-cua-Chien-luoc-phat-trien-kinh-texa-
hoi-20112020/20108/11379.vgp (accessed on June 2, 2018).

3. "Với tinh thần 'lá lành đùm lá rách,' góp phần chia sẻ với những hộ gia đình
còn gặp nhiều khó khăn trong cuộc sống, hỗ trợ nâng cao đời sống vật chất
và tinh thần, tạo điều kiện cho các hộ gia đình có hoàn cảnh đặc biệt khó
khăn vươn lên ổn định cuộc sống." (Field note, official letter posted on a
public bulletin board to collection contributions for a child protection fund.)

4. See coverage of the mobilization for the Fund for the Poor in 2016, *Chính
thức phát động tháng cao điểm vì người nghèo* (Officially kick-starting the
month for the poor in 2016), at https://www.vietnamplus.vn/chinh-thuc-
phat-dong-thang-cao-diem-vi-nguoi-ngheo-nam-2016/411282.vnp, accessed
on June 2, 2018.

5. See for example the discussion of a charity professional about the behavior of
charity recipients, *Hạn chế từ thiện* (Limiting Charity) at https://vnexpress.
net/tin-tuc/goc-nhin/han-che-tu-thien-3679738.html, and the interview
given by a vice minister of the Ministry of Labour Invalids and Social Affairs
on the poor household policy, *Chính sách cho không đang triệt tiêu động lực
thoát nghèo* (Give-away policies are eliminating the [poor's] momentum to

escape poverty), at https://www.vietnamplus.vn/chinh-sach-cho-khong-dang-triet-tieu-dong-luc-thoat-ngheo/417307.vnp. Interestingly, both accounts refer to the tendency of the recipients of charity or poverty benefits to become passive and dependent, to lose the "consciousness to rise" (ý thức vươn lên), and even to compromise their dignity in some instances. The articles were accessed on June 2, 2018.

6. This expression in Vietnamese changes in meaning depending on whether it is a self-assessment or another person's assessment of one's situation. In the first instance, it is often an attempt to "speak bitterness" (kể khổ), which someone might do to attract sympathy or justify a claim on other people's help. In the latter case, it can evoke pity and sympathy for what people have to go through, but sometimes also contempt on the part of the speaker, depending on how it is said and in what context. In the instance described here, the statement dramatizes the family's incapacities in a way that simultaneously attracts sympathy and conveys a sense that the family is a burden on the village.

## Conclusion

1. One must of course keep in mind the environmental impacts of the global recycling industry as a whole and the extent to which material can be recycled until the maximum recyclability is reached. The waste traders, however, undoubtedly play a major role in preventing a large amount of recyclable waste from ending up in the dumpsites.

2. See the educational website *Chúngta.com* (http://www.chungta.com/) for a long list of "books on learning how to be a moral person" (*Sách học làm người*), which includes numerous translations of international bestsellers about how to become successful and how to live as successful persons by authors such as Bill Gates, Stephen R. Covey, and John C. Maxwell alongside books about happiness written by Buddhist-inspired authors.

# REFERENCES

Agarwal, Bina. 1997. "'Bargaining' and Gender Relations: Within and Beyond the Household." *Feminist Economics* 3(1): 1–51.

Agergaard, Jytte and Vu Thi Thao. 2011. "Mobile, Flexible, and Adaptable: Female Migrants in Hanoi's Informal Sector." *Population, Space and Place* 17(5): 407–420.

Ahlers, Anna L. and Gunter Schubert. 2009. "'Building a New Socialist Countryside'—Only a Political Slogan?" *Journal of Current Chinese Affairs* 38(4): 35–62.

Alexander, Catherine and Joshua Reno, Eds. 2012. *Economies of Recycling: The Global Transformation of Materials, Values and Social Relations.* London: Zed Books.

Anagnost, Ann. 2004. "The Corporeal Politics of Quality (Suzhi)." *Public Culture* 16(2): 189–208.

Anderson, Benedict 2006. *Imagined Communities: Reflections on the Origin and Spread of Nationalism.* London: Verso.

Anjaria, Jonathan Shapiro. 2006. "Street Hawkers and Public Space in Mumbai." *Economic and Political Weekly* 41(21): 2140–2146.

Appadurai, Arjun. 1986. *The Social Life of Things: Commodities in Cultural Perspective.* Cambridge, UK: Cambridge University Press.

Arnold, Dennis, and Pickles John. 2011. "Global Work, Surplus Labor, and the Precarious Economies of the Border." *Antipode* 43, no. 5 (2011): 1598–624.

Bakken, Børge. 2000. *The Exemplary Society: Human Improvement, Social Control, and the Dangers of Modernity in China.* Oxford: Oxford University Press.

Bauman, Zygmunt. 1998. *Globalization: The Human Consequences.* New York: Columbia University Press.

Bauman, Zigmunt. 2004. *Wasted Lives: Modernity and its Outcasts*. Cambridge: Polity Press.

Bayly, Susan. 2013. "How to Forge a Creative Student-Citizen: Achieving the Positive in Today's Vietnam."

Beck, Ulrich. 1992. *Risk Society: Towards a New Modernity*. London: Sage Publications.

Beckert, Jens. 2016. *Imagined Futures: Fictional Expectations and Capitalist Dynamics*. Cambridge, Mass.: Harvard University Press.

Berlant, Lauren Gail. 2011. *Cruel Optimism*. Durham, N.C.: Duke University Press.

Berner, Erhard and Benedict Phillips. 2005. "Left to Their Own Devices? Community Self-Help between Alternative Development and Neoliberalism." *Community Development Journal* **40**(1): 17–29.

Binh, Nguyen Thi Thanh. 2016. "The Dynamics of Return Migration in Vietnam's Rural North: Charity, Community and Contestation." In *Connected and Disconnected in Viet Nam: Remaking Social Relations in a Post-Socialist Nation*, ed. Philip Taylor, Canberra: ANU Press: 73–108.

Birkbeck, Chris. 1978. "Self-Employed Proletarians in an Informal Factory: The Case of Cali's Garbage Dump." *World Development* **6**(9–10): 1173–1185.

Boholm, Åsa. 2003. "The Cultural Nature of Risk: Can There Be an Anthropology of Uncertainty?" *Ethnos* **68**(2): 159–178.

Bourdieu, Pierre. 1990. *The Logic of Practice*. Cambridge, UK: Polity Press.

Brandtstädter, Susanne. 2009. "Gendered Work and the Production of Kinship Values in Taiwan and China." In S. Brandtstädter and G. a. D. Santos, Ed. *Chinese Kinship: Contemporary Anthropological Perspectives*. London: Routledge.

Brenner, Suzanne. 1998. *The Domestication of Desire: Women, Wealth, and Modernity in Java*. Princeton: Princeton University Press.

Butler, Judith. 1990. *Gender Trouble: Feminism and the Subversion of Identity*. New York: Routledge.

Butler, Judith. 1993. *Bodies that Matter: On the Discursive Limits of "Sex."* New York: Routledge.

Campkin, Ben and Rosie Cox. 2012. *Dirt: New Geographies of Cleanliness and Contamination*. London: I. B. Tauris.

Chan, Anita. 2011. *Labour in Vietnam*. Singapore: Institute of Southeast Asian Studies.

Cohen, William A. and Ryan Johnson. 2005. *Filth: Dirt, Disgust, and Modern Life*. Minneapolis: University of Minnesota Press.

Denning, Michael. 2010. "Wageless Life." *New Left Review* **66**(November): 79–97

DiGregorio, Micheal. 1994. *Urban Harvest: Recycling as a Peasant Industry in Northern Vietnam*. Honolulu: East-West Centre.

DiGregorio, Michael. 2011. "Into the Land Rush: Facing the Urban Transition in Hanoi's Western Suburbs." *International Development Planning Review* **33**(3): 293–319.

Douglas, Mary. 1966. *Purity and Danger: An Analysis of Concepts of Pollution and Taboo*. London: Routledge & K. Paul.

Douglas, Mary. 1992. *Risk and Blame: Essays in Cultural Theory*. London: Routledge.

Douglass, Mike. 2012. Global Householding and Social Reproduction: Migration Research, Dynamics and Public Policy in East and Southeast Asia. Asia Research Institute Working Paper Series No. 188. Singapore: Asia Research Institute.

Douglass, Mike and Liling Huang. 2007. "Globalizing the City in Southeast Asia: Utopia on the Urban Edge—The Case of Phu My Hung, Saigon." *IJAPS* **3**(2): 1–42.

Dove, Michael. 2011. *The Banana Tree at the Gate: A History of Marginal Peoples and Global Markets in Borneo*. New Haven: Yale University Press.

Drummond, Lisa. 2004. "The Modern 'Vietnamese Women': Socialization and Women's Magazines." In *Gender Practices in Contemporary Vietnam*, ed. L. Drummond and H. Rydstrøm. Singapore: Singapore University Press, Nordic Institute of Asian Studies, 158–178.

Drummond, Lisa. 2012. "Middle Class Landscapes in a Transforming City: Hanoi in the 21st Century." In *The Reinvention of Distinction Modernity and the Middle Class in Urban Vietnam*, ed. V. Nguyen-Marshall, L. Drummond, and D. Belanger. Dortrecht: Springer Verlag: 79–94.

Drummond, Lisa and Helle Rydström. 2004. *Gender Practices in Contemporary Vietnam*. Singapore: Singapore University Press and Nordic Institute of Asian Studies.

Elliot, Allice. 2016. "Gender." In *Keywords of Mobility: Critical Engagements*, ed. N. B. Salazar and K. Jayaram. New York: Berghahn: 73–92.

Endres, Kirsten 2014. "Making Law: Small-Scale Trade and Corrupt Exceptions at the Vietnam–China Border." *American Anthropologist* **116**(3): 611–625.

Endres, Kirsten, and Ann Marie Leshkowich. 2018. *Traders in Motion: Networks, Identities, and Contestations in the Vietnamese Marketplace*. Ithaca: Cornell University Press, Southeast Asia Program Publications.

Eriksen, Thomas Hylland. 2016. *Overheating: An Anthropology of Accelerated Change*. London: Pluto Press

Eriksen, Thomas Hylland and Elisabeth Schober. 2017. "Waste and the Superfluous: an Introduction." *Social Anthropology* **25**(3): 282–287.

Fan, C. Cindy. 2008. *China on the Move: Migration, the State, and the Household*. London: Routledge.

Fassin, Didier. 2009. "Moral Economies Revisited." *Annales. Histoire, Sciences Sociales* **64**(6): 1237–1266

Ferguson, James. 1999. *Expectations of Modernity: Myths and Meanings of Urban Life on the Zambian Copperbelt*. Berkeley: University of California Press.

Ferguson, James. 2015. *Give a Man a Fish: Reflections on the New Politics of Distribution*. Durham, N.C.: Duke University Press.

Folbre, Nancy. 1986. "Hearts and Spades: Paradigms of Household Economics." *World Development* **14**(2): 245–255.

Fredericks, Rosalind. 2012. "Devaluing the Dirty Work: Gendered Trash Work in Participatory Dakar." In *Economies of Recycling: The Global Tranformation of Materials, Values and Social Relations,* ed. C. Alexander and J. Reno. London: Zed Books: 119–142.

Gainsborough, Martin. 2010. *Vietnam: Rethinking the State.* London: Zed Books.

Gammeltoft, Tine. 2015. *Haunting Images: A Cultural Account of Selective Reproduction in Vietnam.* Berkeley: University of California Press.

Gill, Kaveri. 2010. *Of Poverty and Plastic: Scavenging and Scrap Trading Entrepreneurs in India's Urban Informal Economy.* New Delhi: Oxford University Press.

Gille, Zsuzsa. 2007. *From the Cult of Waste to the Trash Heap of History: The Politics of Waste in Socialist and Postsocialist Hungary.* Bloomington, Ind.: Indiana University Press.

Glick Schiller, Nina, Linda Basch, and Cristina Blanc-Szanton. 1992. "Transnationalism: A New Analytic Framework for Understanding Migration." *Annals of the New York Academy of Sciences* **645**(1): 1–24.

Glick Schiller, Nina and Noel B. Salazar. 2013. "Regimes of Mobility Across the Globe." *Journal of Ethnic and Migration Studies* **39**(2): 183–200.

Goffman, Erving. 1956. *The Presentation of Self in Everyday Life.* University of Edinburgh Social Sciences Research Centre. Edinburgh: University of Edinburgh.

Goldstein, Joshua L. 2006. "The Remains of the Everyday: One hundred Years of Recycling in Beijing." In *Everyday Modernity in China,* ed. M. Y. Dong and J. L. Goldstein. Seattle: University of Washington Press: 260–302.

Goodman, Jane E. 2003. "The Proverbial Bourdieu: Habitus and the Politics of Representation in the Ethnography of Kabylia." *American Anthropologist* **105**(4): 782–793.

Gourou, Pierre. 1955. *The Peasants of the Tonkin Delta: A Study of Human Geography.* New Haven: Human Relations Area Files.

Graeber, David. 2001. *Toward an Anthropological Theory of Value: The False Coin of Our Own Dreams.* New York: Palgrave.

Greenhalgh, Susan. 2010. *Cultivating Global Citizens: Population in the Rise of China.* Cambridge, Mass.: Harvard University Press.

Gregory, Chris. 2009. "After Words." In *Ethnographies of Moral Reasoning: Living Paradoxes of a Global Age,* ed. K. M. Sykes. New York: Palgrave Macmillan: 189–201.

Gregson, Nicky and Mike Crang. 2015. "From Waste to Resource: The Trade in Wastes and Global Recycling Economies." *Annual Review of Environment and Resources* **40**: 151–176.

Gupta, Akhil. *Red Tape: Bureaucracy, Structural Violence, and Poverty in India.* Durham: Duke University Press, 2012.

Hann, Chris (2018). Moral(ity and) Economy: Work, Workfare, and Fairness in Provincial Hungary. *European Journal of Sociology*, doi:10.1017/S000397561700056X.

Harms, Erik. 2009. "Vietnam's Civilizing Process and the Retreat from the Street: A Turtle's Eye View from Ho Chi Minh City." *City & Society* 21 (2): 182–206.

Harms, Erik. 2011. *Saigon's Edge: On the Margins of Ho Chi Minh City.* Minneapolis: University of Minnesota Press.

Harms, Erik. 2012. "Beauty as Control in the New Saigon: Eviction, New Urban Zones, and Atomized Dissent in a Southeast Asian City." *American Ethnologist* 39(4): 735–750.

Harms, Erik. 2013. "The Boss: Conspicuous Invisibility in Ho Chi Minh City." *City & Society* 25(2): 195–215.

Harms, Erik. 2016. *Luxury and Rubble: Civility and Dispossession in the New Saigon.* Berkeley: University of California Press.

Hart, Keith and John Sharp. 2015. *People, Money, and Power in the Economic Crisis: Perspectives from the Global South.* New York: Berghann Books.

Harvey, David. 2005. *A Brief History of Neoliberalism.* New York: Oxford University Press

Hayami, Yujiro, A. K. Dikshit, and S. N. Mishra. 2006. "Waste Pickers and Collectors in Delhi: Poverty and Environment in an Urban Informal Sector." *The Journal of Development Studies* 42(1): 41–69.

Hayton, Bill. 2010. *Vietnam: Rising Dragon.* New Haven: Yale University Press.

Herzfeld, Michael. 2005. *Cultural Intimacy: Social Poetics in the Nation-State.* New York: Routledge.

High, Holly. 2014. *Fields of Desire: Poverty and Policy in Laos.* Singapore: National University of Singapore Press.

Hoang, Kimberly Kay. 2015. *Dealing in Desire: Asian Ascendancy, Western Decline, and the Hidden Currencies of Global Sex Work.* Berkeley: University of California Press.

Hoang, Lan Anh and Brenda S. A. Yeoh. 2011. "Breadwinning Wives and 'Left-Behind' Husbands." *Gender & Society* 25(6): 717–739.

Hsu, Carolyn L. 2007. *Creating Market Socialism: How Ordinary People Are Shaping Class and Status in China.* Durham, N.C.: Duke University Press.

Huijsmans, Roy. 2014. "Becoming a Young Migrant or Stayer Seen through the Lens of 'Householding': Households 'In Flux' and the Intersection of Relations of Gender and Seniority." *Geoforum* 51(January): 294–304.

Inda, Jonathan Xavier. 2006. *Targeting Immigrants: Government, Technology, and Ethics.* Malden, Mass.: Blackwell.

Jacka, Tamara. 2012. "Migration, Householding and the Well-Being of Left-Behind Women in Rural Ningxia." *The China Journal* 67: 1–22.

Jacka, Tamara. 2013. "Chinese Discourses on Rurality, Gender and Development: A Feminist Critique." *Journal of Peasant Studies* 40(6): 983–1007.

Jacka, Tamara. 2017. "Translocal Family Reproduction and Agrarian Change in China: A New Analytical Framework." *The Journal of Peasant Studies*, doi: 10.1080/03066150.2017.1314267.

Jamieson, Neil 1993. *Understanding Vietnam*. Berkeley: University of California Press.

Jellema, Kate. 2005. "Making Good on Debt: The Remoralisation of Wealth in Post-Revolutionary Vietnam." *The Asia Pacific Journal of Anthropology* 6(3): 231–248.

Karis, Timothy. 2013. "Unofficial Hanoians: Migration, Native Place and Urban Citizenship in Vietnam." *The Asia Pacific Journal of Anthropology* 14(3): 256–273.

Kipnis, Andrew. 2007. "Neoliberalism Reified: Suzhi Discourse and Tropes of Neoliberalism in the People's Republic of China." *Journal of the Royal Anthropological Institute* 13(2): 383–400.

Kipnis, Andrew B. 2011. *Governing Educational Desire: Culture, Politics, and Schooling in China*. Chicago: University of Chicago Press.

Kristeva, Julia. 1982. *Powers of Horror: An Essay on Abjection*. New York: Columbia University Press.

Kuan, Teresa. 2013. *Love's Uncertainty: The Politics and Ethics of Child Rearing in Contemporary China*. Berkeley: University of Carlifornia Press.

Labbé, Danielle and Julie-Anne Boudreau. 2011. "Understanding the Causes of Urban Fragmentation in Hanoi: The Case of New Urban Areas." *International Development Planning Review* 33(3): 273–291.

Lambek, Michael. 2010. *Ordinary Ethics: Anthropology, Language, and Action*. New York: Fordham University Press.

Latour, Bruno. 2005. *Reassembling the Self*. Oxford: Oxford University Press.

Lefebvre, Henri. 1991. *The Production of Space*. Oxford: Wiley.

Leshkowich, Ann Marie. 2005. "Feminine Disorder: State Campaigns against Street Traders in Socialist and Late Socialist Vietnam." In *Le Vietnam au féminin [Vietnam: Women's Realities)]*, ed. G. Bousquet and N. Taylor. Paris: Les Indes Savantes: 187–207.

Leshkowich, Ann Marie. 2011. "Making Class and Gender: (Market) Socialist Enframing of Traders in Ho Chi Minh City." *American Anthropologist* 113(2): 277–290.

Leshkowich, Ann Marie. 2014. *Essential Trade: Vietnamese Women in a Changing Marketplace*. Honolulu: University of Hawai'i.

Li, Shichao. 2002. "Junk-Buyers as the Linkage between Waste Sources and Redemption Depots in Urban China: The Case of Wuhan." *Resources, Conservation and Recycling* 36(4): 319–335.

Li, Tania. 2007. *The Will to Improve: Governmentality, Development, and the Practice of Politics*. Durham, N.C.: Duke University Press.

Li, Tania. 2014. *Land's End: Capitalist Relations on an Indigenous Frontier*. Durham: Duke University Press.

Li, Tania. 2017. "After Development: Surplus Population and the Politics of Entitlement." *Development and Change* **48**(6): 1247–1261.

Locke, Catherine, Thi Thanh Tam Nguyen, and Thi Ngan Hoa Nguyen. 2014. "Mobile Householding and Marital Dissolution in Vietnam: An Inevitable Consequence?" *Geoforum* **51**: 273–283.

Luong, Hy Van. 1989. "Vietnamese Kinship: Structural Principles and the Socialist Transformation in Northern Vietnam." *The Journal of Asian Studies* **48**(4): 741–756.

Luong, Hy Van. 2010. *Tradition, Revolution, and Market Economy in a North Vietnamese Village, 1925–2006*. Honolulu: University of Hawai'i Press.

Luong, Hy Van. 2018. "A Mobile Trading Network from Central Coastal Vietnam: Growth, Social Network, and Gender." In *Traders in Motion: Identities and Contestations in the Vietnamese Marketplace*, ed. K. Endres and A. M. Leshkowich. Ithaca, N.Y.: Cornell University Press, Southeast Asia Program Publications.

MacLean, Ken. 2013. *The Government of Mistrust: Illegibility and Bureaucratic Power in Socialist Vietnam*. Madison: University of Wisconson Press.

Malarney, Shaun Kingsley. 2002. *Culture, Ritual and Revolution in Vietnam*. Honolulu: University of Hawai'i Press.

Malarney, Shaun Kingsley. 2007. "Festivals and the Dynamics of the Exceptional Dead in Northern Vietnam." *Journal of Southeast Asian Studies* **38**(03): 515–540.

Masocha, Mhosisi. 2006. "Informal Waste Harvesting in Victoria Falls Town, Zimbabwe: Socio-economic Benefits." *Habitat International* **30**(4): 838–848.

Medina, Martin. 2000. "Scavenger Cooperatives in Asia and Latin America." *Resources, Conservation and Recycling* **31**(1): 51–69.

Mehra, Rekha, Thai Thi Ngoc Du, Nguyen Xuan Nghia, Nguyen Ngoc Lam, Truong Thi Kim Chuyen, Bang Anh Tuan, Pham Gia Tran, and Nguyen Thi Nhan. 1996. "Women in Waste Collection and Recycling in Hochiminh City." *Population and Environment* **18**(2): 187–199.

Milgram, B. Lynne. 2014. "Remapping the Edge: Informality and Legality in the Harrison Road Night Market, Baguio City, Philippines." *City & Society* **26**(2): 153–174.

Millar, Kathleen. 2012. "Trash Ties: Urban Politics, Economic Crisis and Rio de Janeiro's Garbage Dump." In *Economies of Recycling: The Global Tranformation of Materials, Values and Social Relations*, ed. C. Alexander and J. Reno. London: Zed Books: 164–184.

Millar, Kathleen. 2018. *Reclaiming the Discarded: Life and Labor on Rio's Garbage Dump*. Durham, N.C.: Duke University Press.

Minter, Adam. 2013. *Junkyard Planet: Travels in the Billion-Dollar Trash Trade*. New York: Bloomsbury Press.

Mitchell, Carrie L. 2008. "Altered Landscapes, Altered Livelihoods: The Shifting Experience of Informal Waste Collecting during Hanoi's Urban Transition." *Geoforum* **39**(6): 2019–2029.

Mitchell, Carrie L. 2009. "Trading Trash in the Transition: Economic Restructuring, Urban Spatial Transformation, and the Boom and Bust of Hanoi's Informal Waste Trade." *Environment and Planning A* **41**(11): 2633–2650.

Ministry of Natural Resource and Environment (MONRE). 2011. Vietnam Environment Report: Solid Waste. Hanoi: MONRE

Moore, Henrietta L. 1994. *A Passion for Difference: Essays in Anthropology and Gender.* Bloomington: Indiana University Press.

Morris, Rosalind C. 1995. "All Made Up: Performance Theory and the New Anthropology of Sex and Gender." *Annual Review of Anthropology* **24**: 567–592.

Mosbergen, Dominique. 2018. What Happens When One Of The World's Biggest Cities Doesn't Recycle. *Huffington Post*, January 27, 2018.

Moses, Kara. 2013. China Leads the Waste Recycling League. *UK Guardian*, June 14, 2013

Muehlebach, Andrea Karin. 2012. *The Moral Neoliberal: Welfare and Citizenship in Italy.* Chicago: University of Chicago Press.

Myers, Fred. 2001. *The Empire of Things: Regimes of Value and Material Culture.* Santa Fe: School of American Research Press.

Nelson, Lise. 1999. "Bodies (and Spaces) Do Matter: The Limits of Performativity." *Gender, Place and Culture: A Journal of Feminist Geography* **6**(4): 331–353.

Nordstrom, Carolyn. 2004. *Shadows of War: Violence, Power, and International Profiteering in the Twenty-First Century.* Berkeley: University of California Press.

Nguyen, Martina Thucnhi. 2016. "French Colonial State, Vietnamese Civil Society: The League of Light [Đoàn Ánh Sáng] and Housing Reform in Hà Nội, 1937–1941." *Journal of Vietnamese Studies* **11**(3–4): 17–57.

Nguyen, Minh T. N. 2015a. "Migration and Care Institutions in Market Socialist Vietnam: Conditionality, Commodification and Moral Authority." *The Journal of Development Studies* **51**(10): 1326–1340.

Nguyen, Minh T. N. 2015b. *Vietnam's Socialist Servants: Domesticity, Gender, Class and Identity.* New York: Routledge.

Nguyen, Minh T. N. 2018. "Money, Risk Taking and Playing: Shifting Masculinity in a Waste-Trading Community in Northern Vietnam." In *Traders in Motion: Networks, Identities and Contestations in the Vietnamese Marketplace*, ed. K. Endres and A.-M. Leshkowich. Ithaca, N.Y.: Cornell University Press: 105–116.

Nguyen, Minh T. N. and Meixuan Chen. 2017. "The Caring State? On Welfare Governance in Rural Vietnam and China." *Ethics and Social Welfare* **11**(3): 230–247.

Nguyen, Minh T. N. and Catherine Locke. 2014. "Rural-Urban Migration in China and Vietnam: Gendered Householding, Space Production and the State." *Journal of Peasant Studies* **41**(5): 855–876.

Nguyen, Minh T. N., Roberta Zavoretti, and Joan Tronto. 2017. "Beyond the Global Care Chain: Boundaries, Institutions and Ethics of Care." *Ethics and Social Welfare* **11**(3): 199–212.

Nguyen, Tuan Anh, Jonathan Rigg, Luong Thi Thu Huong, and Dinh Thi Dieu. 2012. "Becoming and Being Urban in Hanoi: Rural-Urban Migration and Relations in Viet Nam." *Journal of Peasan Studies* **39** (5): 1103–1131.

Nguyen–Marshall, Van. 2008. *In Search of Moral Authority: the Discourse on Poverty, Poor Relief, and Charity in French Colonial Vietnam.* New York: Peter Lang.

Nguyen–Marshall, Van, Lisa Drummond, and Danielle Belanger. 2012. *The Reinvention of Distinction: Modernity and the Middle Class in Urban Vietnam.* Dortrecht: Springer Verlag.

Nguyen–Vo, Thu–Huong. 2008. *The Ironies of Freedom: Sex, Culture, and Neoliberal Governance in Vietnam.* Seattle: University of Washington Press.

Offe, Claus. 1982. "Some Contradictions in the Modern Welfare State." *Journal of Critical Social Policy* **2**(2): 7–14.

O'Malley, Pat. 2004. *Risk, Uncertainty, and Government.* London: The GlassHouse Press.

Otto, Ton and Rane Willerslev. 2013. "Value as Theory: Comparison, Cultural Critique, and Guerilla Ethnographic Theory." *HAU: Journal of Ethnographic Theory* **3**(1): 1–20.

Parizeau, Kate. 2013. "Formalization Beckons: A Baseline of Informal Recycling Work in Buenos Aires, 2007–2011." *Environment and Urbanization* **25**(2): 501–521.

Parizeau, Kate. 2015. "Re-Representing the City: Waste and Public Space in Buenos Aires, Argentina in the Late 2000s." *Environment and Planning A* **47**(2): 284–299.

Pun, Ngai. 2016. *Migrant Labor in China: Post-Socialist Transformations.* Bristol, UK: Polity Press.

Rao, Ursula. 2013. "Tolerated Encroachment: Resettlement Policies and the Negotiation of the Licit/Illicit Divide in an Indian Metropolis." *Cultural Anthropology* **28**(4): 760–779.

Read, Rosie and Tatjana Thelen. 2007. "Social Security and Care after Socialism: Reconfigurations of Public and Private." *Focaal* **2007**(50): 3–18.

Reno, Joshua. 2009."Your Trash Is Someone's Treasure: The Politics of Value at a Michigan Landfill." *Journal of Material Culture* **14** (1): 29–46

Reno, Joshua. 2016. *Waste Away: Working and Living with a North American Landfill.* Oakland: University of California Press.

Resurreccion, Bernadette and Thị Vân Khanh Hà. 2007. "Able to Come and Go: Reproducing Gender in Female Rural-Urban Migration in the Red River Delta." *Population, Space and Place* **13**: 211–224.

Rigg, Jonathan and Albert Salamanca. 2011. "Connecting Lives, Living, and Location: Mobility and Spatial Signatures in Northeast Thailand, 1982–2009." *Critical Asian Studies* **43**(4): 551–575.

Rigg, Jonathan and Peter Vandergeest. 2012. *Revisiting Rural Places: Pathways to Poverty and Prosperity in Southeast Asia*. Honolulu: University of Hawai'i Press.

Rigg, Jonathan, Tuan Anh Nguyen, and Thi Thu Huong Luong. 2014. "The Texture of Livelihoods: Migration and Making a Living in Hanoi." *The Journal of Development Studies* 50(3): 368–382

Rigi, Jakob. 2012. "The Corrupt State of Exception: Agamben in the Light of Putin." *Social Analysis* 56(3): 69–88.

Robin, Françoise. 2009. "The 'Socialist New Villages' in the Tibetan Autonomous Region." *China Perspectives* 3(79): 56–64.

Robinson, Fiona. 2011. *The Ethics of Care: A Feminist Approach to Human Security*. Philadelphia: Temple University Press.

Rofel, Lisa. 2007. *Desiring China: Experiments in Neoliberalism, Sexuality, and Public Culture*. Durham, N.C.: Duke University Press.

Rose, Nikolas S. 1999. *Powers of Freedom: Reframing Political Thought*. Cambridge, UK: Cambridge University Press.

Rydstrøm, Helle. 2003. *Embodying Morality: Growing up in Rural Northern Vietnam*. Honolulu: University of Hawai'i Press.

Rydstrøm, Helle. 2006. "Sexual Desires and 'Social Evils': Young Women in Rural Vietnam." *Gender, Place & Culture* 13(3): 283–301.

Rydstrøm, Helle. 2016. "Vietnam Women's Union and the Politics of Representation: Hegemonic Solidarity and a Heterosexual Family Regime." In *Gendered Citizenship and the Politics of Representation*, ed. H. Danielsen, K. Jegerstedt, R. Muriaas, and B. Ytre-Arne. London: Palgrave MacMillan: 209–234.

Schlecker, Markus. 2005. "Going Back a Long Way: Home Place, Thrift and Temporal Orientations in Northern Vietnam." *Journal of the Royal Anthropological Institute* 11(3): 509–526.

Schneider, Leander. 2014. *Government of Development: Peasants and Politicians in Postcolonial Tanzania*. Bloomington: Indiana University Press.

Schwenkel, Christina and Ann Marie Leshkowich. 2012. "How Is Neoliberalism Good to Think Vietnam? How Is Vietnam Good to Think Neoliberalism?" *positions: east asia cultures critique* 20(2): 379–401.

Scott, James C. 1977. *The Moral Economy of the Peasant: Rebellion and Subsistence in Southeast Asia*. New Haven: Yale University Press.

Sen, Amartya. 1990. "Gender and Cooperative Conflicts." In *Persistent Inequalities: Women and World Development*, ed. I. Tinker. New York: Oxford University Press: 123–149.

Sicular, Daniel T. 1991. "Pockets of Peasants in Indonesian Cities: The Case of Scavengers." *World Development* 19(2–3): 137–161.

Sikor, Thomas and Phuc Xuan To. 2011. "Illegal logging in Vietnam: *Lam tac* (forest hijackers) in practice and talk." *Society & Natural Resources* 24(7): 688–701.

Silverstein, Paul A. 2004. "Of Rooting and Uprooting: Kabyle Habitus, Domesticity, and Structural Nostalgia." *Ethnography* 5(4): 553–578

Stafford, Charles. 2013. *Ordinary Ethics in China*. London: Bloomsbury Publishing.

Stallybrass, Peter and Allon White. 1986. *The Politics and Poetics of Transgression*. Ithaca, N.Y.: Cornell University Press.

Steinmüller, Hans. 2011. "The State of Irony in China." *Critique of Anthropology* **31**(1): 21–42.

Sykes, Karen Margaret. 2009. *Ethnographies of Moral Reasoning: Living Paradoxes of a Global Age*. New York: Palgrave Macmillan.

Taylor, Philip. 2007. "Poor Policies, Wealthy Peasants: Alternative Trajectories of Rural Development in Vietnam." *Journal of Vietnamese Studies* **2**(2): 3–56.

Thompson, Edward P. 1971. "The Moral Economy of the English Crowd in the Eighteenth Century." *Past & Present* (**50**): 76–136.

Thompson, Michael. 1979. *Rubbish Theory: The Creation and Destruction of Value*. Oxford: Oxford University Press.

Thorner, Daniel, Basile Kerblay, and R. Smith, Eds. 1966. *A. V. Chayanov on the Theory of Peasant Economy*. Madison: University of Wisconsin Press.

Thorpe, Nick. 2009. Downturns Hit Romania's Tinker. *BBC News*, January 17, 2009

Tố Hữu. 1961. *Gió Lộng* (Strong Wind). Hanoi: Literature Publishing House (Nhà xuất bản Văn học).

Tong, Xin and Jici Wang. 2012. "The Shadow of the Global Networks: E-waste Flows to China." In *Economies of Recycling: The Global Tranformation of Materials, Values and Social Relations*, ed. C. Alexander and J. Reno. London: Zed Books: 98–118.

Tran, Angie Ngoc. 2013. *Ties that Bind: Cultural Identity, Class, and Law in Vietnam's Labor Resistance*. Ithaca, N.Y.: Cornell University Press.

Tronto, Joan C. 1993. *Moral Boundaries: A Political Argument for an Ethic of Care*. New York: Routledge.

Trương, Huyền Chi. 2009. "A Home Divided: Work, Body, and Emotions in the Post Doi-moi Family." In *Reconfiguring Families in Contemporary Vietnam*, ed. M. Barbieri and D. Bélanger. Stanford, Calif.: Stanford University Press.

Turner, Sarah and Laura Schoenberger. 2012. "Street Vendor Livelihoods and Everyday Politics in Hanoi, Vietnam: The Seeds of a Diverse Economy?" *Urban Studies* **49**(5): 1027–1044.

United Nations Office on Drugs and Crime. 2015. *World Drug Report 2015*. New York: United Nations. http://www.unodc.org/wdr2015/ (accessed on March, 7, 2017).

Veblen, Thorstein. 1979. *The Theory of the Leisure Class*. New York: Penguin Books.

Vu, Thi Thao. 2013. "Making a Living in Rural Vietnam from (Im)mobile Livelihoods: A Case of Women's Migration." *Population, Space and Place* **19**(1): 87–102.

Vu, Thi Thao and Jytte Agergaard. 2012. "Doing Family: Female Migrants and Family Transition in Rural Vietnam." *Asian Population Studies* **8**(1): 103–119.

Vũ, Xuân Dân. 2011. Quy hoạch nghề đồng nát (Planning for waste trading). *Quân đội nhân dân Newspaper* July 05, 2011.

Wacquant, Loïc. 2008. *Urban Outcasts: A Comparative Sociology of Advanced Marginality.* Bristol, UK: Polity

Willis, Paul. 1977. *Learning to Labor: How Working Class Kids Get Working Class Jobs.* New York: Columbia University Press.

Wilson, David C., Costas Velis, and Chris Cheeseman. 2006. "Role of Informal Sector Recycling in Waste Management in Developing Countries." *Habitat International* **30**(4): 797–808.

Wong, Linda. 2005. *Marginalization and Social Welfare in China.* London: Taylor & Francis.

World Bank, Ministry of Natural Resources and Environment, Canadian International Development Agency. 2004. Vietnam Environment Monitor: Solid Waste. Hanoi: WB, MONRE and CIDA

Yan, Yunxiang. 2013. "The Drive for Success and the Ethics of the Striving Individual." In *Ordinary Ethics in China,* ed. C. Stafford. London: Bloomsbury Publishing, 263–288.

Yanagisako, Sylvia Junko. 1979. "Family and Household: The Analysis of Domestic Groups." *Annual Review of Anthropology* **8**: 161–205.

Zavoretti, Roberta. 2016. *Rural Origins, City Lives: Class and Place in Contemporary China.* Seattle: University of Washington Press.

Zhang, Li. 2001. *Strangers in the City: Reconfigurations of Space, Power, and Social Networks within China's Floating Population.* Stanford, Calif.: Stanford University Press.

Zhang, Li. 2010. *In Search of Paradise: Middle-Class Living in a Chinese Metropolis.* Ithaca, N.Y.: Cornell University Press.

Zhang, Li and Aihwa Ong. 2008. *Privatizing China: Socialism from Afar.* Ithaca, N.Y.: Cornell University Press.

Zimring, Carl. 2004. "Dirty Work: How Hygiene and Xenophobia Marginalized the American Waste Trades, 1870–1930." *Environmental History* **9**(1): 80–101.

Zimring, Carl A. 2017. *Clean and White: A History of Environmental Racism in the United States.* Minneapolis: University of Minnesota.

# INDEX

....................

Tables, figures, and boxes are indicated by an italic *t*, *f*, and *b* following the page number.